# THE DUBLIN PUB

## A SOCIAL AND CULTURAL HISTORY

### DONAL FALLON

NEW ISLAND

# THE DUBLIN PUB

First published in 2025 and reprinted in 2026 by
New Island Books
Glenshesk House
10 Richview Office Park
Clonskeagh
Dublin D14 V8C4
Republic of Ireland
www.newisland.ie

Text copyright © Donal Fallon, 2025
Foreword copyright © Dermot Bolger, 2025

The right of Donal Fallon to be identified as the author of this work has been asserted in accordance with the provisions of the Copyright and Related Rights Act, 2000.

Print ISBN: 978-1-83594-024-2
eBook ISBN: 978-1-83594-025-9

All rights reserved. The material in this publication is protected by copyright law. Except as may be permitted by law, no part of the material may be reproduced (including by storage in a retrieval system) or transmitted in any form or by any means; adapted; rented or lent without the written permission of the copyright owners.

Cover image: © Colm Keating, 1986; by kind permission of the photographer.

The author has made all reasonable effort to trace copyright holders, credit correctly and obtain permission to reproduce visual and textual material. Please contact the publisher if any copyright appears to have been infringed.

British Library Cataloguing in Publication Data. A CIP catalogue record for this book is available from the British Library.

Product safety queries can be addressed to New Island Books at the above postal address or at info@newisland.ie.

Set in 11pt on 16pt in Espinosa Nova
Book and cover design by Niall McCormack, hitone.ie
Edited by Neil Burkey, neilburkey.com
Printed by Özlem Print, Turkey, ozlemmatbaa.com.tr
Printed on paper from managed sources.

New Island Books is a member of Publishing Ireland.

*This book is dedicated to the memory of Tommy Smith.*

It was closing time. The barmen in McDaid's were shouting 'Time, gentlemen, please' with an automatic insistence that intimidated nobody. Drinks continued to be sipped slowly and sensually, and the barmen's end of day ritual was, as usual, an unrelieved failure. Yet it would be the barmen who would win in the heel of the hunt, for it was within their power to cut off supplies from behind the counter, forcing us to leave. But that would be later, perhaps fifteen minutes later, and in the meantime, there were things to be said.

**JOSEPH COLE**
*Dublin Magazine*, 1969

A scene from McDaid's on Harry Street, with barman Paddy O'Brien at work. (Fáilte Ireland Tourism Photographic Collection, Dublin City Library and Archive)

# CONTENTS

|    | About the Author | 9 |
|----|---|---|
|    | Foreword *by Dermot Bolger* | 10 |
|    | Introduction | 14 |
| 1  | The Pugilist Publican of the Coombe | 32 |
| 2  | Drinking with Wolfe Tone | 40 |
| 3  | Heaven and Hellfire | 52 |
| 4  | Fenian Conspiracy and the Public House | 60 |
| 5  | Snugs and Mirrors | 72 |
| 6  | Easter Week | 82 |
| 7  | Monto's Revolutionary Pub | 92 |
| 8  | What's in a Name? | 102 |
| 9  | The Dawning of the Day | 110 |
| 10 | Publore | 124 |
| 11 | War on Bass | 128 |
| 12 | The Pub and the Stage: The Flowing Tide | 132 |
| 13 | Lee Miller: In Search of Joyce | 140 |
| 14 | Murals in the Moral Pub | 152 |
| 15 | The Horseshoe Bar | 158 |

| | | |
|---|---|---|
| 16 | A Bird Never Flew on One Wing | 166 |
| 17 | Chapelizod and Beyond | 174 |
| 18 | One of Dublin's Princes | 186 |
| 19 | At the Sign of the Zodiac | 194 |
| 20 | Elizabeth Taylor and After | 198 |
| 21 | 'A Most Unusual Pub' | 206 |
| 22 | The Ballad Boom and After | 214 |
| 23 | From Singing Pubs to Karaoke | 224 |
| 24 | Vienna in Trinity College Dublin | 230 |
| 25 | A Reminder of The Towers | 234 |
| 26 | Coddle, Sandwiches and Tayto Crisps | 240 |
| 27 | Con Houlihan's Dublin | 248 |
| 28 | The Relics of The Irish House | 262 |
| 29 | Signs of the Times | 268 |
| 30 | Art and Tradition in the Castle Lounge | 276 |
| 31 | The Changing Sound of Benburb Street | 286 |
| | Select Bibliography | 294 |
| | Acknowledgements | 300 |
| | Notes | 302 |
| | Map of Some Lost Pubs of Dublin | 316 |
| | Index of Pubs | 318 |

**DONAL FALLON** is a historian and broadcaster from Dublin. He is the creator of the Three Castles Burning podcast and he works as Social Historian at 14 Henrietta Street, a social history museum of Dublin life. His previous publications include *Three Castles Burning: A History of Dublin in Twelve Streets*.
@threecastlesburning

# FOREWORD

**I**n 1977 I made my first and last appearance as a traditional Irish musician in a Dublin pub. O'Donoghue's of Merrion Row, the haunt of musical greats like The Dubliners, Seamus Ennis and Joe Heaney when he passed through town. One of the seven musicians playing there one Sunday afternoon handed me a bodhrán. 'He's eighteen, unemployed, broke and a poet,' he told the others, who nodded and made room. Then he gave me two instructions, 'Firstly, hold the bodhrán like you know how to play it. Secondly, don't attempt to play it or we'll break your neck.' My silent performance was rewarded by a barman ferrying down at regular intervals not seven but eight pints of Guinness, accompanied by thick ham sandwiches. It didn't matter that I couldn't play a note; these things happen in a Dublin pub.

Some months later in another Dublin pub, The Granby, a trade unionist handed me a woollen hat and a donkey jacket to disguise my identity before joining a throng of workers in a nearby hall where I raised my hand, along with everyone else present from Finglas, to vote for continued strike action. It didn't matter that I was still unemployed, with no right to be there; these things happen in a Dublin pub.

Seven years later in another Dublin pub, The International, I met my first wife by chance, an encounter that led to us being together for a quarter century until her death. It didn't matter that she was stunningly good looking and I wasn't; these things happen in a Dublin pub.

All this is just to say that, like a lot of Dubliners, I can map out my life by naming Dublin pubs. Like many who will read Donal Fallon's superb distillation of the evolution of the Dublin pub, I keep encountering ghosts on his wondrous voyage through the licenced premises of my native city.

But this book is an equal joy to read if you are not from Dublin or never got a chance to sup in some of the pubs that Fallon evokes which no longer exist. His book is not just an informative, entertaining guide to the backstory of many famous pubs still with us, but conjures the spirit of establishments that have disappeared but were once a vital part of Dublin's social fabric.

Because often Dublin pubs were not just social meeting places, but central planks of their communities. Dockers seeking a day's work would pack early morning houses in East Wall to discover what ships had docked in the night and which stevedores and coal merchants would be hiring men to unload them at dawn.

In these pages we find artists like Harry Kernoff, whose work brilliantly captured Dublin pub culture; cherished singers like the great song collector Frank Harte in the Strawberry Beds; revolutionaries like Theobald Wolfe Tone plotting insurrection on nights when his diary did not admonish himself for being 'drunk again' in the Eagle Tavern or Brazen Head; poets like Patrick Kavanagh nursing a ball of malt in the bohemian maelstrom of McDaid's; journalists like the legendary Con Houlihan nursing a first drink in Mulligan's after delivering his newspaper column, written in black marker on reams of the white paper in which butchers wrapped sausages; and appearances from Dublin's standing army of eccentrics like The Bird Flanagan, turning up on horseback at the Gresham Hotel to demand a parity of liquid refreshment for horse and rider.

But Fallon also captures the atmosphere of lively pubs that sprang up to serve the population of growing working-class suburbs, like The Embankment in Tallaght or The Towers in Ballymun, where a tradition of ending many nights with a raucous rendition of 'Skippy the Bush Kangaroo', as drinkers formed human chairs to dance along, was, as I can testify, a godsend to future generations of orthopaedic surgeons.

In Joyce's *Ulysses*, Leopold Bloom muses that a 'good puzzle would be cross Dublin without passing a pub'. This feat of cartographic dexterity is beyond me. But it is now perhaps more theoretically feasible than if traversing the nineteenth-century streetscape that Fallon brilliantly conjures up, in which myriad numbers of breweries and distilleries started along the banks of Liffey tributaries, helping to shape areas of the city. Fallon uncovers the meanings behind names of old pubs like Hole in the Wall or the Turk's Head; pays homage to great owners and barmen like the legendary Tommy Smith of Grogan's; delves into the discreet environs of Dublin's first gay pubs like Bartley Dunne's; captures the atmosphere in watering holes for parched thespians like The Flowing Tide; and explores the occasionally uneasy meeting of the waters when the old landed gentry and the nouveau riche mingled in the Shelbourne Hotel's Horseshoe Bar.

All of Dublin life is in these pages, jostling at a counter before the curate calls 'Last orders', swapping anecdotes, songs, propositions of dubious intent and downright lies. This is the finest, most extensive pub crawl you will ever embark on, and all without leaving your armchair. Readers will raise a glass in salutation to its author.

**DERMOT BOLGER**

# INTRODUCTION

MAP SHOWING
DUBLIN'S GREATEST
(PUBLIC HOUSES)

**T**his book is not a history of licensing laws and public house legislation, or the economic trials and tribulations of an industry. Instead, what is presented here is a miscellany of histories drawing on the public house in Dublin and rooted in their social and cultural importance. Some stories are anecdotal, others are set against the backdrop of defining moments of the city.

While several entries open in an era before the modern public house had arrived, all touch on communal drinking in Dublin through the ages, and many are connected to the contemporary city. Over the course of this book, the reader will encounter public houses that were entangled in the drama of the Irish Revolution, pubs that were part of significant social change in modern Ireland and so-called literary pubs.

The pub is a real physical space, but it is also one that emerges time and again in the literature of the city. In his collection *More Pricks Than Kicks*, Samuel Beckett describes a pub interior and its fixtures in minute detail: 'the stools, the counter, the powerful screws, the shining phalanx of the pulls of the beer-engines, all cunningly devised and elaborated to further the relations between purveyor and consumer in this domain'.[1] Entering the door of Grogan's on South William Street, a UNESCO City of Literature plaque is immediately visible, cementing the idea that the public house and Dublin's literary heritage are interconnected.

The author and former politician Stephen Gwynn maintained in his 1938 study *Dublin Old and New*, intended as an introduction to the city for the visitor, that 'Dublin's pubs were, and I suppose are, the equivalent of Parisian cafés. Literary groups, artistic groups, political groups, had their regular or irregular meeting places in them.'[2] Fair enough, but let us not forget the importance of Dublin's cafés, and that literary and social discussion thrived and thrives in a variety of settings. Tony Farmar rattled off the names James Joyce, Arthur Griffith, Paddy Kavanagh, Maud Gonne, Jimmy O'Dea, Micheál Mac Liammóir, Mary Lavin, Terry Wogan and Ludwig Wittgenstein when reflecting on the regulars of one alcohol-free Dublin establishment: Bewley's.[3] To the shock of the occasional visiting writer, not all Irish writers hung around in pubs. When Honor Tracy profiled Peadar O'Donnell, the novelist and editor of *The Bell*, she felt it worth telling her readers that 'a curious thing about Peadar is that he doesn't drink: curious, because most good Irishmen do, and heavily'.[4]

Pubs were not the only space in which people socialised and plotted. Still, their physicality (a land of snugs, dim lighting and wooden partitions), the presence of alcohol and their existence in the 'after-hours' city makes them especially interesting settings in the social story of the capital.

Reminders of Dublin's UNESCO City of Literature status are easily found in the city's public houses. However, the pubs themselves, the Vintners' Federation of Ireland (VFI) have argued, are also deserving of UNESCO heritage status. While seeking to have pubs listed amidst the National Inventory of Intangible Cultural Heritage of Ireland – a necessary first step on that journey to heritage status – Pat Crotty of the VFI has insisted that the pub 'transcends its physical space to become a cornerstone of community life'.[5] Perhaps in seeking such status for our public houses, there is an acknowledgment of a changing Ireland. A report commissioned by the Drinks Industry Group of Ireland noted that, in the period between 2005 and 2022, 'the number of pubs is down by 22.5 per

An interior shot showing the Welcome Inn, Parnell Street. (Courtesy of photographer Andy Sheridan)

cent from 8,617 in 2005 to 6,680 for the most recent period in 2022. This represents a closure of 1,937 public houses across the country since 2005'.⁶

On both sides of the Liffey, Dublin city is dotted with closed former public houses. On Parnell Street, both the Welcome Inn and Conway's (where many a father-to-be eagerly awaited news from the Rotunda) are in a state of physical decay, the latter propped up in place awaiting the redevelopment of Moore Street and its laneway environs. Barney Kiernan's, so important to the chapter in this book exploring photographer Lee Miller, wasn't saved by its importance to *Ulysses*. Hourican's on Leeson Street, once popular with students from the nearby National University on Earlsfort Terrace, has sat empty for almost a decade. Beyond the city centre, the shells of former public houses slowly rot as areas are transformed and house prices rise, like the Horse and Jockey on Inchicore's Emmet Road or the Fassaugh House pub in Cabra. Licences are transferred, buildings gradually fall apart, something else follows. All these pubs and others were once someone's local, and important to the people who lived and worked in their vicinities.

Patrick Conway's public house on the corner of Parnell Street and Moore Lane, January 2025.

Gone without trace are other establishments, as the city streetscapes have been transformed. Alderman Tom Kelly, city representative and local historian, wrote in 1910 of how 'in no other locality in Dublin has there been such a change within recent years as there has been in Patrick Street and its neighbourhood'.[7] Drastic road widening in more recent times has changed Patrick Street and Clanbrassil Street further still, as the city adjusted to increased car traffic. Who would recognise Patrick Street as we see it here, in an image that captures John McCall's public house, a pub that lured James Clarence Mangan and Arthur Griffith in their respective times. When a young Griffith went to the 'quaint old tavern', it was said that 'one could still be shown the actual place once favoured by Mangan, and even occupy his accustomed chair or bench'.[8]

An unrecognisable view of Patrick Street showing John McCall's public house. (Courtesy of the National Library of Ireland)

Alcohol and its consumption has been a feature of the city from its earliest times, of course. Culinary historian Máirtín Mac Con Iomaire has written of 'gastro-topography', and how our maps today reflect our rich culinary heritage.[9] To walk Dublin is to walk streets like Bull Alley, Cornmarket, Cow Lane and Fishamble Street. And let us not forget Winetavern Street, 'a busy drinking spot since the medieval period', now devoid of a public house.

The soldier and author Barnabe Rich, in describing the Dublin of the early seventeenth century, complained of the abundance of taverns in the city. These 'nurseries of drunkenness' were proof that 'the whole profit of the town stands upon ale houses and the selling of ale'. Drinking was unregulated, with taverns seemingly open 'night and day, and in every minute of the hour', even during religious services on Sunday.[10] According to Dublin Corporation records, by 1667 the city was somehow home to more than 1,500 ale houses and taverns.[11] Dublin was more than just a centre of administration; its population increased significantly over the course of the seventeenth century, when it became not merely the largest city in Ireland, but 'indisputably the second city of the British isles'.[12] It was home to perhaps 60,000 people by 1680, and no other city could boast of a similar number of drinking establishments for its population size.

The eighteenth century brought an explosion in brewing and distilling in the city. H. S. Corran of the Guinness Museum describes how the Liberties became the epicentre of these industries:

> The Liberties was always well supplied with water. The nearness of the River Poddle to the east and the Camac to the west, together with the City Basin adjoining what was to be developed into Grand Canal Harbour ensured this. As a result, the industries which grew up during the eighteenth century tended to be those which could take advantage of this useful raw material.[13]

By 1804, the Dublin Directory lists no fewer than fifty-five breweries in the city, and an impressive twenty-five distilleries. Over the course of time, the powerhouse brewery of Arthur Guinness & Sons would absorb 'about ten smaller breweries' premises', while, Corran noted, 'there were eventually three major distilleries left at the end of the nineteenth century'.[14] Alfred Barnard, the English historian of the brewing and distilling industries, would visit the city to chronicle these historic sites of production. 'The porter and whiskey made in Dublin are of high repute,' Barnard told his readers, 'not only in their native country, but in England and the Colonies.'[15] Some of what Barnard describes is not only still familiar, but has grown in stature, like the St James's Gate Brewery. Other producers have disappeared, or have been absorbed into the built landscape. Today, apartments occupy some of the site of

Alfred Barnard
(1837–1918).

the Jones Road Distillery, constructed in the 1870s for D. W. D. (Dublin Whiskey Distillery Company), but Barnard described it as something of a colossus:

> ... it was commenced on the 22nd day of July, in the year 1872, and on the 22nd day of July, 1873, the Company were mashing; thus showing what Irish enterprise is capable of doing. The Distillery buildings are a fine stately work in red brick, some sixty-five feet high; at a distance the place looks like some public building, the architect having given it that character. The chimney stack, one hundred and thirty-five feet high, is also built of red brick, handsomely designed, and of great ornamentation; it rears its

proud head from the centre of the courtyard in front of the gateway, and at a distance looks like a monument built to commemorate the virtues of some dead hero.[16]

Breweries and distilleries were not only significant employers, but a force in shaping the city. Statues of Lord Ardilaun (Sir Arthur Guinness, 1840–1915) and Sir Benjamin Lee Guinness (1798–1868) are testament to the philanthropy of the largest brewing family in the city, who constructed public housing and transformed physical spaces. When the socialist James Connolly wrote a short story set in the city in 1895, he described Dublin as a city where 'the very air is redolent of patriotism and rebellion and Dublin Bay herring', before alluding to how 'you have Christ Church and St. Patrick's Cathedral restored by the rival efforts of two dealers in strong drink'.[17] When it came to Irish alcohol exports, Dublin brewers 'produced about three-quarters of the total output, and accounted for 96 per cent of exports at the outset for the twentieth-century'.[18]

Naturally, drink was readily available in a city that produced it in such quantities, but it was consumed in a wide variety of settings that reflected the class divisions of the city. For the poorest, there was the nineteenth-century phenomenon of the dram shop, a makeshift shop one could step into off the street and down a quick drink of spirits, described thus in one contemporary magazine:

> The Dublin whiskey shops, like the London gin shops, are undoubtedly the cause of much intemperance by affording the poor the opportunity of indulging their depraved taste; but here the likeness ceases, for a whiskey shop here and a gin temple in London are as unlike in all other respects as can possibly be imagined …
> 
> Imagine a small shop at the corner of a street in Dublin, with a doorway on each side of the angle of the house, so that those who wish to cut off the corner may do so at please, and of which privilege not a few avail themselves, for here there are no mahogany

doors, with ground-glass windows to offer an impediment; you can therefore enter the shop without difficulty, should the doorway not be occupied by two or three old women.[19]

The Victorian era transformed drinking in Dublin and across Britain, with significant legislative measures drawn up, aiming to control the selling of alcohol and impose structure on the industry. Culturally, public houses changed too, becoming places that prided themselves on their interiors and sociability. At least partially, this was responding to the emerging strength of the temperance movement, an international movement pushing for moderation or total abstinence from drinking alcohol, 'as drink came to be identified as a major social problem'.[20]

Paul Jennings, leading authority on the public house in English history, pinpoints the 1850s and 1860s as the time 'that one can begin to think of an institution called "the pub", subsuming under that name the various types of drinking place' that had come before.[21] It is to Dublin's good fortune that so many of these Victorian establishments have survived, fully or partially, as explored later. Some of them hark back to earlier times, listing themselves in signage as not merely public houses, but spirit grocers. The practice of allowing a customer to purchase alcohol and groceries on the same premises was condemned in some quarters for creating an environment in which women succumbed to drunkenness. Later, the suffragette newspaper *The Irish Citizen* would argue for the abolition of these relics of the Victorian era:

> Women's societies should agitate for the abolition for the spirit grocer's licence. A large part of the drinking among women is due to this spirit grocer's licence. How many women, and even men, who would shrink from being seen going into an open bar find an excuse to buy something else in order to slake their alcoholic thirst surreptitiously?[22]

A map produced by the Church of Ireland Temperance Society highting the number of public houses in Dublin city centre. (Dublin City Library and Archive)

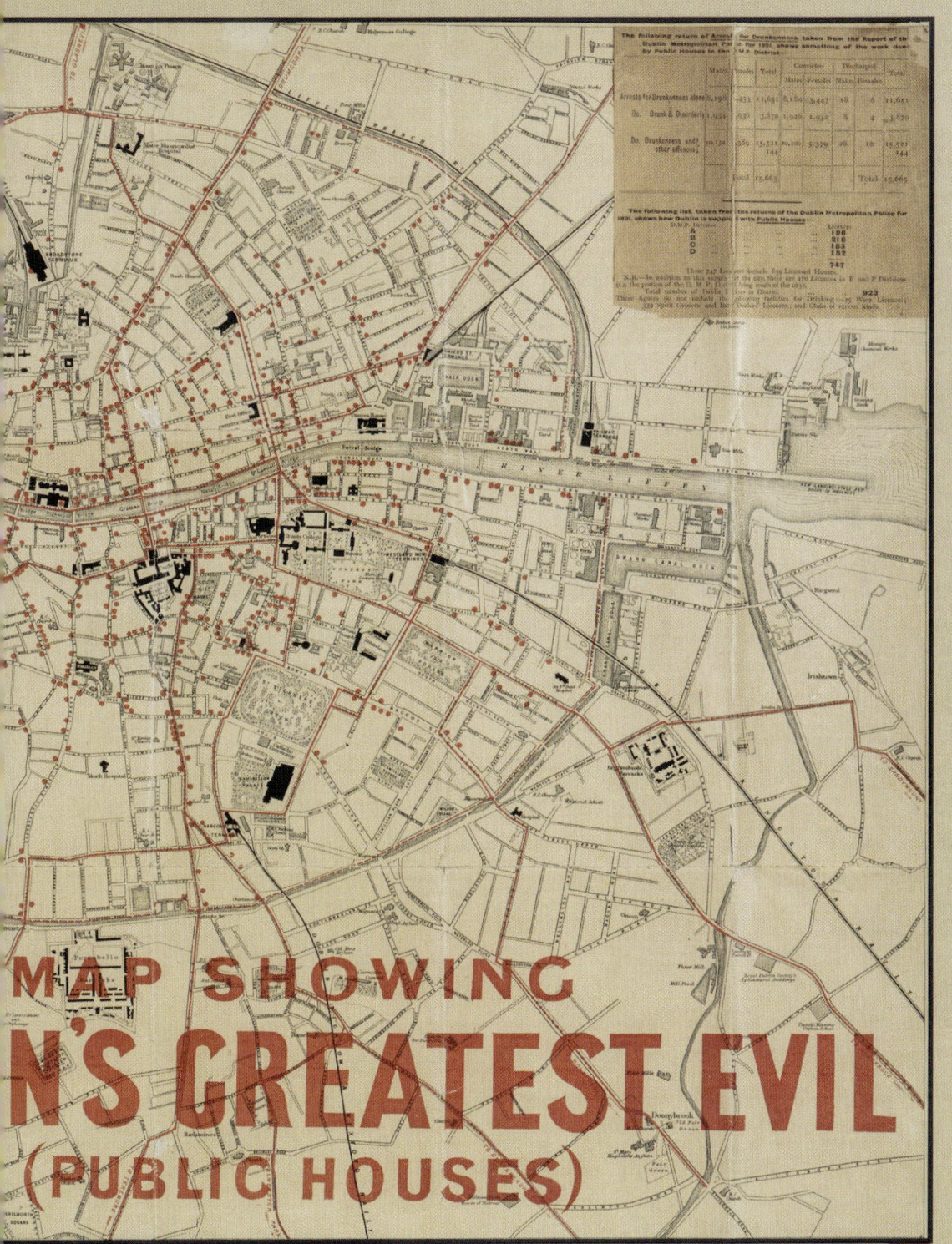

# FATHER MATHEW T.A. ASSOCIATION
## CHURCH STREET.

# IRELAND SOBER
## IS
# IRELAND FREE!

The extraordinary scale of the Irish temperance movement, following on from Daniel O'Connell's movement for constitutional reform and the struggle for Catholic Emancipation, would also shape cultural attitudes to drunkenness in Ireland. The visiting American abolitionist Frederick Douglass would himself take 'the pledge' before Father Theobald Mathew, proudly writing that 'I now reckon myself with delight the fifth of the last five of Father Mathew's 5,487,495 temperance children.'[23] The cause of temperance was not an exclusively Catholic one, as an 1892 map from the Church of Ireland Temperance Society reminds us.

While public houses are primarily places of jovial social recreation, there are also moments of tragedy throughout this story. Pubs can be places that facilitate self-destruction. Brendan Behan would recall a phone call from Seán O'Casey, at the height of his stardom in 1962, who told him to stop drinking: '"Why?" I asked. "Because you have work to do", he replied. "I think he's right."'[24] He was dead within two years. Pubs are also places of vulnerability, demonstrated by the number of killings within them. We encounter

*The primary slogan of the temperance movement in Ireland. (Capuchin Archives)*

Mary Cooney, the much respected owner of the Brazen Head public house. (Photograph by Colm Keating)

death in the public house during the revolutionary period in this book, but in more recent times pub killings have occasionally been a feature of gangland violence in the capital. Though outside the remit of this publication, it would be impossible to write a history of the Troubles that didn't feature public house assassinations and bombings. On occasion, such as the bombing by the Ulster Volunteer Force of the Widow Scallan's pub on Pearse Street during a republican fundraiser in 1994, the capital witnessed a form of violence that was relatively commonplace in Ulster during the conflict. McGurk's, Kelly's, the Four Step Inn, the Mountainview Tavern and the Bayardo Bar are just a small selection of Belfast pubs variously targeted by loyalist and republican paramilitaries during the conflict.

Still, the story told here is overwhelmingly a positive one, passing through subjects as diverse as the folk music revival of the 1960s and the visible emergence of once-marginalised communities in the city from the 1970s onwards. This is a book about pubs, but it is also fundamentally a book about people. When working on this book, mentions of certain public houses in conversation immediately gave rise to the names of people associated with them. The Brazen Head for many was inseparable from Miss Cooney, its one-time proprietor, who resisted any move towards draught beer, serving only large bottles to the singers who flocked there. Writer Benedict Kiely recalled her, with her voice 'crisp, clear, sweet as a blackbird, each word defined and lingered over, and her eyes all but closed, as was the mode once with old people singing in country places'.[25] Likewise, Grogan's is intrinsically tied to the memory of former co-proprietor Tommy Smith, explored later in this book. But on occasion the connection between an establishment and an individual concerns those on the other side of the bar. Mulligan's will forever be linked with the newspaper columnist Con Houlihan, with the pub mentioned in almost all obituaries of the Kerryman, and to whom a secular shrine stands on the premises.[26]

Certainly, these were all individuals of engaging dispositions, but the public house also matters in terms of what it means to people collectively. We see symbols of identity in pubs that mean so much locally, but which a visitor may miss. At the Yacht Tavern on Ringsend's Thorncastle Street, for example, rowing oars take pride of place above the bar, in a community so proud of its proximity to, and inseparability from, the Liffey. While other parts of Dublin have football rivalries (Ringsend also has that in abundance), one of these oars comes from local rowing club Stella Maris (1937), and the other from St Patrick's Rowing Club (1936). These kinds of local symbols can be found in public houses all across the city, connecting them to victories and the occasional heartbreak.

Here's a good question to ask any Dubliner (that is, anyone residing in the city Joyce called 'the Hibernian Metropolis'): what is a pub? Outside of licensing laws, there is sometimes disagreement over what falls into the category of 'pub'. The Bailey, explored in this collection, is perhaps thought of now more as a restaurant than

**An advertisement for John Jameson & Son whiskey designed by the artist Harry Clarke. (Courtesy of the National Library of Ireland)**

By Appointment  to H.M. the King.

# JOHN JAMESON
## Three Star Whiskey.

One reason why J.J. is recognised as
## "IRELAND'S PREMIER BRAND"

ITS WHOLESOMENESS, proved by analysis and by the Medical Faculty when prescribing a stimulant. It increases the enjoyment of food and so promotes digestion and assimilation.

Messrs. JOHN JAMESON & Son Ltd., Dublin.          London Office: 7 Mark Lane, E.C.

a pub, for example. There are other venues that exist in this curious space, where the lines between a bar and a restaurant are blurred. On Mary Street, the former St Mary's Church (a building with a rich history linking it to names as diverse as architect Thomas Burgh, Theobald Wolfe Tone and Arthur Guinness) is today The Church, a popular restaurant-focused space that allows for one of the most unusual pint experiences in the city, amidst memorials to the deceased and a working church organ. When the venue opened in its present guise, in 1997, the *Irish Independent* commented that Dublin had witnessed such curious transitions before:

> Dublin for many years revelled in the fact that it was probably the only city in Europe that could boast a church which was once a pub and a pub which was once a church. The Blessed Sacrament Chapel on D'Olier Street was formerly an oyster bar, while the sometimes notorious McDaid's on Harry Street began life as a place of worship for the Moravian Church.[27]

In as much as this book is concerned with history, I hope it serves as a guide of sorts to the public houses of Dublin today. I make no claim that the pubs here are 'the best' pubs in the city; indeed many of my own favourites aren't present, such are the constraints of any publication when it comes to matters of size or the fine dance of thematically working institutions into the narrative. The proliferation of 'influencers' in the digital realm today, and the monotony of the obsession with finding 'the best pub' or 'the best pint' means that, while the industry is in a moment of flux and pubs are closing in unprecedented numbers, a handful of pubs are increasingly venerated. You will find most of the big-name institutions here, but I hope others are surprising or new to you, and that the absence of a personal favourite won't grate too much.

Some of the types of establishment in this book are rapidly disappearing, with just a handful of early houses remaining in the city. Others are innovative and fresh approaches to what a

This image from the Lawrence Photograph Collection shows St Mary's Church, now trading as The Church bar and restaurant. (Courtesy of the Naitonal Library of Ireland)

licensed premises can be, like Fidelity, which has the feeling of a 'listening bar' one might encounter in Tokyo. Most of the public houses within this book would be considered 'traditional' pubs, but we also encounter spaces where culture takes an important place. Reading earlier books, like pub historian Eamonn Casey's 1992 *Dublin Pub Saunter*, it struck me how much can change in a relatively short period of time. Here is a history of publand, yes, but here is a moment in time as well.

With no little pride I conclude by saying that, if it still exists, and it is in these pages, I have passed through it. Such is the life of the committed researcher.

# CHAPTER 1.

# THE PUGILIST PUBLICAN OF THE COOMBE

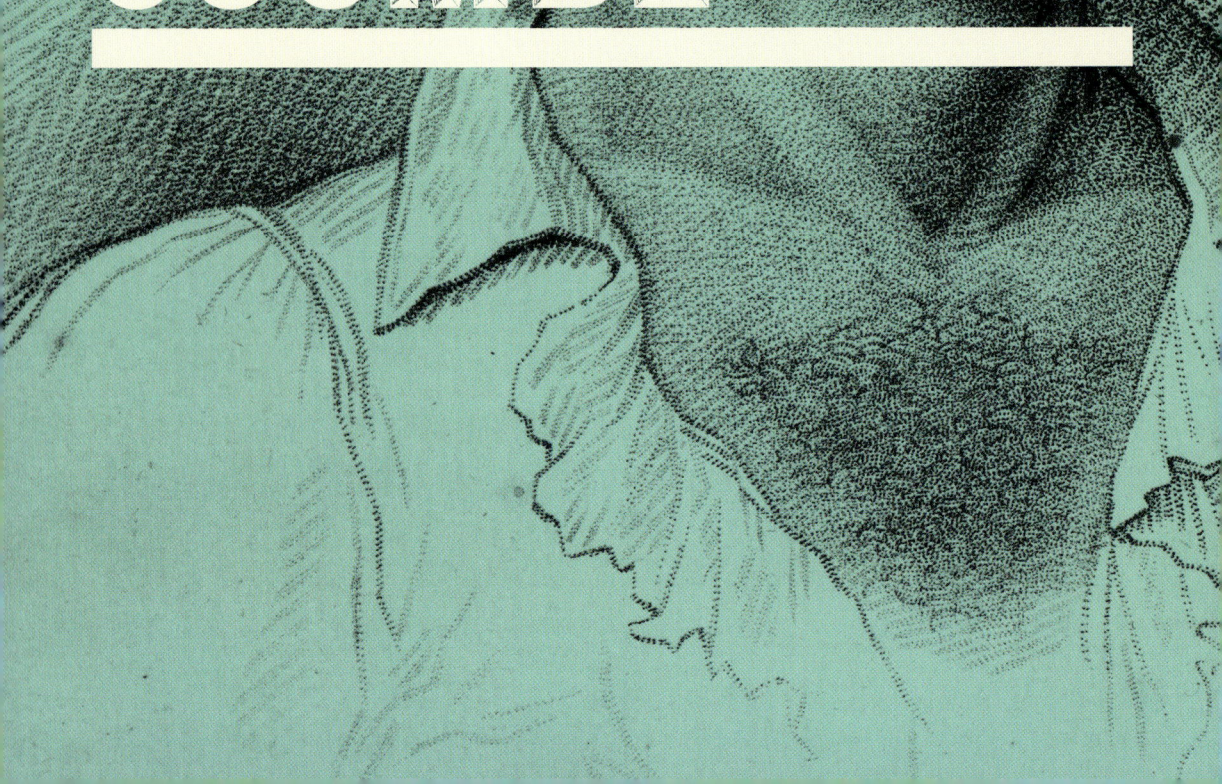

There weren't too many tears shed for the old motor tax office, River House, when the wrecking ball came for it in 2018. On a corner of Chancery Street and neighbouring the much-loved M. Hughes' pub, River House had been repeatedly described in the press as ugly; the *Sunday Times* called it a 'brutalist eyesore'.[1] In his classic study, *The Destruction of Dublin*, Frank McDonald, a champion of good architecture in Dublin of all different schools and styles, described it as an 'incoherent building'.[2] Today, it has been replaced by a hotel and there is no remaining trace of River House or M. Hughes. Gone without trace also is the plaque to the pugilist Dan Donnelly, marking the location of one of his four public houses across the city.

The son of a carpenter, Donnelly was born in 1788 in Townsend Street, going on to become a folk hero and the first Irish-born heavyweight champion boxer. In the true spirit of such folk heroes, stories of his exploits are both iconic and inconsistent. In the *Dictionary of Irish Biography*, sports historian Paul Rouse acknowledged this problem at the very outset of his entry on Donnelly: 'His life is one in which reality and mythology are not easily separated.'[3] The Dan Donnelly who emerges in nineteenth-century histories like *The Life and Battles of Dan Donnelly* is a giant of stature and spirits. 'Dan was all fight,' it begins, 'and being very partial to a drop o' potheen, his combativeness showed itself all the more when the *craythur* got into his upper story.'[4]

Donnelly's fighting prowess is well documented. His victory over English boxer Tom Hall in September 1814 on the Curragh of Kildare was witnessed by a crowd of thousands, and the spot of that victory (and others) is now marked by a memorial and known as Donnelly's Hollow. The Irish victory was met by bonfires on hillsides as Donnelly returned to Dublin but, ominously, the main celebrations occurred in the taverns of the capital when the pugilist eventually made it home. In November 1815 Donnelly snatched victory from the jaws of defeat against George Cooper, a tougher opponent, who Donnelly's biographer notes was nicknamed the Bargeman 'because he worked as a labourer on canal barges', and who a previous opponent described as 'the best natural fighter I have ever worked with'.[5] Donnelly's homecoming is quite the mental image, the *Dublin Penny Journal* recounting:

> We remember well Donnelly's triumphal entry into Dublin after his great battle on the Curragh. That indeed was an ovation. He was born on the shoulders of the people while his mother, like a Roman matron, leading the van in his procession and with all the pride of a second Agrippina, frequently slapped her naked bosom, exposed for the occasion, and exulting exclaimed: 'There's the breasts that

A Henry Brocas engraving celebrating Dan Donnelly. (Courtesy of the National Library of Ireland)

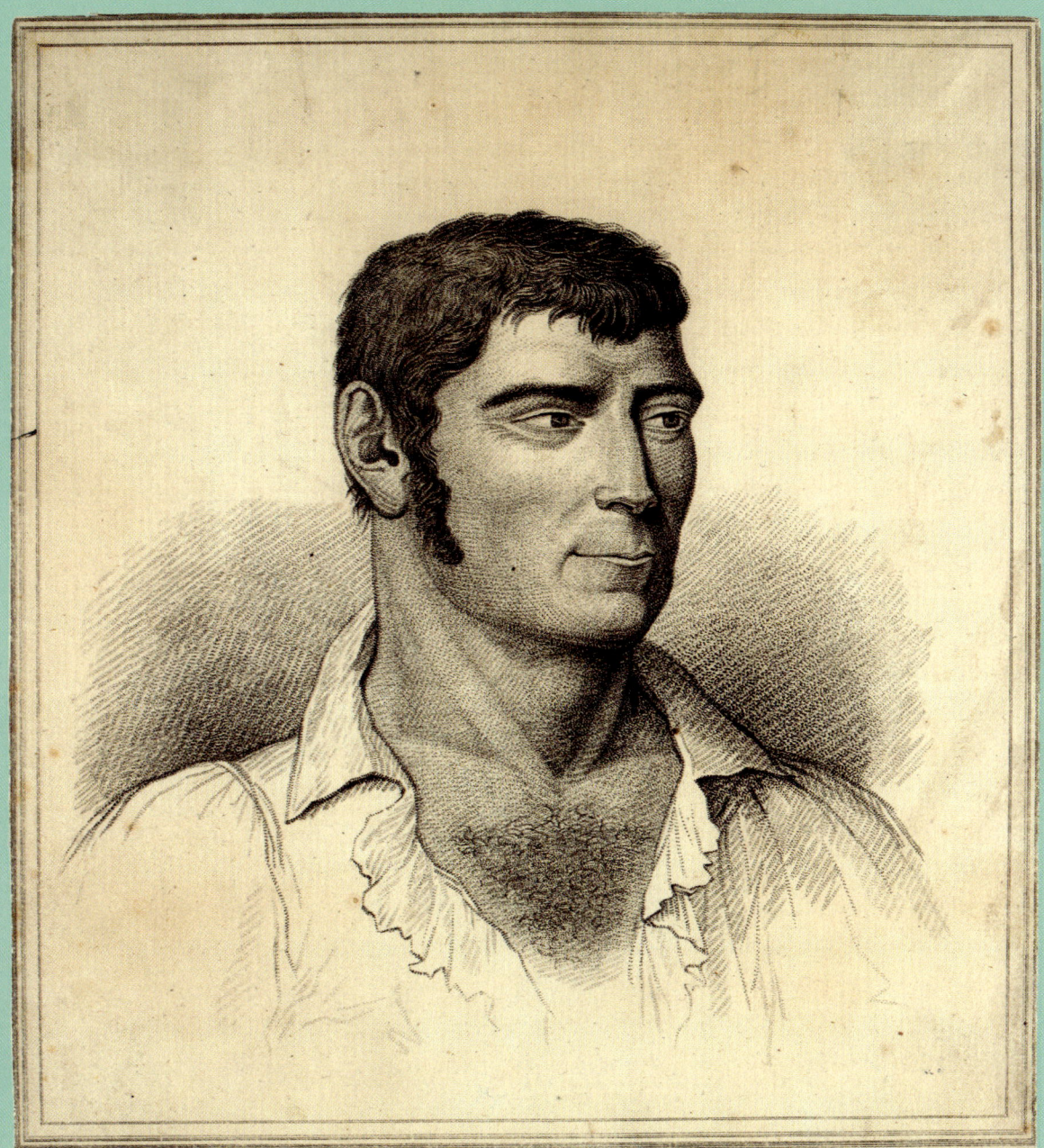

Engraved by H. Brocas

DAN<sup>l</sup>. DONNELLY,
*The Irish Pugilist*

Published by M. Sandford, 45 Henry Street

suckled him; there's the breast that suckled him.' Was the pride of a mother ever more admirably expressed?[6]

Not unlike fighters of more recent times, Donnelly's downfall was perhaps rooted in his success, with the cork rarely put back into a celebratory bottle. Following in the footsteps of many leading English prizefighters, Donnelly became a publican, opening his first premises on Capel Street with the support of a wealthy merchant. Later came a pub on Poolbeg Street, near his Townsend Street birthplace, and one on the Coombe – the only surviving premises today. As his biographer Patrick Myler noted, 'a sober publican might be able to avoid squandering much of his profits, but for someone as gregarious and fond of the bottle as Donnelly, it was a fatal occupation'.[7]

Donnelly's appearance at the Donnybrook Fair in 1819 in some ways typified his celebrity status. In the boxing booth, he put on sparring matches for large audiences, who were disheartened not to see him competing. The fair was a notoriously drunken environment, and one that Dublin's temperance movement had long sought to close. The campaigner James Haughton (dismissively referred to as one of the *anti-everythingarians* by opponents) would recall it as a fair 'so famous in song and at a distance, so notorious in reality!'[8] The fair, by then a centuries-old drinking binge, is immortalised in the ballad 'The Humours of Donnybrook Fair':

> Brisk lads and young lassies can fill up their glasses
> With whiskey and send a full bumper around
> Jig it off in a tent till their money's all spent
> And spin like a top till they rest on the ground.

It was a sad environment for a figure like Donnelly. Within a year he was dead, dying in February 1820 on the premises where River House would later stand. According to *The Life and Battles of Sir Dan Donnelly*, 'it is said that his blood was overheated from drinking

'Buying Ale at the Donnybrook Fair' by Francis Wheatley. (National Gallery of Ireland)

forty-seven tumblers of whiskey punch that Dan had taken on the previous evening, to show some of his companions the insensible effect spirituous liquor had upon his constitution'.[9]

Stories about Donnelly are endless; unsurprisingly, he emerges several times in the Schools' Collection of the Irish Folklore Commission, which recorded thousands of tales from across Ireland in the late 1930s. One child recounted a tale concerning Donnelly and his pub, and talked up the fighting prowess of a local hero:

> Dan Donnelly was a famous Dublin boxer. Big Phil often carted from Dublin as well as from Drogheda and he knew all about Donnelly who ran a public house somewhere in the city.

One day when Phil had some drink taken he challenged Dan in his own pub to fight him. Dan refused for he thought this unknown cartman from Breffni could be no match for him. But as Phil persisted in his challenge, Dan promised to match him next day with the second best man in Dublin. Phil was satisfied and spent that night lying in a barn. A glass of whiskey was the only thing he touched next morning before his fight.

He knocked his opponent unconscious with the second blow.

Dan Donnelly who was present at the fight refused to face Phil after what he had seen of him.[10]

The pub now trading as Fallon's, located at 129 The Coombe, is proud of its connection to former proprietor Donnelly, his image hanging on the wall of what is essentially one room and a (highly sought-after) snug. All in the vicinity of this pub has been transformed since the time of Donnelly, when the street outside was known as Cross Poddle, in reference to the river that runs below it. The area around St Patrick's Cathedral was one of great poverty and unregulated market activity, with everything from slaughterhouses to poorly run dairies amidst the 'unwholesome trades' of the area that troubled Dublin Corporation.[11] It would be philanthropic Guinness money that would later help transform this district, creating the Iveagh Trust housing scheme, St Patrick's Park and the properly regulated Iveagh Market. The bells of the cathedral can be heard from Fallon's pub, and a glimpse of it can be caught too from the stools neighbouring the door, provided you peek up for a look. Owing to the high wooden partition, blocking the view of those outside looking in, this is known as Meerkat Corner.

One thing you won't find in Fallon's is Dan Donnelly's mummified arm. Following his burial in Kilmainham's Bully's Acre, Donnelly's grave was disturbed by graverobbers, a not entirely uncommon scandal in the Dublin of the time. Some called such thieves 'resurrectionists', and money was made by selling cadavers to medical institutions, before the 1832 Anatomy Act brought an end to the morbid but profitable business. There are conflicting tales

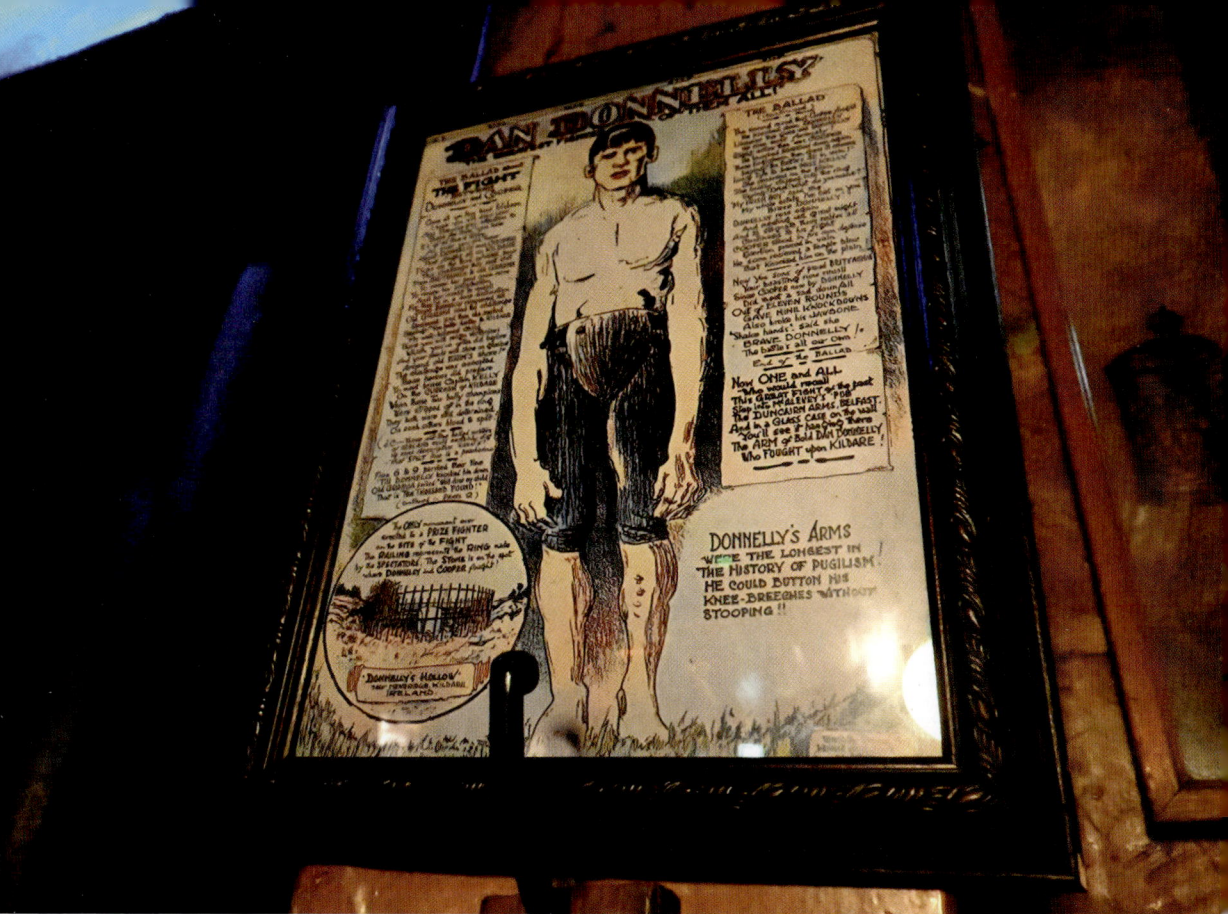

A tribute to Dan Donnelly inside Fallon's today.

on how Donnely's right arm came to be severed and mummified, but its afterlife is a curious and fascinating journey that included display in Belfast's Duncairn Arms and a residency for several decades in Kilcullen's Hideout from 1953. 'It is a pity to dismiss the myth,' his biographer Patrick Myler notes, 'but Dan's preserved arm is not of abnormal length. It matches the measurement of a man of just above six feet, which Donnelly was, when using the guide of an average arm span, from fingertip to fingertip, being about the same as a person's height.'[12] The arm has gone on to tour the world, being displayed in Boston College and even returning for an exhibition in Dublin's Croke Park. With Donnelly's plaque on the since-demolished River House missing, a triumphant return to the Coombe for the arm that beat George Cooper might be a fine commemoration.

## CHAPTER 2.

# DRINKING WITH WOLFE TONE

Amongst the books at home was a copy of Wolfe Tone's *Autobiography*, published by his son in America in 1826 ... I read Tone slowly ... Other leaders, with the exception of Hugh O'Neill, had been abstractions; at school we had read of them in relation to events; they had nothing to do with living. Tone was the first human note; 'drunk again' in his diary meant much: it brought him down to mortal level.[1]

Ernie O'Malley's recollection of reading Theobald Wolfe Tone's diaries in his childhood captures something fundamental about Tone. What emerges from those pages is, as a young Ernie discovered, a human being. We follow Tone as he pursues reform and then revolution, gaining insight into his deepest feelings and closest alliances. We sense his heartbreak at being removed from his family, and his curiosity at the new societies he finds himself moving in, seeking the support of the fledgling French Republic in pursuit of an Irish Republic. To historian Thomas Bartlett, these diaries show us 'his fondness for irony and self-mockery, his impatience with anything that looks like humbug or pretentiousness, and a sense of fun and gaiety that has endeared him to readers ever since'.[2]

Portrait of Theobald Wolfe Tone. (National Gallery of Ireland)

As the social media network formerly known as Twitter began its descent into bothood and madness, one saving grace emerged in 2024 in the form of a page entitled 'OTD Wolfe Tone Diary'. Posting entries on the corresponding date to Tone's observations, many are deeply serious. We also find plenty of nights out:

> July 14 1792 – Generally drunk. – Broke my glass thumping the table. Home, God knows how or when. Huzza!
> October 3 1792 – Dinner, and a great deal of wine. Frivolous day. Generally drunk.
> November 18 1792 – Huzza! Drink like a fish till past twelve. God bless everybody.

On Eustace Street in Temple Bar, the first meeting of Theobald Wolfe Tone's Society of United Irishmen in Dublin is today commemorated by a plaque marking the site of the Eagle Tavern. For the movement, taverns were an important centre of organisation. Before it was driven underground and outlawed, many meetings in establishments like the Eagle Tavern were widely documented affairs. With James Napper Tandy as secretary, the Dublin men passed a constitution that acknowledged how 'the society is constituted for the purpose of forwarding a brotherhood of affection, an identity of interests, a communion of rights, and a union of power, among Irishmen of all religious persuasions, and thereby obtaining an impartial and adequate representation of the nation in parliament'.[3]

At meetings of the Society of United Irishmen and other radicals, toasts were raised in these taverns, and they were occasionally deeply seditious. Tone drank to a toast wishing 'The spirit of the French mob to the people of Ireland', while there could be more radical toasts still, including 'May mankind trample upon royalty.' A toast wishing 'The fate of Louis to all crown'd heads' was a celebration of the French guillotine, but toasts raised to 'King George the Last' revealed the best of Irish optimism and humour.[4]

Plaque commemorating the site of the Eagle Tavern.

The tradition of seditious toasts continued long after the United Irishmen, as evidenced by a file in the National Archives of Ireland concerning 'disloyal toasts made in Dublin public house' some twenty-four years later. Then there was fury at the raising of a toast proposing 'a Bloody end and extermination to all Orangemen' in a Crampton Court public house.[5]

Taverns and coffee houses were becoming increasingly important spaces in the age of the United Irish movement, with historian Timothy Murtagh noting how 'the reading of newspapers in coffee houses and taverns was a central part of the social life of journeymen and apprentices, with the days' events not only read aloud but debated over as well'.[6] The American Revolution had demonstrated the importance of taverns as spaces where the people – and not just their political leadership – could debate political points and find those who shared their own world view. One history of revolutionary America describes how 'accounts from the 1790s contain many reports of taverns filled with Americans singing French revolutionary songs and heatedly discussing the latest political developments in Europe'.[7] The tavern was becoming the parliament of the lower orders. 'Every porter house,' one commentator noted, 'could boast a set of statesmen who, without the aid of education or experience, considered themselves competent to every branch of legislative occupation.'[8]

In Belfast, taverns would quickly carry the names of Dumouriez and Mirabeau, heroes of the French Revolution in the popular mind. This, no doubt, marked out such places to the authorities. While taverns were a vital recruitment ground for the Society of United Irishmen, 'the very public nature of such meetings was probably also the undoing of the organisation'.[9]

In mapping the Dublin taverns frequented by the Society of United Irishmen, a vital tool is the evidence of informers, who kept Dublin Castle abreast of the movement and its protagonists. When the informer Francis Higgins sent a songbook to Dublin Castle, loaded with parodies and patriotic aspirations, he reported that the book was being 'used in taverns, clubs and ale houses where United Traitors frequent'.[10] Informers not only frequented taverns and ale houses, where people talked more freely under the influence of alcohol, but could even come from within the profession. R. R. Madden, historian of the movement, documents a publican who asked his handler to secure payment of his licence for him, 'as he had to give all his money to the brewers and distillers. He adds that his being in business will enable him to do much more good for the cause.'[11]

*An advertisement for Sweetman's Superior Leinster Ale. The Sweetman family were commited members of the Society of United Irishmen and successful brewers in the Irish capital. (Courtesy of the National Library of Ireland)*

# JOHN SWEETMAN & Co's

## SUPERIOR LEINSTER ALE

Whatever the politics of publicans, brewers also held a wide variety of viewpoints. John Sweetman, a member of the Directory of the Society of United Irishmen, would be described as 'an eminent and opulent citizen of Dublin, of an old and highly respectable family'.[12] His Francis Street Brewery was used by the movement as a meeting place, and was the successor to an earlier Sweetman's Brewery beside St Stephen's Green. Sweetman would be arrested at his brewery in March 1798. The Sweetman family – Catholic and republican – could not be further removed culturally from the nearby brewery of Arthur Guinness & Sons.

The pub most synonymous with the movement today is the Brazen Head on Lower Bridge Street, where heroic images of Tone and Emmet – many produced for the 1898 centenary of the 1798 rebellion – abound. Only The Lord Edward at Christ Church, opposite St Werburgh's Church and the final resting place of Lord Edward Fitzgerald, presents a greater assortment of 1898 memorabilia. That year lit a fire in the heart of the young and would-be revolutionary generation, Irish Republican Army (IRA) leader Seán Moylan later recalling how 'the '98 Centenary brought my first vivid lessons in Irish history ... In my mind's eye I saw the Wexford pikemen and the swift fierce onslaught of the French.'[13] It was also a good year to be in the printing business, as the walls of The Lord Edward attest.

On a street that was home to the leading United Irishman Oliver Bond, the Brazen Head was the scene of a lucky escape for some in the movement, when information channelled by one informer led to a raid on Bond's house, as most of the Leinster leadership of the movement met in March 1798. The Wexford representatives, Ruan O'Donnell notes, 'had delayed in the nearby Brazen Head pub long enough to hear the commotion across the street and slipped away with incriminating papers which would have proved the strength of the organisation in their native county'.[14]

At the time of the Lower Bridge Street raid, Tone was in Paris. There he met the English-born radical Thomas Paine, author of *The Rights of Man* and an honorary member of the Society of United

A view of the Brazen Head that is little changed today. (Fáilte Ireland Tourism Photographic Collection, Dublin City Library and Archive)

Irishmen. Tone found Paine to be 'vain beyond all belief, but he has reason to be vain, and for my part I forgive him'. Tone also felt it worth noting that 'he drinks like a fish, a misfortune which I have known to befall other celebrated patriots'. In England, radicals would in time bestow names like The Rights of Man on taverns, though praising Paine too loudly in his own lifetime brought real risk.

Following the crushing of the 1798 revolt and the death of Theobald Wolfe Tone, the revolutionary movement would retreat into the shadows, re-emerging with Robert Emmet's 1803 insurrection. Lore had it that Emmet availed of the Brazen Head as a centre of operations, plotting the subsequent uprising at least partially there and availing of a room that provided him a glimpse of who was approaching the inn, yet by then the institution was very much under the watchful eye of the Castle authorities. Instead, Emmet's movement was to retreat into a series of depots and hidden offices within the warrens of the Liberties, successfully

Colm Keating's photo of former owner Miss Cooney at the Brazen Head. Musician Alph Duggan sits on the other side of the bar.

evading the authorities until bad luck and misfortune forced his men into premature action.

Still, the writer James Plunkett would write in the 1970s of how the Brazen Head 'has retained the aura of its past in a distinctive way. It whispers of conspiracies.'[15] For Myles na gCopaleen – a writer whose real name was Brian O'Nolan and who also wrote under the pen name Flann O'Brien – it was the 'one-time resort of Robert Emmet and the United Irishmen. Here, the most random spit will land on ten centuries of antiquity.'[16] A history of the haunted inns of Britain and Ireland speaks of the Brazen Head and 'the patriot's ghost', a claim repeated in a guide to paranormal Ireland, which says that Robert Emmet is 'reported to still wander the upper floors of the inn'.[17]

On Thomas Street, the White Bull Inn and the Golden Bottle were two other taverns owned by members of the movement. And those seeking the ghost of Tone instead of Emmet may find him at the Tailors' Hall on Back Lane, near Christ Church, a venue where he made many memorable speeches. A public house and restaurant in recent times, Tailors' Hall was long the venue for meetings and assemblies in the city, before falling into disarray. In 1983, the *Irish Times* complained:

> For well over a year now, Tailors Hall has stood empty, cold, damp and open to the elements, the windows open, doors broken and with many break ins. It is a sitting target for anyone who wished to burn it down and for those who wish to vandalise it.[18]

An intriguing (and hostile) account of a United Irish meeting at the venue survives, the writer recalling that 'the very aspect of the place seemed to render it adapted for cherishing a conspiracy. It was in the locality where the tailors, skinners, and curriers held their guilds, and was the region of the operative democracy.' On hearing Tone speak, the outsider 'set him down as a worthy, good-natured, flimsy man, in whom there was no harm, and as the least likely person in the world to do mischief to the state'.[19]

# IN THE BRAZEN HEAD (extract)
**Gerard Smyth**

Under the image of the rebel on the scaffold,
perhaps on the very spot where the plot was hatched,
we sat in a corner of the Brazen Head,
spent long evenings until we came to the dregs,
sharing the company of men of all trades,
fellow-travellers in from the cold, in from the rain,
from nights of frost and the four winds passing
through places soon to be rubble, sites of desecration.
We sat in a Cupid's corner, eavesdropping
on raw music in the backroom: banjo and whistle,
and the balladeers swilling songs
from the cup of tradition: Boulevogue, The Foggy Dew.
All the listeners keeping time, tapping the tunes.

From *The Fullness of Time: New and Selected Poems*
(Dedalus Press, 2010)

# CHAPTER 3.
# HEAVEN AND HELLFIRE

*I have not observed the wit and fancy of this town so much employed in any one article as that of the contriving variety of signs to hang over houses where punch is to be sold ... The animals are sometimes one black lion, and sometimes a couple; sometimes a single eagle and sometimes a spread one; and we often meet a crow, a swan, a bear or a cock, in the same posture ...*[1]

**J**onathan Swift spent plenty of time inside taverns and coffee houses, but this 1732 observation on their exterior signage is an important observation. This list could bring us with the Dean of St Patrick's Cathedral on a walk through the city streets as they once were, passing the Cock and Punch Bowl on Charles Street, the Black Lion on Blind Quay, the Crown and Punch Bowl in Temple Bar and other establishments.

*Drapier's Letters*, a series of pamphlets in which Swift defended Irish industry and currency against English infringement, had brought him the status of a champion of the common people: 'At every street corner, broadsheets and ballads in his honour were sold. Every tavern had its club to celebrate the Drapier, and every convivial meeting rang with choruses in his honour.'[2] Each year, bells would ring and bonfires blaze brightly in the capital to mark Swift's November birthday.[3] When the authorities considered charging Swift with sedition, they were informed in no uncertain terms that 'a substantial army would be needed to storm the grounds of St Patrick's and make the arrest'.[4] Part of what we now call the Liberties was Swift's domain, falling under the jurisdiction of the cathedral. He would write to his friend Alexander Pope:

> I am Lord Mayor of 120 houses, I am absolute lord of the greatest cathedral in the Kingdom, I am at peace with the neighbouring princes – the Lord Mayor of the City and the Archbishop of Dublin; only the latter, like the King of France, sometimes attempts encroachments on my dominions.[5]

The Dean would likely also have encountered taverns named in his own honour – or honouring his pen name – as he walked through the city. His biographer Leo Damrosch notes that 'taverns sprang up called the Drapier's Head, with signs showing Swift in clerical garb'.[6]

Not only did Swift enjoy a drink, he firmly believed in the medicinal benefit of alcohol, writing to a friend of drinking 'a bottle of French wine myself every day ... the only thing that keeps me out of pain'. As Tara McConnell notes in her wonderful entry in the landmark *Irish Food History: A Companion*, Swift jokingly referred to claret as 'Irish wine', not for its origin, but as a nod to the penchant for it amongst his clique.[7] Martyn Cornell, beer historian (a fine profession) and author of a title that is a contender for the best-named book in the genre with *Around the World in 80 Beers*, suggests Swift as the likely author of a denunciation of English porter in the *Dublin Daily Advertiser* of October 1736, when readers were told that it was made of 'the worst Malt, which is sent from all parts of the Country for that Use, and consequently nothing but Gin exceeds it for Badness'.[8] On beer – like trade – Swift was a patriot.

Given his long association with the Liberties, Swift's name remained a fashionable choice for taverns and, later, public houses. To subsequent patriots he remained an inspiration and was evoked in speeches to the College Green Parliament as a defender of Irish interests. There were new heroes in Ireland to name taverns after, like the Dr Franklin Tavern in Belfast, which honoured Benjamin

Franklin, but the Drapier remained eternal. Into recent times, Swift's name has been found with The Dean Swift on Francis Street, while Swift on the corner of Thomas Street and Bridgefoot Street has also returned the Dean to Dublin 8.

Internationally, Swift is honoured with the Swift Hibernian Lounge in New York City, just a short stroll from McSorley's Ale House. Given that one of Swift's causes in his own lifetime was defending Ireland's economy and currency (the Drapier bitterly opposed the introduction of copper halfpence and farthing coins into Ireland), it is fitting that that the depiction of Swift presented in the branding of the NYC bar comes from the £10 Series B banknote, introduced by the Central Bank of Ireland in 1978.

In Swift's time, some behaviour within the walls of Dublin's drinking establishments troubled him and other men of faith. The Blasters, a forerunner to the infamous Dublin Hellfire Club, were explicitly condemned by Swift for blasphemous behaviour and inflammatory iconoclasm. David Ryan, author of a history of these clubs, rightly notes that such groups intended to outrage and shock: 'parties external to the club were also disposed to exaggerate and amplify its supposed diabolism. Innuendos and half-truths concerning its activities circulated in Dublin's social circles, with some proclaiming that the Earl of Rosse "dealt avec le diable". Such rumours provided abundant fuel for the popular press.'[9] They have continued to provide abundant fuel for the imagination of Dubliners too; despite no evidence that the Hellfire Club ever met there, the ruin on Mountpelier Hill continues to attract ghost tours and those seeking out the paranormal.

In reality, Dublin's 1730s Hellfire Club met in Cork Hill's Eagle Tavern (not to be mistaken with the nearby birthplace of the Society of United Irishmen, which later carried the same name). In a time before the existence of what we now call Lord Edward Street, neighbouring Cork Hill was a hive of activity, populated by printers, coffee houses and members' clubs. Dublin's pre-eminent local historian J. T. Gilbert described its drinking scene in his history of the capital:

> The taverns on Cork Hill were The Globe ... The Hoop (1733), in which a musical society used to hold their meetings; The Cock and Punch Bowl (1735), where a Masonic Lodge assembled on every second Thursday; and the Eagle Tavern, one of the most noted in Dublin ... Richard Parsons, first Earl of Rosse, and his associate, James Worsdale, the humorous painter, were reported to have established a 'Hell-fire Club' in the Eagle Tavern about the year 1735.[10]

Ryan's digging unearthed a group of poorly behaved and violent hedonists, acting out even to the point of murder. The brutal killing of an ill sedan chairman, who was set ablaze by the out-of-control Lord Santry, is a factual event that has gone on to be a genesis of mythology and folklore elsewhere. Satanic iconography (such as a Chippendale table described as having 'an unmistakeable carved resemblance on one side of his Satanic Majesty and ... for supporters, which terminate in what look uncommonly like cloven hoofs'[11]) was seen as a provocation and intended primarily as two fingers to the societal norms of the day. In truth, the Hellfire Club comprised violent men protected by their social class and privilege. In understanding Dublin's Hellfire Club and others like it, we might better see in them 'a form of male bonding, where young bored rich people took on libertine and provocative behaviours inspired by Enlightenment radicalism'.[12] To toast Satan was one thing, but to believe in him would be another entirely.

Situated beside the Eagle Tavern, Lucas's Coffee House was at the time a notorious duelling hotspot, with Gilbert describing how 'the yard behind which was the scene of numerous duels; on such occasions the company flocked to the windows to see that the laws of honour were observed, and to lay wagers on the probable survivor of the combatants'.[13] Duelling was considered something of a gentleman's sport, the lawyer and parliamentarian Jonah Barrington remembering in his memoir that:

> It is nearly incredible what a singular passion the Irish gentlemen (though in general excellent tempered fellows) formerly had for

*Jonathan Swift, Dean of St Patrick's Cathedral and toast of many a Dublin ale house. (National Gallery of Ireland)*

fighting each other and immediately becoming friends again. A Duel was indeed considered a necessary piece of a young man's *education*, but by no means a ground for any future animosity with his opponent: – on the contrary, proving the bravery of both, it only cemented their friendship.[14]

Some viewed coffee houses as dangerous places of sedition, where men plotted and schemed against the existing order. The presence of pamphlets and newspapers troubled the authorities, who felt revolutionary or reformist movements could emerge from these premises. When Charles II sought their closure in the London of the 1670s, their defenders pointed to alcohol as a far more dangerous substance:

> It is wine and strong drinks make tumults increase;
> Choc'late, tea, and coffee are liquors of peace:
> No quarrels nor oaths amongst those that drink 'em;
> Tis Bacchus and brewers swear, damn 'em and sink 'em!
> Then, Charles, thy edicts against coffee recall:
> There's ten times more treason in brandy and ale.[15]

Did coffee houses represent a sober alternative to the alehouse? One account of the London scene describes the coffee houses as spaces where 'other beverages such as chocolate, sherbet, tea, ale, beer etc. according to the season' could be enjoyed.[15] While some coffee houses offered alcohol and others did not, the proximity of Lucas's to the many taverns of Cork Hill and its immediate environs ensured it operated as a sort of extension of them. Both the Hellfire Club's tavern of choice and the trigger-happy Lucas's are now gone without trace, as the Wide Streets Commission transformed Cork Hill and its surroundings.

The men who formed the backbone of the Dublin Hellfire Club were not the last to play up to such imagery. Before the modern transformation of the cathedral and its surroundings, nearby Christ Church Cathedral was bordered by narrow laneways and alleys, giving a busyness to the cramped streetscape around it. A section of this district was christened 'Hell', described later by historian Éamonn MacThomáis as 'a small area of taverns and bed-and-breakfast establishments in the Monto style'.[17] In Gilbert's history of Dublin, he quotes the recollections of a visitor to the district:

> This was certainly a very profane and unseemly soubriquet to give to a place that adjoined a Cathedral whose name was Christ Church; and my young mind, when I first entered there, was struck with its unseemliness. Yes, and more especially when over the arched entrance there was pointed out to me the very image of the Devil, carved in oak ... This locale of Hell, and this representation of his Satanic majesty, were famous in those days even beyond the walls of Dublin.[18]

'Hell' was established enough to appear in John Rocque's 1756 map of the city, while its infamy extended beyond Dublin, appearing in the poetry of Scotland's national bard, Robert Burns:

> But this that I am gaun to tell,
> Which lately on a night befell,
> Is just as true as the deil's in hell,
> Or Dublin city.[19]

Closer to home, the Dublin Liberties Whiskey Distillery has named whiskeys 'Oak Devil' and 'King of Hell' in acknowledgement of the area and its lore. Another 'Hell' nearer to the site of the modern-day distillery was considerably less frightening, with the intersection of Dean Street, Patrick Street, New Street and Kevin Street earning the title 'The Four Corners of Hell' owing to the presence of a public house (Kenny's, Quinn's, O'Beirne's and Lowe's) on each corner.[20] Situated right beside Swift's cathedral, it would perhaps appeal to his wit that only one pub occupies the widened intersection now, taking the name The Fourth Corner.

# CHAPTER 4.
# FENIAN CONSPIRACY AND THE PUBLIC HOUSE

**T**he Irish Republican Brotherhood (IRB) lived in the shadows. As a secret society and oath-bound organisation dedicated to the establishment of an independent democratic republic, it operated in a manner not unlike the underground revolutionary societies that existed in a larger urban metropolis like Paris or Berlin in the second half of the nineteenth century. Operating in clandestine 'circles', a member of the organisation was never intended to know who else had taken the oath to the movement beyond those in their immediate group. The Dublin Castle informers had played their part in dismantling the earlier Society of United Irishmen, but this Fenian movement intended to prove themselves a much tougher adversary in the fight for an Irish Republic. It was an organisation that moved quickly and decisively. Just a handful of men met on Dublin's Lombard Street on St Patrick's Day 1858; within nine years, there would be an attempt at revolution in Ireland under their flag.

The Fenian movement, historian Owen McGee noted, 'attempted to recruit people from all social classes and cultivate an egalitarian spirit within its organisation, both to sustain its political resolve and to make a political impact, allowing artisans and labourers, for example, to hold higher positions in the organisation than members of various middle-class professions'.[1] Here was a movement with barmen, not just bar owners, in its ranks. Unsurprisingly, the public houses of Dublin would become entangled in the conspiracy, being a space in which classes mingled and labourers talked freely.

Public houses may seem a decidedly unsuitable location to discuss the business of revolutionary politics. A cynic may even suggest it says something particular of Irish revolutionaries. There is, alas, nothing uniquely Irish about the use of a pub backroom for such serious discussions. On a visit to London in 2024, a friend insisted we visit The Three Johns in Islington. It ticked a lot of London pub boxes, from craft beer to burgers. What separates this pub from the ones around the corner is the fact that the Bolshevik and Menshevik split, which would shape the Russian Revolution to come, had occurred in the back bar in 1903, with both Lenin and Trotsky in attendance. On the other side of the world, alcohol played enough of a role in the American Revolution to inspire Adrian Covert's history, *Taverns of the American Revolution.*

Several public houses associated with the Fenian movement remain in the city, with The Long Hall on George's Street perhaps the most significant. Acquired by the Fenian Joseph Cromien in 1864, the premises carried the name Parker's from a former owner. The veteran Fenian John Devoy would recall in his memoir that 'there were never less than twenty of our men in his place in the evening and often there were as many as fifty, some of whom carried revolvers; so it would take a strong force of police to arrest a man there'.[2]

The Long Hall's entry door sits on George's Street, but at its rear is Dublin Castle and Ship Street, home to British army barracks in the nineteenth century. The proximity of the public house to the centre of British rule and a garrisoned presence of soldiers may seem a hindrance, but for the Fenian movement it also offered opportunities. Keen to infiltrate the ranks of the British army in Ireland, the movement sought to meet soldiers on an individual basis, with sympathetic public houses a favoured location. Patrick O'Leary, himself a veteran soldier of the American-Mexican War, was an enthusiastic recruiter of soldiers into the movement. His recruitment technique has been described as 'simple, but effective; IRB men in the army introduced their friends, to minimise the risk of betrayal'.[3] To his contemporaries, O'Leary was better known as 'Pagan O'Leary', owing to his hostility to the Christian churches. In John Devoy's brilliant recollections of the movement, we are told:

> His eccentricity took the form of a sort of religious mania. He hated Rome and England with equal intensity, and his queer notion was that after driving out the English, Ireland should return to the old Paganism. He was not really a Pagan, but an anti-Roman Catholic ... The Pagan had his particular grievances against St. Patrick, which made him drop the name. He claimed that the Apostle of Ireland had demoralized the Irish by teaching them to forgive their enemies.[4]

The Pagan was, John O'Leary remembered, 'during all this time a strict teetotaller'.[5] Beyond his eccentricities, he was respected in the movement for his ability to recruit. So many of the men stationed in Inchicore's Richmond Barracks had joined the movement that Devoy would recall 'our men were in the majority'.[6] On James's Street and Thomas Street, a network of clandestine public houses allowed these men a space to meet with Fenian recruiters like the Pagan O'Leary, beyond the gaze of their military officers. There was logic to the selected locations, as 'we selected public houses owned or managed by friends, and changed them frequently when we had reason to believe we had attracted too much attention'.[7]

Following the American Civil War (1861–5), a new kind of Fenian was concerning the authorities on the streets of Dublin. Described as 'Americanised Celts', their distinctive facial hair and imported fashions caught the attention of many, and so did their swagger. To one contemporary:

> I found that for every one who came from New York, three came from Massachusetts. They seemed to me to court arrest, for they were singularly rude and insolent, swaggering through the streets, jostling the passers-by, and walking at a rapid pace three or four abreast when the footpath was crowded during the fashionable hours for promenading or shopping.[8]

While many of these veterans were Union soldiers, a small minority had fought for the Confederacy. The most dynamic of them all was Colonel Thomas J. Kelly, who had fought with the Union's 10th Ohio Regiment and who was dispatched to Ireland to inspect the military capabilities of the movement at home. As he lived on Grantham Street, The Bleeding Horse would become his public house of operations. It quickly became one of the pubs described in a courtroom as 'known to the police to be the rendezvous of Fenians throughout the city'.[9]

The experience of the veterans of the Civil War offered opportunities to the movement. Devoy remembered introducing some of them to men the Fenians had recruited from the British army, to teach them specific lessons on what form war would take in future. Customers enjoying a drink in one city-centre pub, right beside what is now the National Gallery of Ireland, had no clue what was occurring over their heads on one occasion:

> … in the private parlour of Peter Curran, over his public house in Clare Lane. Here I gathered about twelve men each from the Fifth Dragoon Guards and the Tenth Hussars for a conference with Captain McCafferty, who had been an officer in Moseby's

The veteran Fenian John O'Leary, depicted here by John Butler Yeats, detailed in his memoir the importance of public houses to the movement. (National Gallery of Ireland)

Guerrillas in the Confederate Army … in a few brief words and with a very quiet manner, he told them what could be done by insurgent cavalry under existing circumstances in Ireland.[10]

Throughout 1866, the authorities gradually moved in on the Fenian movement. Cromien was arrested at his premises, suggesting that informers had made their way into the pub we now call The Long Hall. His mugshot survives, along with the description of him as 'spirit-retailer, Kept a meeting house for the Fenians in Dublin'. These images, showing some of the first prisoners in Ireland to be photographed in such a way, represent a critical moment in the history of photography here, concerned primarily with the purpose of state intelligence.[11]

The public house went from a place of recruitment to one of paranoia throughout the repression of 1866. At Hoey's on Bridgefoot Street, a well-known meeting place for the movement, an informer was shot during trials, 'but though hit by three bullets none of them touched a vital spot and he was not killed'.[12] The press reported that a raid at Pillsworth's public house on James's Street 'resulted in the capture of eighteen persons charged with Fenianism. No fewer than eleven of them were soldiers. The rest were civilians of the artisan class. Three of them were armed with loaded revolvers.'[13] Amongst the arrested men was John Devoy. The same report noted that the authorities were furious at the 'too common practice of soldiers attending certain public houses in Dublin known to be the resort of Fenian agents, and have accordingly given orders in dictating several of such places which soldiers are henceforth forbidden to enter'.[14] The pub, which had long been of interest to the authorities, was described in a police report as a place where 'desperate and determined men met nightly … for treasonable purposes'.[15] The primary appeal of this particular pub was that 'a large room at the back of the pub had two exits, one of which went through the adjoining building so that those who secretly met there felt they could escape in the event of the raid'.[16]

When the Fenian insurrection did come in March 1867, it happened in a very different terrain from Dublin city, with fighting in the hills around Tallaght and what were then sleepy rural villages like Stepaside and Glencullen. In the repression which followed, public houses were raided across the city. In one raid on a Camden Street pub, the arrested men included several bricklayers, a wood carver, a tailor's porter, an engine fitter, a bookkeeper and a clerk.[17]

Cromien would remain an active Fenian in the United States, but his departure from Dublin marked the end of the public house he had run as a revolutionary centre of sedition. Later owners would all bring their own mark to the pub, with Patrick Dolan responsible for much of the fitting in the early 1880s that survives to this day within The Long Hall.

Joseph Cromien, proprietor of what is now The Long Hall, photographed in Mountjoy Prison. (New York Public Library)

Joseph Cromien, Spirit-retailer, kept a meeting house for the Fenians in Dublin.

At the same time as Dolan was refitting his public house, Fenians were again plotting revolution in Dublin establishments. The very word 'Fenian' in late nineteenth-century political discourse recalled not the insurrection of 1867, but the Phoenix Park assassinations of May 1882, an event that shook the British political establishment and almost led to the downfall of a government. Lord Frederick Cavendish and Thomas Burke, Chief Secretary and Under Secretary for Ireland, while strolling in the Phoenix Park, were stabbed to death by members of the Irish National Invincibles, best described as a secret-society-within-a-secret-society.[18] As in earlier times, publicans had been recruited into the movement, with Dorset Street publican James Mullett sworn in on the plot.

The chief meeting place of the Invincibles was Wrenn's on Dame Street, a public house located literally across the street from the epicentre of British rule in Ireland, within sight of the Palace Street gates of Dublin Castle. Today known as Brogan's, the pub still has its distinctive appearance, owing to the surviving entrance to the neighbouring Crampton Court laneway.

Wrenn's achieved a certain infamy because of its connection to the killings. During the trials of the Invincibles, in which the testimony of informers led to the hanging of five men in Kilmainham Gaol, Wrenn's was repeatedly raised as a centre of the conspiracy. As late as 1969, a guidebook to the pubs of the city noted that 'it was also the last pub in which the Invincibles had a drink before leaving for Phoenix Park'.[19]

One of the finest historical images of a Dublin public house shows the premises, photographed by Thomas H. Mason & Sons photographers, as the 'public house where the Invincibles had met'. The photograph is a fantastic Dublin time capsule, not least for the style of the generally curious Dubliners who stand in front of what was then O'Brien Bros. We also see the name of Dan Lowrey, the creator of the Star of Erin music hall and theatre, a site today known as the Olympia Theatre. In Lowrey's 1880s music hall, his

J. Mullet's public house, a meeting place for the Invincibles. (Courtesy of the National Library of Ireland)

'particular brand of Irishry was tinged with the memory of the peasant Pikeman of the past and the wearing of the green'.[20] In its more recent incarnation, The Dubliners took to the stage of the Olympia on many occasions, belting out songs like 'Take Her Up To Monto' that speak of the Invincibles and their actions, and how 'it wasn't very sensible to tell on the Invincibles'. These words were sung just a few metres from the public house where the Phoenix Park plan was partially hatched.

In the 1860s and again in the 1880s, the public house was a core place of importance to the Fenian movement. Though quieter years followed, public houses remained entangled with the movement. In Phibsborough, The Hut has been noted as 'a haunt of advanced nationalists' in the closing years of the nineteenth century.[21] The later revolutionary generation could, on occasion, be dismissive of what had come before and the drinking culture around it. Dan Breen, one of those said to have begun the Irish War of Independence in January 1919, would speak of how:

> My father, I believe, was also nationally disposed and his people had all been Fenians, but the impression I gained was that he belonged to a type of Fenian who did more talk than anything else … I have heard it said of the people that he represented that they were great fellows for talking and drinking and doing very little after that but, on the other hand, I suppose there was little they could do in their day.[22]

But talking and drinking could, as The Long Hall and Brogan's remind us, sometimes lead to much more.

The pub at 75 Dame Street, now home to Brogan's, was photographed owing to its connections to the Invincibles story. (Courtesy of National Library of Ireland)

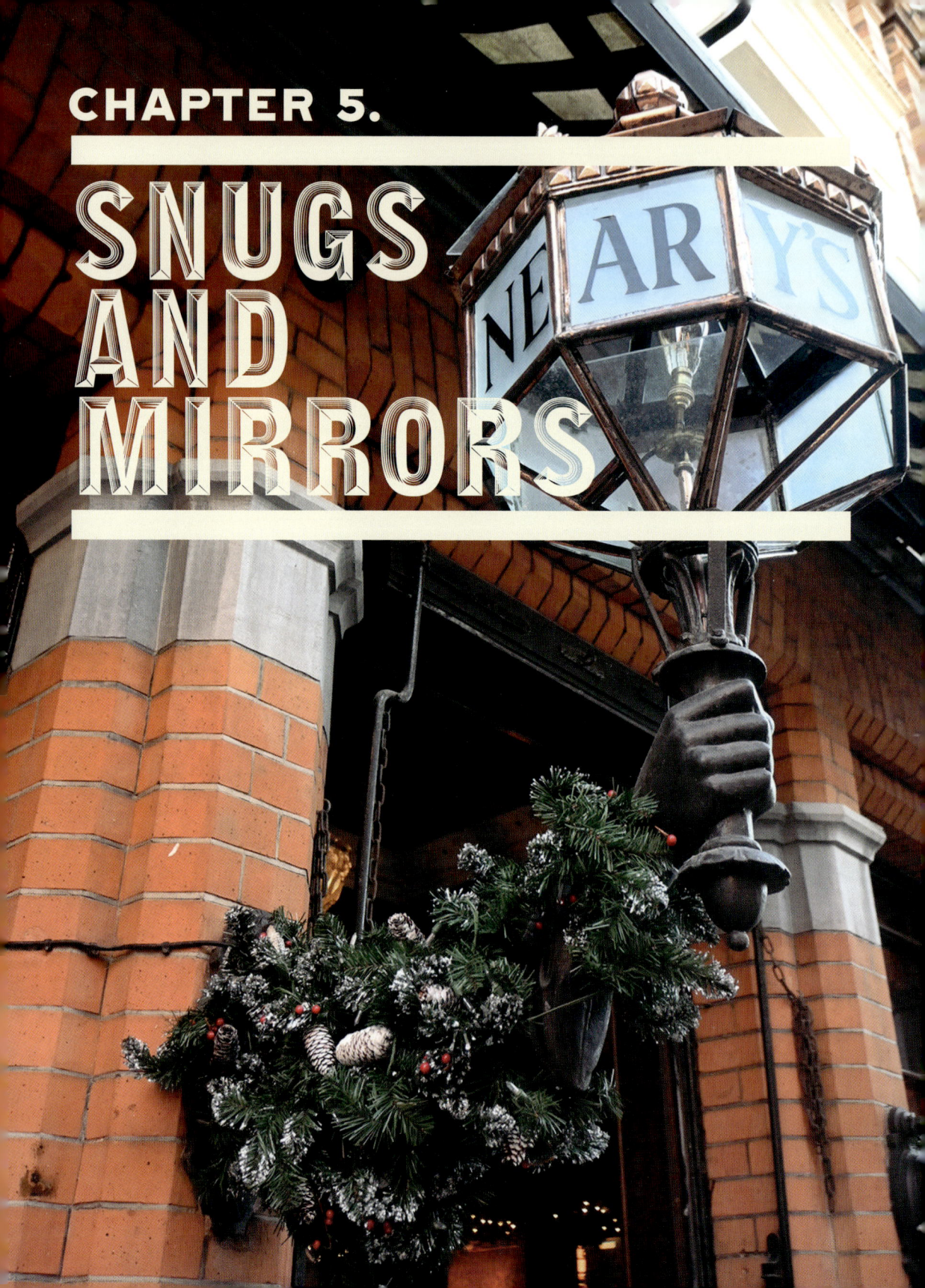

# CHAPTER 5.
# SNUGS AND MIRRORS

**T**he impressive thing about some of Dublin's most highly regarded public houses aesthetically is not that they survived the revolution, but rather that they survived the 1970s. In early 1981, the *Irish Independent* complained of the new kind of pub, sometimes emerging in the shell of the old. Gone was the bar; the lounge had arrived:

> You could land an aeroplane in the middle of the lounges ... What has happened to the old fashioned, cosy intimacy which characterised public houses in the past? From the mid-fifties they succumbed to cheap plastic modernity or at least too many of them did. To the Victorians goes the honour of inventing the pub ... The customers were almost incarcerated in mahogany-built snugs, but they were cosy nooks for pleasurable imbibing, conversing or even doing business.[1]

One of the most striking features of any Dublin public house exterior are these decorative lamp standards at Neary's.

A public house interior does not have to be Victorian or Edwardian to be appreciated. The stylised motifs and sleek lines of the Art Deco period have lent a beautiful modernist touch to public houses across these islands, while ornate plasterwork and more from the Georgian era has survived in places. For a city that has shaken off most mentions of Victoria (The Patriot's Inn in Kilmainham, located right beside the gaol, was once The Victoria Tavern in her honour), Dublin is still rightly proud of the Victorian pubs it houses. Yet there is little agreement on just how many pubs in the capital fit the criteria, while a complete list may be impossible to compose, as elements have been lost even if some fabric remains.

Certainly, such pubs exist well beyond the city centre. Cleary's public house on Inchicore's Sarsfield Road, dating from the middle of the nineteenth century, has a distinctive cast-iron railing on its parapet, the words 'THE GREAT SOUTHERN & WESTERN RAILWAY HOUSE' still clear today. It is a reminder that the railway itself was one of the great advances of the Victorian age, and something that facilitated the expansion and connectivity of Irish cities. In his history of the Victorian city, historian Michael Barry rightly points out that, for Dublin, this period consisted of 'the formative years in which were created the foundations of the modern city'.[2] Not all changes were good, and Dublin conceded much ground economically to Belfast, but we are still surrounded by the nineteenth century. The rise of the townships, Dublin's first suburbs, was truly transformative for life in the capital. Some of the city's best-preserved Victorian-era pubs are found in areas that were once considered beyond the city itself.

Taking George Orwell's description of the perfect pub, we find something not unlike some of the celebrated Dublin public houses discussed here. For him, writing in 1946, it was a place whose:

> ... whole architecture and fittings are uncompromisingly Victorian. It has no glass-topped tables or other modern miseries, and, on the other hand, no sham roof-beams, ingle-nooks or plastic panels

An archival view of John Kehoe's public house on South Anne Street. (Fáilte Ireland Tourism Photographic Collection, Dublin City Library and Archive)

masquerading as oak. The grained woodwork, the ornamental mirrors behind the bar, the cast-iron fireplaces, the florid ceiling stained dark yellow by tobacco-smoke, the stuffed bull's head over the mantelpiece – everything has the solid, comfortable ugliness of the nineteenth century.[3]

There is little in the way of 'ugliness' to my mind in what Orwell describes, and much of it is still familiar. Absent from his appraisal, however, is the snug – to many a quintessential feature of the nineteenth-century pub. 'The old conception of the intimate type of pub with quiet snugs is dying a rapid death,' the *Irish Examiner* told readers in 1964. Despite the best efforts of some, many have survived.

What defines a snug? These wooden compartments, generally to the side of the bar, often contain a hatch through which communication with bar staff and the ordering of drinks is possible. Many snugs were – and are – also capable of being locked from within, thus ensuring privacy, something added to by high panels or frosted glass. The best examples – one of which survives at Kehoe's pub on South Anne Street – even included separate entrances from the street.

These separate entrances remind us that public houses also sold more than just alcohol in the Victorian era; with many public houses also operating as grocers and tea merchants, these doors allowed women to shop on the premises without having to enter the bar environment. Drawers behind the bar in several Dublin public houses still attest to this dual purpose, while differences in the height of bar and grocery counters – noticeable for example

(L) A match striker inside the snug of Walsh's of Stoneybatter. (With thanks to Rory Mulvaney)

(R) Separate entrances to snug and bar are still visible at Kehoe's on South Anne Street.

Entrance to the snug inside The Palace bar, Fleet Street.

in Stoneybatter's Walsh's — also remind us that one business could play multiple roles, even in the lives of a family.

In popular memory, snug spaces facilitated women within the male preserve of the public house, but there were others who wished to avail of the privacy of such a space. There are references to snugs in the testimonies of those who participated in the Irish Revolution, as places where clandestine meetings could be held.

Other touches of the Victorian age in public houses can include match-strikers alongside counters (there are particularly good examples at Ryan's on Parkgate Street) and the presence of gas lamps, a reminder of another great advance of the nineteenth century. Such lighting created what public house historian Eamonn Casey describes as 'distinctive yellow haloed light shimmering and casting flittering shadows over deep grained mahogany walls'.[4] Even today, lighting (or the lack thereof) can create distinctive atmosphere in a public house space. Nothing can empty a pub like the switching on of the 'big light'.

These pubs also boast fine craftmanship in the form of decorative features like stained-glass windows and fine clocks; in the case of The Long Hall, its beautiful Wekler & Schlegel clock has been described as giving one 'the illusion of being in a Victorian train station'.[5] Pubs also abounded with beautiful advertising mirrors and branded stained glass, a popular form of advertising in the Victorian age, with particularly good examples surviving at Gaffney & Son in Fairview and The Palace on Fleet Street. In both, we see D. W. D. promoted; the Dublin Whiskey Distillery on Jones Road was established in 1872.

Mosaic tiled floors are now a rare feature of public houses, but a beautiful example can still be found at The Swan on Aungier Street, depicting the bird that gives the public house its

A rare advertising mirror for D. W. D. whiskey at Gill's pub, Russell Street.

Mosaic detail at entrance to The Swan, Aungier Street.

name, complete with the knocks and damage of time. With their countertops, partitions, mosaic tiled floors and fine clocks, J. P. Donleavy would argue that 'except that they left every customer pissing in debt, most Dublin pubs if they resembled anything at all, resembled banks. Stout mahogany doors, frosted glass windows etched with legends, "Whiskey Bonders, Sherry Importers"'.**6**

There is no uniform style of 'Victorian pub'. Some of the pubs mentioned existed within what had previously been residential dwellings, or in buildings that still housed people. To sit upstairs in Kehoe's on South Anne Street is to enjoy a pint in what was once the living quarters of a family. Other public houses were purpose-built, or rebuilt. The Stag's Head, at a site acquired by successful merchant George Tyson, was designed lavishly by the architect Alfred Ignatius McGloughlin of Great Brunswick Street (now Pearse Street), opening in its present form in 1895. Tyson sought a pub that might bear 'favourable comparison with the best establishments of its kind either in London or in any other part of England'.**7** McGloughlin later worked as an architectural draughtsman for the team behind the construction of New York's landmark Singer Building, and his Dame Court pub is testament to his ability as an architect. With its stained glass, mahogany counter

An advertising mosaic for The Stag's Head, Dame Street.

complete with polished stone top, fine joinery and wall-mounted stags' heads, it is the kind of Victorian interior Orwell would recognise from his description of the perfect pub.

If the Victorian-era snug was all about sneaking into the pub and not being seen, it shouldn't be entirely surprising that pubs with the very opposite intention would also emerge in time. In 1994, as Ireland was on the verge of the Celtic Tiger, the *Sunday Independent* noted:

> ... pubs like The Globe and Thomas Read's have changed all that. Here the idea is to see and be seen. Huge windows of clear glass give onto the street so that everyone knows you're there and, more important, you can keep an eye on what's going on in the street.[8]

Now, the snug is very much back in fashion. Rather than stripping them out, there are good examples of newly added snugs in the city, for example at the King's Inn and The Flowing Tide. It's a great thing to hear a friend is at the pub ahead of you, the pints already ordered. It's a blessing when they've got the snug.

Stained-glass windows are one of the many touches that make The Stag's Head interior so memorable. (Courtesy of photographer Andy Sheridan)

# CHAPTER 6.
# EASTER WEEK

A view towards the destroyed Middle Abbey Street and The Oval. (From Thomas Johnson Westropp collection. Courtesy of the Royal Irish Academy)

**T**he Oval, near the intersection of Middle Abbey Street and O'Connell Street, has always recalled for me Michael O'Riordan's memoir of the Spanish Civil War. One of those in the ranks of the International Brigades, who had gone to Spain in support of the Spanish Republic and in opposition to the coup of Franco, O'Riordan had no illusions about where popular support lay in 1930s Ireland. The Brigadistas returned home to Westland Row train station largely unnoticed:

> A curious crowd of onlookers at the station watched as the returning volunteers and the welcoming party formed up in marching order, and led by a single piper, set out for Abbey Street corner, where on a lorry in the midst of a downpour stood Father Michael O'Flanagan. To the small audience he spoke the words of welcome to those back from Spain. The meeting over, the participants adjourned to The Oval Bar to drink, relax and exchange all the news that had built up in Spain and Ireland.[1]

Twenty years earlier, it was fighting closer to home that worried the proprietor of The Oval. Established in 1820, the pub found itself an unwilling protagonist in the story of the Easter Rising, like many of its neighbouring businesses. A walk from the Abbey Street Luas stop to The Oval reveals the scale of destruction in the area. At Spar, a plaque recalls that the premises was previously home to the Royal Hibernian Academy (RHA), where more than 500 pieces of art were destroyed. Much is still owed to the RHA's Keeper, Joseph Malachy Kavanagh, who ran from the burning building, saving the charter, some important documentation and the president's medal. On the other side of the street, the Permanent TSB occupies the former Hibernian Bank, totally reconstructed in the aftermath of the rebellion and now carrying a memorial plaque to a Volunteer killed in the fighting. The Oval also boasts a plaque on its exterior, noting that the pub was rebuilt after the Easter Rising.

John J. Egan, proprietor of The Oval, had acquired the premises in 1902. Over the course of a year he refitted the pub, before reopening in 1903. The challenges of the Rising proved more substantial, however, and it would be six years before the doors opened once again.

As was the case for The Palace on Fleet Street, The Oval benefited from the presence of many offices around it connected to the newspaper trade. Independent House was home to the *Irish Independent*, *Evening Herald* and other titles, while the *Freeman's Journal* was one of several other newspapers that called Middle Abbey Street home.

For The Oval and businesses like it, the first threat to overcome was not the artillery shells raining down on the street, but the fires started deliberately by looters. If children behaved predictably in looting Lawrence's toy shop and Noblett's sweet store, adults were just as predictable in what lured them to smash a glass window. On the tenth anniversary of the Rising, a Volunteer would recall in the pages of *An tÓglach*:

A commemorative plaque at The Oval, Middle Abbey Street.

The looters had pillaged a public house opposite the GPO in Henry Street, and a woman offered the Volunteers some bottles of stout. These were refused by all except one man, who took a bottle and had it to his lips when an officer appeared on the scene and smashed it to pieces. Having referred to the order on the subject he announced that the next men found taking a drink without permission would be shot without warning. Such measures had their effect.[2]

The leaders of the Easter Rising were haunted by what had occurred on the streets of Dublin during Emmet's rebellion on Thomas Street in 1803. The historian R. R. Madden would describe the 'motley assemblage of armed men, a great number of whom were, if not intoxicated, under the evident excitement of drink'.[3]

Now, drink would be kept away not only from the rank and file, but also from the citizenry. A traveller enjoying a drink in a public house near Amiens Street station would describe to a reporter the shutting down of the establishment on the first day of the Rising, and how a pub was emptied of costumers:

> No closing was ever obeyed in the Metropolis with such alacrity. When proceeding through the doorway, a glance back showed the men with rifles turning on the taps, and a minute or so later barrel after barrel of stout was rolled out, and the contents emptied in the gutter. He understood this happened universally in the centre of the city.[4]

Around O'Connell Street, the same scene was playing out in different bars. The Ship on Lower Abbey Street – which gets several mentions in *Ulysses* – would be destroyed in the fighting, a Ladbrokes bookies now occupying its rebuilt site. The pub had long been known as a popular meeting place for nationalists, with one later recalling going there to catch a glimpse of Arthur Griffith, being in awe of the 'small, broad-shouldered, stockily built man with a large moustache, drinking stout with a few friends' who they found in a corner.[5] Now, the same premises was being emptied of customers in the name of the Irish Republic. It was a source of pride to one Volunteer that 'a few of the men I was in company with, although hardened drinkers, were stationed in The Ship Tavern, and had the taking of anything that was there, but not touch anything and refused the offerings of the barmen'.[6]

Drink played its role in the drama on Sackville Street that day. Seán O'Casey described the sight, as 'through broken windows, all the treasures of India, Arabia and Samarkand were open before them ... All who were underdressed before were overdressed now, and for the first time in their frosty lives the heat of good warm things encircled them.'[7]

The 1916 Proclamation is displayed on the outer wall of Dame Tavern, Dame Lane. Initially a commemorative feature for the centenary year, it has become a permanent addition to the laneway.

As public houses were being systematically emptied around Sackville Street, one beside the Grand Canal was becoming an important strategic position in the fight. At Davy's (still trading as the Portobello Bar), a member of staff who also happened to be in the ranks of the Irish Citizen Army was among those who seized the premises. Given the pub's proximity to the Rathmines barracks, the Volunteers hoped to frustrate efforts by soldiers to enter the city. There is plenty of humour in how Max Caulfield describes the taking over of the premises, as young bar worker Jim Joyce quits his job in the most spectacular style:

Joyce strutted forward masterfully. 'Old Davy', putting down the pint, banged the counter with his fist and roared 'I'm giving you a week's notice, Joyce!' 'And I'm giving you five minutes, Mister Davy!' shouted Joyce, raising his rifle and opening fire at the bottles on the shelves. As Davy ducked in terror, glass showering around him, his customers ran for their lives.[8]

Enforcing the closure of public houses was one thing, but keeping the public out of them afterwards proved more challenging, especially as the fighting itself intensified and resources had to be directed elsewhere. Things were still relatively calm on Tuesday, when, a Volunteer remembered, 'some women handed bottles of stout to the members of the Citizen Army occupying the windows of the GPO'.[9] These were promptly emptied.

By the Thursday, the fourth day of the proclaimed Irish Republic, the clear danger of being on the street was still not enough to keep some Dubliners at home. Leslie Price, a member of Cumann na mBan, recalled how 'I turned into Parnell Street and came up to a public house in front of the Rotunda, Conway's I think, at the corner of a laneway. People were drinking away. They had looted the public house.'[10] For many years, a plaque on the closed-down Conway's would erroneously claim to be the site of Patrick Pearse's surrender at the end of the Rising. The real action there that week was much less heroic.

Wisely, Dublin Fire Brigade's Chief Officer, Thomas Purcell, had removed his men from the line of fire, and could only watch what he termed 'the Great Fire' take hold from the vantage point of the observation tower at Tara Street fire station. When it was relatively safe to return his men to the streets of the capital, he looked to brewers and distillers for help, knowing that they maintained their own fire services owing to the dangers of production. The job at hand was to save Jervis Street Hospital:

> I was informed that the fires were spreading closely in the direction of the hospital, that sparks were raining on the glass roof of their

veranda, and they said that if I could not do something to stop the fire's course then I must make immediate arrangements for the removal of the patients.

To the firemen's credit, they one and all declared that they would save the hospital, even under the bullets. We immediately hurried our available force out, recovered our engines and other apparatus from O'Connell Bridge, and started on for the big fight. I also called for the assistance of any available men and apparatus from Mssrs. Powers' Distillery and Guinness's Brewery. Both sections kindly responded to the appeal, and sent men and means which I ordered to work at various points. We fought during all Saturday night, stopping the fire where it was possible to stop it, and saved the hospital.[11]

In such a crisis, public houses were far from the priority of Purcell and his men.

For the Dublin Reconstruction Committee, which included City Architect C. J. McCarthy, the task of reconstructing the Sackville Street area began almost immediately, but encountered external obstacles that slowed progress. It was reported in May 1917 that The Oval was one of thirty-four buildings for which plans had been approved. The great challenge was posed by the world war:

In view of the state of affairs and the urgency of material for war work, the deputation were urged not to give any encouragement to the use of any more timber than was absolutely necessary, and they were asked to impress upon builders, architects and others that in their own interest and with a view to getting their work forward they ought wherever possible reduce the amount of timber to a minimum.[12]

Built to the designs of architect L. A. McDonnell (also responsible for Dublin Zoo's Haughton House and the beautiful elaborate shopfront at 10 Anglesea Street in Temple Bar), The Oval was restored to former glories. Another McDonnell building, Nagle's at 25 North Earl Street (now the site of Madigan's) was a public house that had a particularly bad experience during the Rising, with looting and arson. It's almost certain the bottles of stout that were handed to the Volunteers in the window of the GPO came from there. The raiding of Nagle's was something of a spectacle, historian Padraig Yeates noting that 'when the looters had partaken of the ardent spirits some of them beat each other with bottles so violently that they were under necessity of having their wounds dressed in hospital'.[13]

Some public houses were lucky, even as the shells rained down around them. At 33 Henry Street, the Tower Bar (today Lush cosmetics shop) sat right beside Henry Place, scene of the dramatic evacuation of the GPO garrison towards the end of the rebellion. Frank Burke remembered that, 'as the street was being swept by machine gun fire from the Mary Street direction, we had to make a dash across in ones and twos into Henry Place'.[14] Despite its proximity to the action, and the fact that looters helped themselves to the Tower Bar's contents, the building still survived the week. A few short years later, in the days of the Black and Tans, the young poet Austin Clarke would be on the premises when the pub was raided. Jostled, searched and sent on his way, it nonetheless gave him a taste of what it must have been like to live the life of a revolutionary:

> After ten minutes, nothing seditious was found ... As we left the public house, we saw to our surprise that a large crowd had gathered outside. Instantly it divided and, chatting nonchalantly, we sauntered past the admiring throng until we got around the corner where we burst out laughing. For twenty seconds we had felt the thrill which Éamonn de Valera, Sean Lemass and other heroes have known so often.[15]

Tower Bar, Henry Street. (G. & T. Crampton Photograph Archive, University College Dublin Library)

## CHAPTER 7.
# MONTO'S REVOLUTIONARY PUB

**I**n the Mansion House on Dawson Street, official portraits of those who have held the office of lord mayor of Dublin gaze down on the visitor. For reasons of space their time on the wall is limited, as someone new steps into the role with each passing year, displacing a former lord mayor.

Only two former holders of the office are permanently honoured. Kathleen Clarke, Dublin's first female lord mayor (1939–41), is shown wearing the 'Chain of Conscience', refusing to wear the chain of office emblazoned with the face of King William III. Elsewhere, we find Alfred Byrne. Ten-time lord mayor of the city, he is undoubtedly the name most synonymous with the office. Known as the 'Shaking Hand of Dublin', an obituary noted how 'his passage through the city was an almost continuous salutation. He knew everyone, and nearly everyone knew him'.[1]

Before entering politics with the Home Rule movement of the day – which campaigned for self-government for Ireland within the United Kingdom of Great Britain and Ireland – Byrne was a barman and later, from 1909, a publican, overseeing the Verdon Bar on Talbot Street.[2] Adoration for Byrne was not universal; the labour leader James Larkin would accuse him of using drink to win votes, and of supporting those who blacklegged against his union during disputes. To Larkin, he was 'Mr. Bung Byrne, of the scab shelter, the Verdon Bar'.[3] For the teetotal Larkin, who had campaigned against the paying of dockers and other labourers in public houses, the publican Byrne was one of those who embodied a nationalism he detested.[4] 'Publicans,' Larkin's newspaper *The Irish Worker* insisted, 'run this city, govern this city … everything is made subservient to the interest of the drink seller.'[5] While Larkin was broadly adored by those who wore the red hand badge of his union in the north inner city, his crusade against the public house was one issue on which many in the rank and file broke ranks. A contemporary recalled that 'more than one drunken docker went head first down the steps of Liberty Hall with Larkin the propelling force'.[6] In the north inner city, both Larkin and Byrne held sway, sometimes even in the same hearts.

By 1918, Byrne was more than a city councillor, representing the Irish Parliamentary Party in the Westminster Parliament. However, in that year he learned that victory at the ballot box was not always guaranteed. With the General Election, the first since before the First World War and the Easter Rising, a sweeping victory for the youthful Sinn Féin marked a nail in the coffin of the Irish Parliamentary Party. It was, in the words of one contemporary observer, the 'triumph of the young over the old'.[7]

Thomas Leahy, a member of the Irish Citizen Army who pounded the pavements for Sinn Féin in the General Election, recounted how:

> Alfie Byrne was the sitting member and Phil Shanahan the proposed. We had all our work cut out in that Ward, for it was the biggest industrial area in Dublin, composed mostly of the ex-British soldier element, whose wives looked on Alfie Byrne

## HARBOUR DIVISION.

# VOTE FOR PHILIP SHANAHAN

**[SINN FEIN CANDIDATE]**

**AND STRIKE A BLOW FOR COMPLETE INDEPENDENCE**

Printed by The Gaelic Press, 30 Up. Liffey St., Dublin, and published by Michael A. Corrigan, Solicitor, 208 Great Brunswick Street, Dubli... tion Agent for Philip Shanahan

*An election poster for publican Philip Shanahan from the 1918 General Election. (Courtesy of the National Library of Ireland)*

as a tin god; so, knowing what was in front of us, we got a very strong group of men and women to organise an election committee and Phil himself worked hard, not for himself, but for the Republic. As he often reminded his followers, he was a soldier and not a politician.[8]

A soldier, yes, but also a publican. Philip Shanahan – born in Tipperary in 1874 – had gone out in Easter Week to have 'a crack at the English'. He would discover that his licensed premises, on the corner of Foley Street and Corporation Street in the heart of a district known as the Monto, could come to play a more significant part in the Irish Revolution than his own involvement in the physical fight. It offered a place for planning, holding meetings and storing arms.

The name of the district derived from Montgomery Street, its physical heart and a street renamed by a Dublin Corporation keen to confront its unsavoury reputation. By the time of the Irish Revolution, the area was in decline, as the Corporation had begun constructing public housing within it and demolishing the past to make way for the future. The writer Seamus de Burca recalled that 'prostitutes were driven into the back rooms and alleys'.[9] In truth, brothels were still visible and sometimes even prominent, but there was a broader social mix emerging, and a clear plan of transformation.

The Monto – in the mind of Irish nationalists at least – thrived because of the garrison presence in Dublin. The British army, the fictional Leopold Bloom tells us in *Ulysses*, was 'an army rotten with venereal disease'. In the song 'Hey Johnny McGory', we meet a wandering soldier, who has (mostly) returned from the First World War:

> Hey, Johnny McGory
> Tell me where's your glory gone
> I saw you up in the Monto
> With your old leg gone
> A dirty Flanders bullet
> Sure it left you half a man
> Hey, Johnny McGory
> Where's your old leg gone.

Geography points to other factors that influenced the district beyond the British army; with a nearby train station at Amiens Street, and the docks in close proximity, the Monto was in a place of transience, as red-light districts often are. De Burca captured that brilliantly, recalling an earlier time when the district was at its height, and certain times of year would bring more and more men to it:

> Punchestown or Fairyhouse Races Week brought a spate of jovial summer visitors in Derby and boater [popular hat styles], and they drove to the brothels in open carriages. Country businessmen and gentleman farmers, tipsy and jealous of their 'good name', came in closed cabs when darkness had fallen. Soldiers strolled into the districts in twos, threes and droves to seek their fleeting pleasures. The half-circular fanlights of the flashy houses on one side of the street bore the names of their various madams: May Oblong, Mrs. Hayes, Mrs Sheppard, Mrs. Mack.[10]

Sex drove many men to Monto, but so did the opportunity to drink outside normal licensing hours. Frank Wearen, who grew up around the area, told oral historian Kevin C. Kearns that 'the owner of a kip house, she'd always have a bottle or two of whiskey hid so if you wanted a drink, or you wanted to treat your woman to a drink, well, she had the drink for you – and you paid the highest price for it'.[11]

Shanahan's pub became a popular meeting place for republicans during the War of Independence (1919–21), who met primarily in the drawing room over the establishment, while the public bar downstairs offered opportunities too. Luke Kennedy, a member of the Irish Republican Brotherhood, recalled that 'we procured quite a large number of arms by purchasing them from British military. A lot of British soldiers [frequented] Phil Shanahan's public house and it was there most of the contacts were made.'[12] Dan Breen would recall how careless soldiers might leave items of value behind them in the Monto:

> The lady prostitutes used to pinch the guns and ammunition from the Auxiliaries or Tans at night, and then leave them for us at Phil Shanahan's public house. I might add that there was no such thing as payment for these transactions, and any information they had gave us.[13]

The pub was especially popular with Tipperary republicans owing to Shanahan's own background. One recounting being there in November 1920, as the war was reaching the height of its drama, and on the eve of Bloody Sunday:

> Suddenly, a fine big athletic looking fellow bounded in and spoke to Phil and was introduced to us. This was Mick Collins whom I met then for the first time. He impressed me as a man full of energy and competence and he talked casually with us while he drank a bottle of stout.[14]

For arms and messages, Shanahan's was a vital connection between those fighting the war in the rural terrain of Tipperary and County Dublin. There were dramatic days in the public houses of Monto and the surrounding area during the War of Independence, with Shanahan's raided by Auxiliaries on several occasions. A December 1920 report noted that 'this is about the fifth time that Mr. Shanahan's house has been raided, and on no occasion was anything found there'.[15] Nearby, in February 1921, an informer was shot dead in Hynes' pub at the intersection of Railway Street and Lower Gloucester Street. That he was the brother of a well-known brothel owner in the district said much about this world of intrigue and whispers.

Philip Shanahan opposed the Anglo-Irish Treaty – a deeply contentious agreement reached between the United Kingdom and the budding Irish Free State, which, though narrowly approved by Dáil Éireann, still subsequently led to the Irish Civil War between the pro-Treaty Free State and anti-Treaty IRA. Public houses became entangled in the fighting, with one republican recalling how his unit 'held posts in Davy's public house, Portobello Bridge, commanding the approaches to and from Portobello Barracks and also a public house known as The Swan, Aungier Street'.[16] On Aungier Street, fierce fighting between Free State soldiers in Fanagan's undertakers and republicans in The Swan ensured that

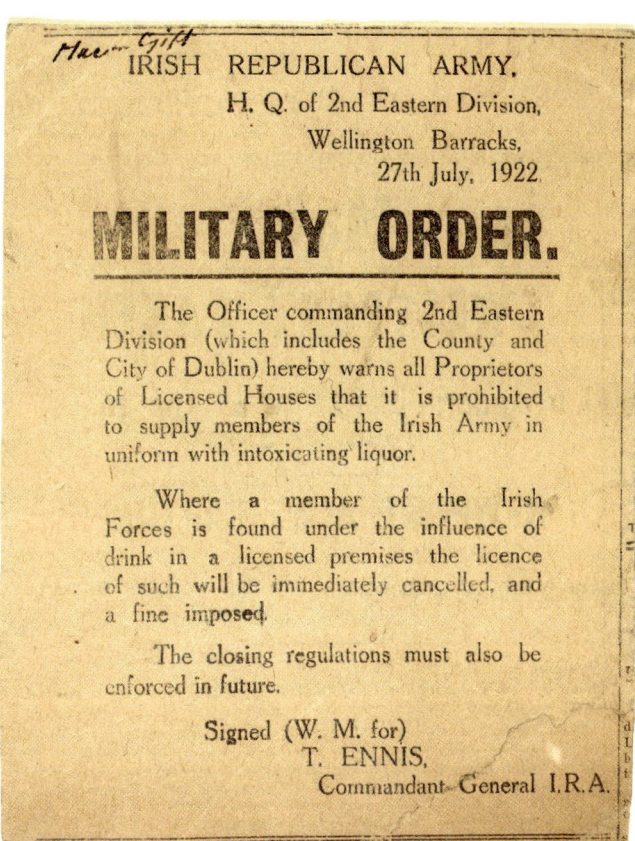

During the Civil War, Free State military authorities issued an order designed to keep their men out of public houses. (National Library of Ireland)

for many years afterwards bullet damage – now near impossible to see following restoration work – was still visible in the façade of one of Dublin's Victorian gems. Members of Cumann na mBan later recalled how, at 15 South William Street, in the pub we now know as Grogan's:

> ... word came in from a sniping post, a public house called Bowe's at the corner of William Street and Coppinger Row, that the two snipers at that post had evacuated it, leaving their arms behind them, and they sent word to Dawson Street to have their arms collected and put into safe keeping. ...
>
> We went to the house next door, round in [South] William Street, where we found a friendly man who showed us up to the skylight which we got through and on to the roof of the public house. Its skylight was a bit small and only my sister, who was small, was able to get through. She went down and opened the door of the public house for the rest of us. We had to search the whole of the house for the arms and at last we found the two loaded rifles in an office.[17]

The conflict also demonstrated the vulnerability of public house workers. People seeking retribution against those who worked in the bar trade generally knew where they worked and when they would be there. Dying For A Pint, an excellent online historical project chronologising deaths in Irish public houses, points to the case of anti-Treaty republican Michael Neville, a young barman at Mooney's on Eden Quay who was abducted from his place of work by three men. His body was later found dumped in a Killester cemetery.[18]

Shanahan's premises avoided direct involvement of this kind in the conflict, something that may well reflect the broad esteem in which Philip Shanahan was held by both factions. Nonetheless, the business suffered immensely in the new state, as did his mental health. Former comrades would remember visiting him on hearing that the pub was closed, and finding:

> ... a pitiful sight. Around the wall of the famous 'room above' were pictures of the Howth gunrunning, Dick McKee and Sean Treacy. But there was no furniture except a solitary chair. And the giant himself was in agony with sciatica, his old enemy. Shanahan could only talk of the old days and old friends ... two neighbouring women of the poorest class brought him food.[19]

Perhaps an unexpected act of generosity came from W. T. Cosgrave, then President of the Free State Executive Council, and now considered the first Taoiseach. While on the opposing side of the Civil War divide, Cosgrave had great sympathy for the plight of Shanahan, owing in no small part to his own family maintaining Burke's pub on James's Street, today still operating under the name of Kenny's. Patrick Cosgrave, his uncle, was shot dead in Burke's during the conflict in October 1922, when the premises was raided by republicans.[20] At Shanahan's, Cosgrave 'restocked the bar and had the licence restored' on hearing of the hard times the Tipperary publican had fallen on.[21]

By then, the Monto district had been transformed, following the symbolic march upon it by the Legion of Mary in March 1925 and the near simultaneous raiding of the area by Gardaí. With that, Monto would fade from the consciousness of the city for a period, though George Desmond Hodnett's

916 Commemoration Souvenir

**A commemorative postcard for the meeting of the First Dáil. Philip Shanahan is circled in the back row of the group.**

satirical 'Take Her Up To Monto' would change all that in the later ballad boom. As Caroline West notes in her recent history of the district, the Monto 'has been preserved in pockets of knowledge, paragraphs here and there, newspaper reports, oral folklore, and family history'.[22]

Shanahan died in November 1931, an obituary recalling how his name 'was a household word in the stormy days of the Anglo-Irish conflict'.[23] Physically, the Monto has all but disappeared, with Mabbot Lane a rare survivor in a district where street names were deliberately erased and erased again in the hope of eradicating history. Thanks to the efforts of the North Inner City Folklore Project, a plaque marks the site of Shanahan's.

## CHAPTER 8.
# WHAT'S IN A NAME?

### 1: THE BIRD FLANAGAN (*Rialto*)

Willie 'The Bird' Flanagan was a well-known Dublin character and practical joker. In his history of the Gresham Hotel, Ulick O'Connor related how, in 1907, a pony appeared in the foyer of the hotel; in the saddle was The Bird Flanagan, who requested a drink for the pony.¹ The writer Padraic Colum believed that, owing to the scale of Dublin, such reputations became widely known, as 'a character's doings and sayings would be repeated from coterie to coterie, losing nothing in drama or humour in the repetition'.² To John Ryan, whose pub The Bailey is examined elsewhere in this collection, The Bird Flanagan was nothing short of 'the patron saint of Dublin characters'.³

### 2: HOLE IN THE WALL (*Blackhorse Avenue*)

Previously known as Nancy Hand's, this public house sits right beside an entrance to the Phoenix Park, one of Europe's largest city parks. While an article from the time the pub was sold in 1971 claims the pub 'got its name from a large aperture in the Park wall before the gate at Blackhorse Avenue was erected', the more popular local lore is that the name is derived from the practice of serving soldiers based in the Marlborough Barracks through a hole in the wall.⁴ Forbidden from leaving the park, they were still technically within it. Whatever about the garrison's proximity, the occasional president has had no problem leaving the confines of the park for a pint, with Seán T. O'Kelly a regular of sorts in the 1950s.

### 3: KITTY O'SHEA'S (*no longer open*)

While there have been pubs named in honour of many nationalist leaders, Kitty O'Shea's at Grand Canal Street honoured Katharine

Katharine Parnell remains better known as Kitty O'Shea. (Fáilte Ireland Tourism Photographic Collection, Dublin City Library and Archive)

O'Shea, the Essex-born partner of Irish Parliamentary Party leader Charles Stewart Parnell. Married to the Member of Parliament Captain William O'Shea – but separated from him from around 1875 – the scandal of her relationship with Parnell played out publicly and led to the fall of Parnell in 1890. As the Home Rule movement questioned its own path ahead, and who should lead the party, a hostile MP quipped: 'who is to be the mistress of the party?'[5] In 'Come Gather Round Me Parnellites', W. B. Yeats alluded to Katharine O'Shea:

> But stories that live longest
> Are sung above the glass,
> And Parnell loved his country
> And Parnell loved his lass.[6]

## 4: YE OLDE GRINDING YOUNG (*no longer open*)

A decaying pub front now over many years, this premises near the Harold's Cross Bridge last traded as the Man of Achill. Thankfully, it was one of many Dublin views the American artist Flora Mitchell felt worthy of depicting, in a work that can be seen in the website of the National Gallery of Ireland. Mitchell is now best recalled for her book *Vanishing Dublin*, in which she outlined her belief that 'to walk in Dublin brings the realisation that soon it must become just another city of concrete and glass, colourless and stereotype'.[7] She had a keen eye for public houses, especially those connected to the literary heritage of the city, but here is a 'local' establishment. The *Irish Digest* described this pub name as 'surely the strangest inn title in Ireland' in the 1950s. The answer to what it actually means is to be found in a publication from decades earlier (1906), which describes how the sign of the pub then depicted 'a mill, something like a threshing mill, and at one side was an old couple, man and woman, entering in, while at the other side emerged a gallant young soldier and a buxom maid'.[8] From this strange folktale of the old being reborn came the name.

The premises of Ye Olde Grinding Young, now delapidated.

## 5: THE BLOODY STREAM (*Howth*)

In an 1893 edition of the *Journal of the Royal Society of Antiquaries of Ireland*, we read of a Howth battle in 1117:

> Sir Almericus Tristram vanquished the Danish and Irish inhabitants of Howth. The neighbouring stream, always known as the 'Bloody Stream', is crossed by Evora Bridge. The battle is described as having been fought 'beside a bridge, as they landed.'[9]

The primary battle fought here today is against the DART timetable, as the pub sits right below the station. While in Howth, walk the pier to avail of the chance to see the footsteps of King George IV from 12 August 1821, recorded by stonemason Robert Campbell. One of his party recalled how 'the passage to Dublin was occupied in eating goose-pie and drinking whiskey, in which his Majesty partook most abundantly, singing many joyous songs'.[10]

## 6: THE BLEEDING HORSE

(*Upper Camden Street*)

As you enter The Bleeding Horse, look down. At one entrance, a stone plaque commemorates the appearance of the pub in *Ulysses*. At the other, we find words from the writer of gothic stories Joseph Sheridan Le Fanu, recalled on his Mount Jerome headstone as 'Dublin's Invisible Prince'. In *The Cock and Anchor*, his 1845 novel set in Dublin, we read of when 'two horsemen rode up to the Bleeding Horse'. While these words are on the plaque, the longer description of the inn from the book describes 'the inn door, over which hung a painted panel, representing a white horse, out of whose neck there spouted a crimson cascade, and underneath, in large letters, the traveller was informed that this was the genuine old Bleeding Horse'.[11]

'Joseph Sheridan Le Fanu' by Brinsley Le Fanu. The writer of ghost stories and supernatural tales evoked Dublin's public houses in his work. (National Gallery of Ireland)

A strong mythology exists around this name, connecting it to the Battle of Rathmines in August 1649, when forces loyal to the Commonwealth of England defended Dublin from an Irish army led by the Earl of Ormond. In the chaos of battle, it's said that a fleeing wounded horse arrived at the location of the inn in a panicked state. In some local variations, the story even takes on a supernatural dimension, with the horse haunting the pub![12]

Far more likely is that the pub is named after the practice of horses being bled owing to equine diseases. As one practitioner wrote in 1825, 'in almost all the internal diseases of horses, bleeding is the essential remedy; and the earlier and more freely it is employed, the more effectually will it generally be found'.[13]

### 7: THE TURK'S HEAD (*Parliament Street*)

Those who feel Temple Bar has too many drinking establishments today should consult J. T. Gilbert's 1859 history of the city, which paints a picture of what was a boozy quarter even in the eighteenth century. At Fownes Street, there was the Shakespeare Tavern. Throughout the district at various times in the century he lists the Punch Bowl, the Raven and Punch Bowl, the Crown and Punch Bowl, the Dog and Duck ('noted for good ale'), the Eagle Tavern (explored elsewhere in this book), the Horseshoe and Magpie ('the accustomed resort of the theatrical performers') and the Turk's Head Chop House.[14] If these names all seem very visual, remember the high levels of illiteracy at that time, and thus the importance of a strong and memorable visual signage. Though in a different location, the Turk's Head is a nod to those earlier times.

### 8: THE MORGUE (*Templeogue*)

First licensed in 1848, the lore around this public house is connected to the Dublin & Blessington Steam Tram No. 10, which passed right by the pub. Morbidly enough, the route earned the moniker 'the longest graveyard in Ireland' from Dublin wits, owing to the number of pedestrian fatalities along it. In his history of Tallaght and its surrounding areas, Albert Perris suggests the name was 'due to the practice of erecting wooden crosses at the side of the tracks where tragedies had occurred'.[15]

Perris points to local lore suggesting that the Tempelogue Inn became known as The Morgue, 'due to the frequency of inquests held there arising from tram-line fatalities'.[16] With the absence of a sufficient number of dedicated coroner's courts, pubs were often utilised for inquests, being large enough to host officials, witnesses and others. Charles Dickens wrote of this practice in *Bleak House*: 'The coroner frequents more public-houses than any man alive. The smell of sawdust, beer, tobacco-smoke, and spirits is inseparable in his vocation from death in its most awful shapes.'[17] More fanciful local lore has it that the tram passed so close to the pub itself that on several occasions drunken revellers leaving the pub were struck by it, their bodies returning to the premises sooner than they may have hoped. Local wits joked:

> The Battle of Ypres was only a sham
> Compared to the rush for the Blessington tram!

Similarly, the Deadman's Inn on the Lucan Road likely owes its origin to the same practice. Historian Éamonn MacThomáis recalled how 'an old man who said he was born next door to the Deadman's told me how it got his name. He said that his father told him that many men were killed on the Lucan Road and that their bodies were brought to the pub where the inquest was held.'[18] Another story links the name to the detested Lord Norbury, known as the 'hanging judge' in eighteenth-century Dublin.[19]

At the Poddle in Kimmage, the origin of the name The Stone Boat is visible.

## 9: THE STONE BOAT
*(Kimmage or Crumlin, depending on who you ask)*

Commenting on how well Daniel Day-Lewis captured the character of Christy Brown, producer Noel Pearson remembered, 'I used to take him up almost every Sunday morning to the Stone Boat in Crumlin. He is very shrewd ... that's how he got the accent.'[20] Brown remains a fondly remembered local of The Stone Boat. Despite its nautical theme, the name of the pub is derived from the nearby physical stone tongue or boat (a nearby housing estate is called Tonguefield) where the River Poddle's stream is divided. Much of the Poddle continues onwards, eventually meeting the Liffey in the city. The location at which they met was historically known as Dubh Linn. The nearby Four Provinces pub, a home of traditional music, produces Poddle Lager in honour of the river that (partially) gives Dublin its name.

## 10: THE HAIRY LEMON *(Stephen Street)*

Pete St John is best recalled for 'Dublin in the Rare Old Times', but his song 'The Mero' was an all-inclusive list of Dublin street characters from yesteryear. In it we meet Dolly Fawcett, who ran a shebeen/brothel of sorts over decades in the form of the Café Continental near the intersection of Bolton Street and Capel Street. A verse that always baffled me as a child begins:

> Me uncle had a wolfhound that never had to pee
> But Hairy Lemon snatched it, down on Eden Quay

To unravel that, Hairy Lemon was the nickname bestowed on a Dublin dog catcher in the 1940s. Added to The Bird Flanagan in Rialto and Dudley's on Thomas Street (a nod to Thomas Dudley, or 'Bang Bang', who staged mock shoot-outs on the streets of Dublin with a key in hand), the question can be genuinely asked: could any other city produce such an assortment of pub names rooted in the characters who inhabited it?

# CHAPTER 9.
# THE DAWNING OF THE DAY

**O**ne rapidly diminishing type of Dublin public house is the so-called 'early house', the name bestowed on establishments that are permitted to open their doors at seven o'clock in the morning. More than any other category of public house in the city, the mapping of these establishments immediately reveals a geographic logic. Located primarily around the historic market areas of the city on the northside and near its docker communities on the southside, these pubs were intended to provide for a city centre workforce who operated in a different time zone entirely from the rest of Dublin. As most were rising for breakfast, these men and women were on their second pints.

The early house doesn't generally feature prominently in the memory of the city. When it does emerge, it tends to mark tragedy. Take Bill Kelly's classic memoir, *Me Darlin' Dublin's Dead and Gone*, where there is an almost ominous sense of doom as he describes Brendan Behan's love for the bars around the markets: 'These had an added advantage. They opened at seven in the morning. In the following months, he introduced them to me.'[1]

I have sat in public houses at seven o'clock in the morning before, with the all-important detail being that these establishments

**Detail of Molloy's early house on Talbot Street.**

were hardly a short stroll from the Liffey. In one such 'kneipe' – a name bestowed on traditional drinking houses in the city of Berlin – a regular told me the bar was open 365 days of the year, and had not locked its doors for twenty years until the pandemic forced it into a temporary hibernation. Nothing I encountered in that pub convinced me otherwise. A pint at seven o'clock in such an establishment is the end of the night. In Dublin, however, it is very much the dawning of the day.

Of the remaining (sometimes disputed) early houses in the capital, several are located in the area immediately bordering the historic fruit and vegetable market opened by Dublin Corporation in 1892. A beautiful red-brick building that would be more at home amidst the Victorian architecture of Belfast, the market building largely ceased functioning in 2019, but the area more broadly remains a busy market environment. Names like Jackie Leonard's (located in neighbouring Anne Street North) carry enormous weight around there, as Kate Leonard had been one of the very first traders in the area to take up a stand in the market building when it opened.[2] There is unbroken continuity in the working lives of several family dynasties around those streets, from florists to fruit importers.

Capel Street's early houses catered to these market workers, but there were others even closer to the market buildings. When Kevin C. Kearns undertook his landmark 1996 oral history, *Dublin Pub Life & Lore*, Billy Sullivan from the nearby Mary's Abbey told him:

> There was three in Arran Street: there was Donoghue's and Roberts's and Corbett's. Now this is going back to the twenties. And the Daisy Market dealers, they'd drink in Corbett's public house at the corner of Little Mary Street, next to Many Penny Yard. He'd serve women no problem. They'd wear shawls. They'd have a glass of porter, a gill, and a baby Power's and that was one and eight pence. Oh, some of them'd drink you under the table.[3]

Slattery's public house on Capel Street. (Image courtesy of the Irish Architectural Archive)

Today, Corbett's has traded shawlies for Swifties, trading as the popular Hacienda, a seemingly must-visit pub for international stars. It no longer opens at seven o'clock in the morning, and keeps its own unique opening hours. Resembling a Spanish white-stone cottage externally, the Hacienda Market Bar generally opens at 8 p.m. Ringing a bell to seek admission (which can just as easily be refused) and passing through the entrance brings you into a space where the walls are adorned with pictures of the slightly recognisable, genuinely famous and even the infamous who have gone before. A short walk away, Slattery's and The Boar's Head are

The Hacienda, formerly a popular early house with market workers. Today, the building is surrounded by hotels in a rapidly changing built landscape.

all that remain locally of the early houses. Whether these strictly qualify as early houses now is a subject of some debate, as they open later in the morning, albeit still before other city-centre establishments.

In nearby Smithfield, Delaney's and The Cobblestone on North King Street were both early houses, though these catered to a different kind of market worker. With neighbouring Stoneybatter colloquially known as 'Cowtown' owing to the importance of the cattle market in former times, these pubs catered primarily to men who herded livestock. A young Edna O'Brien, working as a pharmacy assistant in suburban Cabra, recalled this market environment as something that 'brought back the reek and constraints of home', as 'at Hanlon's Corner I would have to dismount because of all this commotion, the drovers shouting and belting the poor beasts that slithered, their wet scutters and everywhere and bus drivers honking their horns impatiently'.[4] The journalist Gene Kerrigan remembered the same scene, and how 'the cattle were tended by cowboys on bicycles, men with overcoats and hats, furiously pedaling this way and that'.[5] Bicycles and sticks stacked against the wall of a public house at seven in the morning is no longer a familiar Smithfield sight.

The oral history work of Kearns gave these unique pubs their place, but they more often appeared in the newspapers as a sort of curious human interest story, or at times when rumoured regulation seemed to put their future in peril. Con Houlihan frequented a number of them. In 2008 he told his readers:

> In Dublin's sub-language they are known as the Early Houses. This in loose translation means pubs that open their doors about half-past seven in the morning. Those fortunate people who are privy to all knowledge tell us that they were instituted to make life easier for milkmen and market gardeners. That was in the days of horse power and pony power: the good people who bring us the milk and the vegetables no longer need the early houses. And yet they are as much part of our culture as ever.[6]

Yet since 2008, more than half of the remaining such establishments have closed their doors, or have been reinvented as something else. In the same year that Con penned this article, the *Sunday Independent* reported that 'the future is plain for early-house drinkers as Government plans ban'.[7]

Looking especially forlorn along Dublin's Liffeyside is The Chancery, though its painted sign remains, depicting a distinctly alert rooster in front of a Dublin cityscape at dawn. The name is derived from its proximity to the Four Courts, as with the Legal Eagle, but while the latter pivoted towards good-quality grub and reinvention as a restaurant, The Chancery has sat empty for a number of years.

In 2003, *Slate* magazine (free, frequently libellous and sadly missed) ran a feature on the early houses of the city, including an image of a crowd waiting to gain admission to The Chancery on a Saturday morning, as a Dublin bus passes by. Readers were told that 'this place fills up very quickly on a Saturday. If you arrive much later than 8.30, you will probably have to wait outside until a few people leave.'[8] With what one newspaper described as 'two friendly but hefty bouncers and a thumping bass line', waiting to get into The Chancery could feel more akin to starting a night than ending it.**⁹**

In this peculiar relationship between nightlife and morning drinking, The Chancery wasn't entirely unique. On the other side of the Liffey and towards the docklands, there is today nothing about the Starbucks at 1 George's Quay that suggests its former life as The White Horse, an early house that was particularly popular with journalists owing to its proximity to a number of newspaper offices, especially the *Irish Press*. Later, when drinking cultures changed, The White Horse was rechristened The Dark Horse, operating from 7 a.m. until noon at weekends, and hosting electronic music events. In 2012, *The Dubliner* described how the 'all-night revellers in fashionable runners are a far cry from the dockworkers and night-shifters early house licenses [*sic*] were devised for'.**¹⁰**

As The White Horse, the bar had hosted punk rock concerts in the early 1990s, with Green Day performing there in 1991. The Hope Collective – a Dublin-based collective who put on DIY gigs in the capital – lost £50 on the gig. On a 2017 visit to Dublin to perform in a considerably larger venue, Billie Joe Armstrong visited the site, tweeting: 'ugh. it's now a Starbucks ... sorrow. I have a great memory of playing there. No one was allowed to dance in fear of the roof caving in. Everyone was so friendly.' Graduating from punk to techno, the pub remains a curious footnote in the stories of several music scenes. Similarly, Ned's on Townsend Street (replaced by a hotel) hosted an early morning night called 'The Early Shift' before its closure in recent times.

Still, in their heyday there were far more market workers than dancers keeping the doors of early houses open, and changing labour better explains the decline of the early house than changing recreation in the city. When the market building closed in 2019, and when the exodus of wholesalers into the suburban industrial estates began, there simply wasn't the same level of morning activity in the markets – nor in the nearby public houses. As a result, many did not endure.

Nothing about this branch of Starbucks would suggest its former life as the early house known as The White Horse.

Gone is The Capel, for example, located on Little Britain Street in the heart of the markets district, replaced by Bar 1661. Reflective of the changing nature of the public house and the rise of the cocktail bar, this bar champions the historic Irish spirit poitín (in a legal and regulated way, far removed from the unlabelled fizzy drinks bottles full of moonshine some may recall from different times). Gone too is nearby M. Hughes of Chancery Street, lamented in a moving documentary tribute by Brendan Gleeson, who remembered it as a special place for traditional music sessions. In the morning, it did a good trade of market workers and those from the legal system, nestled as it was behind the Four Courts. An obituary of Michael

The painted signage of M. Hughes remains a reminder of a once thriving early house in the markets area.

Hughes, the much-loved proprietor of the establishment, noted that 'the bar's early morning opening was often availed of to brace nerves of litigants facing the stress of legal examination'.[11] Those doing the questioning were often found there too.

Still, the fruit and vegetable market remains standing, with much talk about potential future uses. Extensive refurbishment is intended to bring the market back to life in 2026, though its purpose will be different from before, likely pivoting towards something akin to Lisbon's Time Out Market or London's Borough Market in Southwark, where a hybrid of wholesale and retail stalls bring locals and visitors alike.

What about on the southside? Just a short stroll from the Liffey docklands, two of Dublin's final early houses trade at The Windjammer and The Pádraig Pearse. As the economic decline in Dublin's docklands began before the more gradual decline in the markets area, the number of early public houses there started dwindling earlier. When the *Evening Herald* investigated the decline of such pubs in 1986, in a piece entitled 'The Unholy Hour', the proprietor of The Windjammer noted how 'ten or fifteen years ago there were about twenty early houses in this area, now there's only about ten'.[12]

In a city of very little historical industry, the docklands was a thriving place of early morning activity, although work was often precarious and irregular. What Kearns once described as a 'world of masts, funnels, towering cranes, barges, carts, horses ... a hundred sounds becoming a symphony of dockland' was also a place where men loaded and unloaded ships as they were required. Glass and steel have won the day over many of the public houses that dotted Liffeyside.[13]

The downfall of Dublin's docklands as a major employer was the arrival of containerisation – a system of freight transport using shipping containers – something that marked a dramatic decline in the number of bodies needed by companies working in importing and exporting goods. By 1982, the *Evening Herald* would tell readers that 'containerisation has played a major part in sounding the death knell of the Dublin docker – reduced from 1,300 in 1971 to their present level of 520'.[14] More startling still, that number comes from a front-page story on the axing of another 270. The docklands once had the feeling of a city on the edge of the city, with its own traditions, folklore and identity. These days, the Dublin Dock Workers Preservation Society does much to capture the memory of those proud and proletarian times.[15]

For the all-important research aspect of this book, I visited the last of the seven o'clock establishments. The Pádraig Pearse is named in honour of a signatory of the 1916 Proclamation, and one of the executed leaders of the rebellion, raised only a short distance away from the public house on what was then Great Brunswick Street. In his own lifetime, he was strictly Patrick Henry Pearse or Pádraig Mac Piarais, never settling for the halfway house of a hybrid, bilingual name.[16] That detail is considerably less important than this one: he was a teetotaller.

While a Tripadvisor reviewer found The Pádraig Pearse to be '*Ungemütlich, nicht sehr freundlich*' ('uncomfortable, not friendly'), on any visit here that I've made the atmosphere has been friendly, and it feels like a fast-disappearing and important thing in the city

– not in the sense of being an early house, but instead a genuine 'local'. Pubs like it were once a common feature of the inner city, but more often recall suburbia now.

An important detail a visitor could easily miss on the wall of the Pádraig Pearse is a price list from Widow Scallan's, a pub which sat on the other side of Pearse Street and was the target of an Ulster Volunteer Force attack in May 1994. Pubs, often thought of as a third space removed from work and home life, were frequently targeted over the course of the three-decade conflict, especially in border areas. The Widow Scallan's is now a coffee shop, a reminder of the change brought about locally.

A short walk from The Pádraig Pearse, The Windjammer on the corner of Townsend Street and Lombard Street was a little busier on the morning I visited it, with a table of patrons deep in discussion about the day's racing ahead. The journey from one premises to the other brings the stroller past two distinctive 1930s modernist public housing schemes designed by Herbert George Simms. They carry the names Pearse House and Markievicz House, linking them to the struggle for nationhood. While the pub nearest Pearse House is The Pádraig Pearse, The Countess on Townsend Street has been a slowly decaying ruin for many years.

There are lots of factors in the decline of public houses in this area of the city, but one is undoubtedly the movement of people outwards from the city centre core. Following the collapse of a tenement house on Fenian Street in 1963, a plaque on a block of flats notes that 'within a decade the population of Westland Row parish had fallen from 20,0000 to less than 6,000'. Containerisation was one drastic change in the lives of people here, but suburbanisation was another.

The Windjammer has quite a unique origin story for a Dublin public house, having been financed and constructed for the Beamish & Crawford Brewery in the 1940s. A windjammer, a twenty-first-century Dubliner would be forgiven for not knowing, was the name bestowed upon nineteenth-century commercial sailing ships with several masts, and the name naturally nods to the near-dockside location of the pub. In a time when breweries also dabbled in the public house trade, pubs would be synonymous with particular brands, a system that is still relatively common in other places. In London, Samuel Smith's pubs still serve only Samuel Smith's beers. For the Cork brewery, pubs like The Windjammer were important advertising in the capital, where the influence of Guinness was everywhere felt.

Crossing over the Liffey at the Talbot Memorial Bridge allows the stroller to pass two memorials. First, a life-size bronze statue of a Dublin docker at work, created by Dony MacManus. He looks like just the kind of hard-working man you'd encounter in one of these institutions forty years ago. Dating from 1999, the height of the Celtic Tiger era, it was unveiled at a time when this area was changing drastically, more associated with the letters IFSC than ITGWU, or anything else a docker would have worn on their union badge. Describing his artwork, Dony says 'this work celebrates the working men of the Dublin docklands, on the backs of whom the city was built'.[17] Further along I pass a memorial to Matt Talbot, known as Venerable Matt Talbot. He was a working-class Dublin labourer who spurned alcohol, having battled addiction, becoming instead a symbol of faith and temperance. When Talbot died on his way to Mass on the streets in June 1925, it was discovered that his body was wrapped in chains, a symbol of his religious devotion. In *Father Ted*, he became 'Matty Hislop. He was a notorious drunkard who found God and then decided to punish himself for his sins.'[18] Still, the statue reminds me of the significant impact of the temperance movement in the city of Dublin in times past, and the broad support it enjoyed from movements as diverse as cultural nationalism, the Church, trade unionism and more. Talbot, readers of the bestselling 1925 book *The Life of Matt Talbot* were told, represented the best of the 'true types of our people and not the wretched degenerates which a so-called National Theatre presents to the world as types of Catholic Ireland'.[19] Though a northsider, Talbot now stands on the other side of the river. When the statue was unveiled in 1989, the speaker said that 'he would have been out of place near the Financial Services Centre. He is more at home here on the Southside docks where he worked.'[20]

I pass Connolly Station, where the bar no longer opens at seven in the morning, dropping out of the shrinking club. Separating it from the others, an out-of-city train ticket was once required to gain access, with seasoned drinkers knowing which satellite town routes were the cheapest admission into the club. On Good Friday, at a time when pubs were still required to close their doors on that day, the special dispensation accorded to the train station bar ensured that a remarkable number of empty seats were to be found on apparently fully booked train trips.

Only Molloy's on Talbot Street is a 7 a.m. early house on the northside nowadays, with Slattery's on Capel Street opening its doors at 9 a.m., and The Boar's Head normally turning the key at 10 a.m., a full thirty minutes before regular business can commence elsewhere. Molloy's, right alongside the railway bridge that crosses over Talbot Street, has a beautiful Victorian-era façade, with decorative cast-iron features and carved keystone faces adorning the front of the pub. One shows a Chinese face, an *Evening Herald* feature in the 1970s reminding us what this might symbolise:

> It seems to date back to about 1860, when the firm were not only publicans, but tea, coffee and spice merchants as well ... The keystone showing a citizen of what used to be known in Europe as 'the Celestial Empire' recalls that tea came very recently into Dublin history.[21]

**Details of Molloy's early house on Talbot Street.**

Everything about this pub is a visual treat, including glass mirrors advertising distilleries which have long been lost, and a snug that pubs anywhere would envy. Clearly, a few prefer it to the train station bar, their suitcases suggesting that Connolly Station is the next stop for some here.

Akin to stepping out of a cinema at lunchtime, the light certainly hits differently when you emerge – a little tipsy – from a morning excursion like this one. Indeed, one barman would tell a curious journalist that 'if we want to move people along who have had a bit too much we pull up the blinds. They react like vampires at the purging shaft of light coming in through the window.'[22]

Clearly, these institutions are part of a dying breed, and the picture is the same elsewhere. Despite vast differences in scale, the number of early houses in London does not greatly exceed that here – indeed it will soon fall below it. While the Fox & Anchor by Smithfield Market still opens its doors at seven o'clock, London's pubs now prefer to open later and close earlier than their Dublin equivalents in almost all cases. We'll always have Berlin.

# CHAPTER 10.

# PUBLORE

**P**ubland, at least partially, is built on publore. Sometimes a story is a total fabrication, but on more occasions there is a grain of truth to it, though time and the retelling of a tale has shifted details.

Take the story of the actor Alan Devlin, who *did* indeed storm off the stage of the Gaiety Theatre during a performance of *H. M. S. Pinafore*, his radio microphone still attached. Devlin's action, *Theatre Ireland* lamented at the time, 'is known widely in the profession as "the Irish disease", which should make us think'.[1] The image of Devlin telling his audience 'fuck this for a game of soldiers', before disappearing into Neary's to order a pint, that the audience heard every moment of, is one of the enduring stories of Dublin drinking.[2] Alas, Devlin only made it to Sinnott's, in front of the theatre. In a comment on an online blog, Terry Lawlor, who was onstage that night, corrected the tale:

> He eventually said 'fuck it, I can't do it, I'm going home'. And proceeded to walk through the auditorium, stopping to explain himself to an audience member, and out the front door and across the road to Sinnott's, not Neary's which is at the back of the Gaiety. It's true that he ordered a drink, but the audience didn't hear the exchange. The sound guy could hear it in his cans, but he had cut the channel to the PA.[3]

A portrait of the young W. B. Yeats by John Butler Yeats. (National Gallery of Ireland)

The story has perhaps done no harm for Neary's, where most people still place it. Devlin, a much-loved actor despite it all, returned to the role on the West End a few short years later. When questioned on allowing him onto the stage of London's Old Vic after storming off the Gaiety, the director said he admired the 'style and gusto' Devlin had brought to the role of Sir Joseph Porter.[4] Indeed.

Another great story concerns the poet W. B. Yeats, said to have shunned the public house at every opportunity, only to be brought to Toner's in the company of Oliver St John Gogarty. Having ordered a sherry, the story has it, he departed quickly, telling Gogarty something to the effect of 'I have now seen a pub so would you kindly take me home.'[5] This story is painted on the panelling within the snug of the pub, immortalising it for ever.

What is the origin of this tale? All credit to the broadcaster W. R. Rodgers, who produced a brilliant series of radio broadcasts (later published in print) entitled *Irish Literary Portraits* for the BBC, in which he interviewed the survivors of an extraordinary literary generation. The writer known as Brinsley MacNamara told Rodgers of Yeats:

The name of former proprietor Thomas Neary remains visible on Chatham Street.

> The only thing he never really got used to was the fact that poets and writers might be found sometimes in the public houses of the town, and he never ventured into one of them. There's a story that Yeats once approached Fred Higgins and he said 'Higgins, do you know I have never been in a pub in my life and I'd like to go into a pub.' So Higgins came to me and he asked me what was the most likely pub now to which we might bring Yeats without horrifying him by what he'd see there in the shape of literature and other

things. And we decided on one pub, and Higgins went along with him there, and they called for some mild drink and Yeats looked around and he said, 'Higgins, I don't like it. Lead me out again.'[6]

If it was the poet F. R. Higgins who accompanied Yeats on this fact-finding mission, Yeats could have picked a better companion. In the same series, Frank O'Connor recounted that Higgins 'was always getting hit by somebody in a pub, and it was usually in an argument about what he used to call "pouettry"'.[7] Poets sometimes fared little better in The Palace, where Edna O'Brien later recalled the tale of the arrival of a celebrated poet from afar causing ructions:

> When Louis MacNeice, who lived in London, dared to breach their circle, Kavanagh mocked him, singing 'Let you go back and labour for Faber and Faber' to the tune of 'The Bard of Armagh', the evening descending into blows between rival poets and their foot soldiers.[8]

**Detail visible in the exterior of Toner's public house, Baggot Street. (Fáilte Ireland Tourism Photographic Collection, Dublin City Library and Archive)**

Of course, that tale too has variations in the telling. As for Yeats in the snug, Con Houlihan later placed the tale in Mulligan's, identifying F. R. Higgins as the poet who had accompanied Yeats. When it came to the pub, Houlihan noted, the story 'added to its fame, if in a rather negative way'.[9]

It's unlikely a Dublin public house would have shaken Yeats too much, what with the Rhymers' Club in London, of which he was a member, meeting at Ye Olde Cheshire Cheese, a celebrated inn just off Fleet Street in Wine Office Court. The pub was not a totally alien concept to Yeats, as this was an environment in which poetry was recited and booze flowed freely: 'None of us can say who will succeed, or even who has or has not talent. The only thing certain about us is that we are too many.'[10]

Both draught and bottled Bass are advertised proudly on the front of this Liffeyside pub. (G. & T. Crampton Photograph Archive, University College Dublin Library)

**T**hese days, Bass is little more than a memory in Dublin publand. While advertising mirrors and signs for the ale remain, more than a century of brewing on Belfast's Glen Road came to an abrupt end in 2005, leaving Irish pubs free of the once-popular ale on draught. Politics and Bass may instantly bring to mind former Taoiseach Bertie Ahern – who even mentions the ale in his autobiography – but decades earlier the ale was entangled in a political storm of sorts.

Ten years on from the Civil War, men were storming public houses in Dublin once more. In 1933, the year 'drew to a close to the sound of scuffles over ale kegs', as the IRA went to war on those selling Bass ale.[1] Pubs were raided, publicans threatened, shots fired, and the far-right paramilitary Army Comrades Association – better recalled as the Blueshirts – was dragged into the debacle.

Within the broader context of a 'Boycott British' movement and economic war with Britain, the campaign against Bass was one of the most visible and public manifestations of the tension. The sights and sounds of trashed public houses attracted much press attention, but the wisdom of the campaign was questioned even by some who had partaken in it. Patrick Byrne, on the left of the organisation and soon to leave it (feeling the IRA was increasingly directionless politically) later recalled:

Because of some disparaging remarks the Bass boss, Colonel Gretton, was reported to have made about the Irish, the IRA leadership took umbrage and sent armed units out into the streets of Dublin, Cork and elsewhere to raid pubs, terrify the customers and smash perfectly good stocks of bottled Bass, an activity in which, I regret to say, I was engaged ... Peadar O'Donnell scathingly described it as a 'heedless stunt', and Cumann na mBan leader Sheila Humphreys later admitted that it was a 'terrible waste of time and energy.'[2]

The campaign against Bass began in December 1932, with men calling on publicans in the city, telling the owners of pubs to 'cease selling Bass ale, and to endeavour to dispose of their stocks of ale by a certain period'.[3] Proving there was more to the campaign than words, the press reported on a daytime raid just ten days before Christmas, 'when a party of young men held up a lorry, carrying ale, in Commons Street, Dublin, not far from the warehouse of Messrs. Bass, Ratcliff and Gretton. The contents of the barrels were tipped into the roadway, and when they had been emptied they were sprinkled with paraffin oil and set on fire.'[4]

The IRA's interference with the supply of Bass led the Blueshirts to directly intervene, providing a guard to delivery vehicles, as 'sixteen men, eight forming an escort to each lorry, marched along the footpath from the quays to the stores, but no attempt was made to interfere with the convoy. Members of the ACA later escorted delivery of Bass's ale to a number of licensed vintners in the city.'[5]

Pubs became the centre of campaigning in early 1933, when 'bands of young men entered licensed premises, and jumping over the counters, smashed all the bottles of Bass's ale they could lay their hands on ... earlier in the day bodies of youths smashed Bass's glass advertising signs in several licensed premises'.[6] There was a brazenness to the extent of the campaign; on one night in September 1933, armed men visited John Curran's (75 Meath Street), Bambrick's

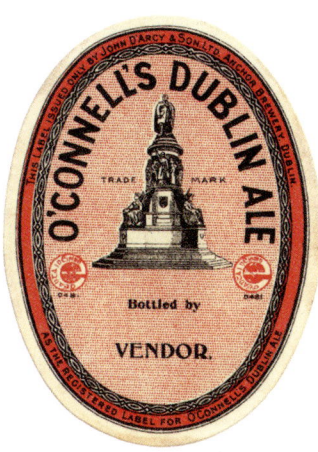

Label for O'Connell's Dublin Ale brewed by D'Arcy's Anchor Brewery before it became Watkin's Brewery in the late 1920s. (From the collection of Niall McCormack)

on Patrick Street, George Farrelly's and McDonald's on Summerhill, J. J. Higgins on Merrion Row and J. Connell's in Stoneybatter.[7] In response, the press reported that Gardaí in lorries 'patrolled Dublin streets last night, their duty being, it was stated, to protect public houses against Bass raiders'.[8] The proprietor of the Deadman's Inn, near Lucan, was taken 'at the point of a revolver' and brought to the Featherbed Mountain, forced to walk back home wearing clothing bearing the slogan 'Boycott Bass'.[9]

Never known to miss an opportunity, rival breweries began advertising their ales in newspapers like *An Phoblacht*, that were reporting on the ongoing IRA campaign. One front page advertised no fewer than three ales: there was Joy Dublin Ale from the Mountjoy Brewery, encouraging readers to 'Support Dublin Labour'. Cairnes Ale told readers to 'Buy Irish!' There was even O'Connell's Ale, carrying the historic image of Daniel O'Connell, and produced by Watkin's Brewery. One wonders what O'Connell would have made of men upending Bass delivery trucks or attacking Dublin public houses.

Beyond the IRA, whose war on British goods also included the burning of Cadbury's delivery trucks, there were others who advocated public house patriotism. In his history of the Pioneer movement in Ireland, Diarmaid Ferriter notes how Taoiseach de Valera suggested, 'in keeping with his own protectionist philosophy, that Ireland should drink more of its own beer'.[10] That was a sentiment the advertisers in *An Phoblacht* would wholly support.

If the economic tensions between Ireland and Britain had any real impact on the alcohol industry, it wasn't to be measured in smashed pub windows. The acquisition by Guinness of the Park Royal Brewery near London, a move designed to 'offset the burden of protective tariffs', would impact on the scale of the brewery as an employer in its home city.[11]

Thousands of gallons of Bass ale were smashed on the roadsides of the country during the campaign, before the IRA quietly abandoned it in 1934.

# CHAPTER 12.
# THE PUB AND THE STAGE: THE FLOWING TIDE

**M**uch has changed since George Moore complained at the beginning of the last century that 'all modern stained glass is so utterly bad and so beastly ugly that it is simply throwing away money trying to improve it – in fact, the sooner it dies the better'.[1] A walk across Dublin city introduces a visitor to the brilliance of Harry Clarke, Michael Healy, Evie Hone and other artists who would come to prominence in the aftermath of Moore's disparaging remarks. Many of the finest artworks are found in places of worship, reflecting the fact that churches – Catholic or otherwise – were the primary patrons of the art form in twentieth-century Ireland.

Some of my favourite stained-glass artworks, however, are found in The Flowing Tide on Abbey Street, where we see a series of works that show us familiar Dublin views of the past and present, including Nelson's Pillar and the Custom House. Amidst the landmarks are actors, painters, labourers, street traders and a very happy man holding a pint of porter. In a nod to the location of the public house, we see tragedy and comedy, reminding us that The Flowing Tide was – and is – very much an actor's pub.

The windows are the work of Tony Inglis, a film art director born in Dublin in 1911, and a graduate of the Metropolitan School of Art. Inglis later received an Academy Award nomination for his work on *The Man Who Would Be King*, John Huston's 1975 film starring Sean Connery and Michael Caine. His works in The Flowing Tide, beautifully illuminated and immediately visible as you enter the premises, are surely one of the great artworks of Dublin publand.

The story of The Flowing Tide is inseparable from that of the Abbey Theatre, the national theatre. Founded in 1904 by Edward Martyn, Lady Gregory and W. B. Yeats, the theatre is deeply synonymous with the latter, though as the writer Edward Kenny rightly noted, it was not 'the creation of any one person or small group of people. It was the product of a period – the product of a period of great intellectual activity, and of a generation dedicated to the national ideal'.[2] Although the public house pre-dated the theatre itself, the Abbey would shift the clientele and character of the establishment, something still clear from the theatre posters and artworks that adorn the walls of the pub now. Stepping inside its snugs, we see sketches of acting royalty like Donal McCann, Gabriel Byrne and Siobhán McKenna. The link between the world of stage and snug is made perfectly clear. By comparison, the actor Breffni McKenna would tell the *Irish Press* in 1990 of the changing culture in London theatreland with some horror: 'After the show drinking has disappeared there. It is down to a glass of wine or Perrier now. Less wear and tear. Most actors now get their kicks in the gymnasium.'[3]

For the founders of the Abbey, the new theatre was intended to mark a break with the popular theatre that had long reigned before it. Here would be a theatre that reached into the Irish past, and aimed to shape identity in the present. It was a time when, as the actor Máire Nic Shiubhlaigh remembered:

> The revival had just begun to gather momentum. Dublin bristled with little national movements of every conceivable kind: cultural,

*The Flowing Tide is visible in this 1972 view of Marlborough Street. (Courtesy of the National Library of Ireland)*

artistic, literary, theatrical, political. I suppose a generation arriving amidst the bickerings of parliamentarians, of Parnellites and anti-Parnellites, had turned from politics and begun at last to seek a national expression elsewhere. Everyone was discussing literature and the arts, the new literature that was emerging.[4]

In this emerging theatre, the Abbey presented a world that was recognisable to the audience. The Irish public house was a part of this world, playing a central role in several productions. Significantly, the two most controversial plays of the early life of the Abbey Theatre both featured public houses prominently. In J. M. Synge's *The Playboy of the Western World* (1907), we meet the protagonist Christy Mahon – who claims to have killed his father – in Michael James Flaherty's fictional public house in

Mayo. Later, Seán O'Casey's *The Plough and the Stars* caused ructions in 1926, as the prostitute Rosie Redmond gave her review of the unfolding Easter Rising in a public house near the fighting; the freedom the rebels were fighting for was a 'freedom that wouldn't be worth winnin' in a raffle!' With the early Abbey Theatre, the pub had arrived as a backdrop for theatrical performances, and it has remained there ever since.

Both productions are associated with 'riots', though *The Playboy* can make a greater claim to the honour of a riotous reception. 'A large section of the Dublin public,' the *Belfast Newsletter* told their readers, 'has taken offence because they consider it not true to Irish life and caricaturing to the peasantry of the West.'[5] The writer Mary Colum recalled attending the production on the night when Yeats defended the work of Synge, and as 'a motley mixture of workmen, students and bourgeoisie in evening dress filled the theatre, most of them with denunciatory speeches ready to deliver'.[6] Lore surrounding The Flowing Tide doing a roaring trade over the run of *The Playboy* is plentiful, suggesting the pub was a shelter from the high drama playing out across the street, and spilling onto it.

While I couldn't find reference to the pub in any of the press coverage of the trials that followed the disturbances (the aforementioned Mary Colum's father-in-law was one of those fined, taking the 46-shilling lesson over a month in jail for disorderly behaviour), the newspaper archives did produce some weird and wonderful moments for the pub in the courts. In 1908, a clergyman from the neighbouring Methodist church objected to

The barman is ready to intervene in this poster for a play by Dion Boucicault. (Courtesy of the National Library of Ireland)

**SUPPORT ABBEY THEATRE AGAINST ORGANIZED INTERRUPTION UPHOLD RIGHT OF EVERY MAN TO HEAR AND JUDGE FOR HIMSELF**

A poster from the time of the so-called 'Playboy Riots' at the Abbey. (Courtesy of the National Library of Ireland)

the continued licensing of the premises, on the basis that 'the house was resorted to by loose women, and was badly conducted'.[7] The publican, Denis Hayes, lived to fight another day. A few years later, the pub appeared in the courts again, when the police arrested a thief (a hotel waiter working nearby, presumably on a detour on the way to work) on the premises, penning a note that was discovered on the counter:

Dear Sir – Your whiskey is excellent. So are your cigars; but your money I like best. Ten to one you won't catch me. I am sorry I cannot divulge my name, but I may on the next visit.[8]

The looters of Easter 1916, explored in detail elsewhere in this book, left no such note of sarcastic apology behind them, but did successfully make off with more than the fumbling waiter had. In the compensation claims of Denis Hayes after the Rising, we learn of five dozen bottles of Sandeman's port wine, three bottles of Hennessy's brandy (three-star), forty dozen stout, ten dozen Bass, four boxes of cigars and two dozen bottles of Powers Three Swallow whiskey as amongst the produce liberated from the premises. This was small fish for Hayes, who also had to contend with the exterior and interior of the premises being 'damaged by rifle fire'.[9]

Into recent times, The Flowing Tide wasn't quite the nearest watering hole to the national theatre, an honour that instead befell The Plough, a curious name given the 1926 response to *The Plough and the Stars*. While one critic recalled 'the good old days in the Abbey when you could pop across the road to The Flowing Tide … during the break', actors tended to make for The Plough, directly opposite the theatre.[10] Disagreement over the serving of a late

drink could lead to entire productions switching loyalties from one corner pub to the other. In a 2010 blog heralding the arrival of Theatre Upstairs – an independent, non-funded theatre space dedicated to showcasing the best new Irish plays – in The Plough, Colin Murphy noted that 'there was a record for the quickest journey from curtain call on stage to the bar at The Plough, and some actors were known for fitting in a quick pint between scenes'.[11] Both pubs were utilised by writers and actors as places of work as well as leisure; when Pierce Brosnan was in town in May 1992, toying with the idea of a film exploring the life of boxer Jack Doyle, the press reported 'he visited The Flowing Tide pub for a meeting with Angeline Ball who he is interested in casting'.[12] Scripts were dissected in both, a barman from The Plough telling

An example of the magnificent stained glass on display in The Flowing Tide. Here we see the Custom House and a variety of Liffeyside workers.

me of finding and returning more than one in his time.

From The Flowing Tide, it is only a short stroll to the Liffey itself, the likely origin of the name. A theory that the public house is named in honour not of the river, but of Prime Minister William Ewart Gladstone, is sometimes repeated.[13] Denouncing opponents of Irish Home Rule, Gladstone told the House of Commons that 'the ebbing tide is with you and the flowing tide is with us'. The very words 'the flowing tide' were frequently evoked with the name of Gladstone in the late nineteenth-century press, and Gladstone's broad popularity in Ireland meant that there were even proposals to erect a statue of him in Dublin. While a statue by John Hughes was commissioned for the city, it instead ended up in Wales, with one of its trustees proposing that, 'if at some future date, the political situation in Ireland makes it possible to erect the statue in Dublin, it should be released and presented to Ireland as originally intended'.[14] The name The Flowing Tide never adorned the pub in the age of Gladstone or even in the generation which followed. Perhaps, if Gladstone's vision had succeeded, the looting and shooting would all have been averted.

Not only has the Abbey brought the pub to the stage, it has also brought the stage to the pub. In the washout summer of 2017, the theatre toured Roddy Doyle's *Two Pints*, bringing the work to twenty-three Irish pubs, including Tigh Neachtain in Galway and Blakes of the Hollow in Enniskillen. Logistically, the easiest nights of the tour were surely 6–8 July: at The Flowing Tide.

# CHAPTER 13.
# LEE MILLER: IN SEARCH OF JOYCE

**S**tanding on the bar counter in The Palace is generally discouraged, and would go against the general Victorian ambience of the establishment. Such behaviour might fly deeper in the bowels of Temple Bar, where stag and hen parties reign supreme, but on this part of Fleet Street there is a general calmness prevailing. The Palace is the kind of establishment that has televisions but knows when to use them. With the exception of the native games, or an Ireland rugby international, they're not generally switched on. There is no piped music. In earlier times, when I was beginning to learn my way around Dublin's public houses, The Palace struck me as a place where civilised people went to read a newspaper. Some of these civilised people had names, like Seamus Heaney, and others I vaguely recognised as former writers of the broadsheets they were clutching in their hands.

Jacques-Emile Blanche painting of James Joyce, 1934. (Courtesy of the National Gallery of Ireland)

In 1946, the American photographer Lee Miller felt no qualms in mounting the bar counter in pursuit of the perfect shot. 'Not only did I drink at the sacred Men's Bar,' she would recall, 'but I stood on it as well, straddling the partition between bars.'[1] Miller's images of The Palace would appear in *Vogue* magazine, illustrating an article by C. P. Curran on his friend James Joyce.

That Miller was alive at all was fortuitous. A former model who had reinvented herself as a photographer at the forefront of the situationist art movement, Miller had been working for the British edition of *Vogue* when the Second World War broke out. Under the stewardship of editor Audrey Withers, the magazine would come to play its own part in the 'Keep Calm and Carry On' feeling that swept across blitzed Britain. When bombs fell on the British capital, the magazine was sometimes produced from a 'wine-cellar basement', and it successfully withstood paper rationing, distribution problems and more besides. The message of the magazine was clear:

> Last year women were running households. This year they are running canteens, voluntary organisations, service units – and taking orders as well as giving them. Last year time was no object: this week, next week, sometime … This year time is of the essence of the contract.[2]

Not content with photographing the home front, Miller took advantage of her American citizenship by applying to US forces for accreditation as a war correspondent. Arriving in France in the near immediate aftermath of the D-Day landings, she discovered that the country was far from at peace. Present at the Battle of Saint-Malo, where besieged fascist forces vigorously defended fortified positions against Allied forces, she would describe the 'sickly death rattle' of the bombs, and the sight of smoke, 'belching, mushrooming and columning'.[3] There were several lucky escapes, but when the fighting did dissipate, fresh horrors revealed themselves across newly liberated Europe. Miller would

A view of The Palace Bar by Lee Miller for *Vogue*. © Lee Miller Archives, England 2025. All rights reserved. leemiller.co.uk

photograph the Dachau and Buchenwald concentration camps, with some of these images later appearing in the American edition of *Vogue*. These images remain haunting, and were amongst the most damning evidence of German crimes published in the Western media. On leaving Dachau, she wrote that 'the sight of the blue and white striped tatters shrouding the bestial death of the hundreds of starved and maimed men and women had left us gulping for air and for violence, and if Munich, the birthplace of this horror was falling, we'd like to help'.[4]

Miller arrived in Munich in time to be photographed in Adolf Hitler's apartment on the day the fascist leader ended his life in a Berlin bunker. David Scherman of *Life* magazine captured the shot of Miller in the bathtub of the man who had torn a continent apart, her mucky boots in shot. It is a defining image of the fall of Hitlerism, but the brutalities of Hitlerism were not something Miller found easy to move on from confronting. 'She was a peacetime casualty,' Scherman remembered. That meant clinical depression, bouts of heavy drinking and what today would be called PTSD. One imagines that the Dublin assignment was a welcome one, far removed from the war and its aftershocks.

In C. P. Curran, *Vogue* had an author who knew Joyce better than perhaps anyone still in Dublin. Curran is also present in the photograph of a young Joyce graduating from the National University of Ireland, standing beneath a tree now found in the gardens of the Museum of Literature Ireland. Curran had also photographed one of the most recognisable images of the writer, standing in the garden of the Curran family home. We see a young Joyce with hands in his pockets, head cocked slightly to one side, an everyman's cap sitting on his head. Curran recalled that the photograph 'has a certain humorous bravado in dress and carriage'; when Joyce was asked what he was thinking when the shot was taken by Curran, he wryly replied 'something about borrowing five shillings from the photographer'.[5] In truth, he had borrowed considerably more than that over the years.

Shane Sutton's mural of James Joyce in the north inner city nods to Con Curran's photograph of the writer.

Miller's photographs of Joycean Dublin would run alongside Curran's article, and brought the photographer on a journey through sites as diverse as Belvedere College, Glasnevin's Prospect Cemetery, Mountjoy Square and the Phoenix Park. Contrary to popular belief, *Ulysses* had never been banned by Ireland's gung-ho Censorship of Publications Board, but the work had not been widely available or engaged with in a significant way at home until a revival of interest in the author in the 1950s. At Belvedere College, the rector told her of the sad case of the 'freak writer … who had lost his faith. He had come from the background of a drunken dissolute father – had no security in his home and "came a cropper".'[6]

There was an inevitability that Miller would find herself photographing public houses. What makes a pub a Joycean pub? Within the pages of *Ulysses*, there are passing references to public houses, including The Oval Bar and The International (then Ruggy

O'Donoghue's), but there are also key moments that centre drinking establishments, both licensed and unlicensed. Pubs are found in *Dubliners*, including Mulligan's on Poolbeg Street, which confusingly boasts a plaque showing the date of *Ulysses*, rather than basking in the glory of its centrality to the 'Counterparts' story in *Dubliners*.

For every pub that boasts Joyce as a former regular – real or imagined – it is far more likely the premises was familiar to John Stanislaus Joyce, his father. When James Joyce described the more than fifteen homes of his Dublin childhood as the 'haunted inkpots' of his youth, he was capturing the precarious and uncertain nature of growing up in a household where the pursuit of drink dominated John's life. Joyce's brother recalled their father as someone who 'had a jolly time of it with his hard-drinking friends of that hard-drinking generation'.[7] However, perhaps an anecdote in Curran's memoir captures the turbulence better:

Patrick Tuohy's depiction of John Stanislaus Joyce. (Courtesy of the National Library of Ireland)

> Another tale told of a night's drinking with friends when he had been living far out beyond Clontarf. Helpless and protesting, he was pushed into the last Dollymount tram and put in charge of the conductor. Faithful to his trust and in spite of all protests, the conductor allowed him to alight only when at midnight they had reached Dollymount. His friends met him the next day and made due inquiries as to how he got home. His language was more than usually fearful; unknown to them, a day or two earlier and in customary haste, he had moved camp to Phibsboro, a quite other quarter of the city.[8]

Another loyal friend, Padraic Colum, recalled Joyce's father as 'well known in the Dublin bars, the restaurants and the racecourses; he had the sort of status in the city that a man who has frittered away his prospects in the name of good fellowship can have in any easy-going social milieu'.[9] In Dublin lingo, then and now, he was a 'character'. For James Joyce, his youthful pockets were not deep enough to spend as much time in public houses. Even later, when fame arrived at his door in Paris, one of the most celebrated barmen of that city would recall him as a 'white-wine-totaler ... he leads a very retired life and never visits bars'.[10]

Miller may have been wandering more in the footsteps of father than son, but her journey still brought her to The Palace. This had become the dominant literary pub of the 1940s, owing in no small part to the gregarious presence of the *Irish Times* editor R. M. Smyllie, and the company he assembled and attracted. One regular, Brian O'Nolan (writing as Flann O'Brien), would describe the pub in the early 1940s in the pages of *The Bell*:

> The Palace Bar in Fleet Street is the main resort of newspapermen, writers, painters and every known breed of artist and intellectual. Porter is served willingly everywhere in the house, and in fancy tankards. The clients range from the tiniest elfin intellectual to a larger editor, alive and in good condition.[11]

The Palace could be an intimidating social environment. When Tony Gray, a young journalist who had joined the *Irish Times* in 1940, first visited, he found a 'motley collection of Dublin intellectuals, businessmen, civil servants, college lecturers, actors and members of the legal profession'.[12] To Patrick Kavanagh, who would in time depart The Palace for the more ramshackle McDaid's, it was a place where men discussed 'such significant matters as George Moore's use of the semi-colon and what English journals paid for book reviews'.[13]

While Miller would encounter a coldness towards Joyce in his alma mater, the feeling in The Palace was different. Here, 'unlike the Jesuits, the owner, Mr. Flynn, is very proud that Joyce is associated in memory with his place'.[14]

The pub Miller describes is still recognisable, with a long front bar and a separate back bar space. As now, the women's toilets are located below the back-room bar, which is no issue today but proved a challenge then. The front bar, Miller notes, 'was gentlemen only ... In order to get to the back room, where ladies are allowed, you have to pass thru this bar and do so practically on tip-toe.'[15] We know that Miller's pictures were taken on a Sunday, and the time at which she shot them:

> Mr Flynn arranged to open the pub for me during Holy Hour (between 2.30 and 3.30 all pubs in Dublin are closed to give the staff a chance to go pray). On Sundays, the pubs are scarcely open at all and we took it over, he invited all these characters to come along to be in the pix ...

The inside of The Palace, architecturally, is unaltered. Elsewhere, however, Miller provides us with an interior view of a public house that was otherwise undocumented: Barney Kiernan's on Little Britain Street. The painted-over façade of this pub remains, blue and deteriorating slowly, with signage just about visible in the window. Located just off Capel Street and beside the Green Street courthouse, Barney Kiernan's was the centre of the action in the Cyclops episode of *Ulysses*, where a narrow-minded zealot and barfly, The Citizen, confronts Leopold Bloom on questions of faith and national identity.

In earlier times, it was one of a network of busy pubs that dotted the markets area. Miller noted that, 'on the back streets behind the Four Courts are a lot of pubs, written about and occupied by Joyce ... the neighbourhood is incredibly shabby now, but once, perhaps even in Joyce's time, the houses were lovely'.[16]

Barney Kiernan's on Little Britain Street today. It is for sale, and the property agent notes 'the surrounding area is currently in the process of wide-scale regeneration and redevelopment'.

Instead of residents of houses – lovely or otherwise – it was market workers, barristers and others who supported the establishments that dotted the district.

The proximity of the pub to the courthouse that had doomed Robert Emmet and a litany of other 'men who died for Ireland' had long given it a peculiar atmosphere. The Brazen Head could boast that the United Irishmen had schemed there, but in Barney Kiernan's things were more macabre. An article on the pub in 1947 noted that 'other historic bric-a-brac on view here included the tankard used allegedly by Robert Emmet's executioner, hangmen's ropes, gyves, chains and instruments of torture from old Newgate Prison ... These museum-pieces have since disappeared, doubtless removed as mementoes as the premises passed from one owner to another.'[17] Lee Miller walked into an establishment where 'everything in the place is a souvenir of some kind or other'.[18] In her photographs, we see a print of The Invincibles proudly on display, the Fenian assassination team that had struck in the Phoenix Park in 1882, rocking the British political establishment. They meant more to some of the locals, such as 'the old bird sitting in the back room [who] is one of the regulars from Joyce's day. He remembers him well but is not vastly interested as his favourite people are all the political assassins etc.'[19]

Lee Miller's Dublin photographs stand on their own merit and would remain a remarkable snapshot of 1940s Dublin even if their creator remained a mystery. She was not the last photographer to attempt to capture the city of *Ulysses*; when the photographer Erich Hartmann visited Dublin in 1964, he felt he already knew the city deeply, such was his admiration for the writings of Joyce. Yet the journey Miller had taken, and her artistic beginnings in the Paris of surrealism, deeply shapes her work. As her son Antony Penrose notes, 'children and ordinary people populate the frames in a way that Joyce, in common with the surrealists, celebrated the marvellous that is to be found in the ordinary'.[20]

Quite rightly, a print of one of Miller's shots of The Palace has pride of place in the establishment's snug. Her name is more widely recalled today, thanks to the trojan publishing efforts of Antony and the Lee Miller Archives, and the 2024 biopic *Lee*, starring Kate Winslet.

On the other side of the Liffey, the fortunes of the other establishment she photographed could not be more different. Barney Kiernan's, also known as the Court of Appeal, has sat idle for decades. A listing on a commercial real estate website correctly describes it as a site of literary importance, going on to note:

> The building retains some of the original elements of the shopfront of the famous pub Barney Kiernan's, and with the potential for increased tourism activity in the area with the renovation of the Victorian Fruit Market and numerous hotels under development, these cultural connections could greatly benefit a future commercial use at the premises.[21]

In a future Dublin, could Barney Kiernan's become a Bloomsday stop of pilgrimage? Stranger things have happened in publand.

Had Miller come to Dublin a few years later, she might have found The Pearl and not The Palace, as the pub on the other side of Fleet Street (long demolished on a site now occupied by a hotel, having first been purchased by the Bank of Ireland) became the local haunt of R. M. Smyllie and his set, moving the drinking even closer to the offices of the *Irish Times*. In this new environment, women came to greater prominence. Later, pioneering female journalists like Nell McCafferty, Mary Kenny and Maeve Binchy were all regulars at The Pearl, the latter telling journalist Cathal O'Shannon that 'I've only been in the *Irish Times* for four years but I suppose I've been here twice a day.'[22] When Binchy interviewed Samuel Beckett in 1980, the topic drifted to Smyllie, The Palace and The Pearl:

> 'My memory of him was that he ran his newspaper from the pubs and that there were circles around him, listening to what he wanted to do and running away to do it. He used to drink in The Palace. Is The Pearl still there?'
> 'No, it's been bought by the bank,' I said.
> 'The bank', said Beckett thoughtfully, 'the bank. How extraordinary.'[23]

# CHAPTER 14.
# MURALS IN THE MORAL PUB

Detail from one of the murals in Davy Byrne's. Many of the individuals depicted in the various murals are former regulars of the pub, including the painter Harry Kernoff and Davy Byrne himself.

The artist Cecil Ffrench Salkeld's life began in India's Assam region in July 1904. A reminder of the complexity of Ireland's place in the colonial world, his father was a member of the Indian Civil Service. Today, he is buried in Dublin's Glasnevin Cemetery, along with numerous members of his distinguished family, including his mother Blanaid Salkeld, an actor, poet and important publisher of bohemian literature. From their garden shed at 43 Morehampton Road, a small wooden hand press brought to life poetry, pamphlets and prose from the mother-and-son team, under the name Gayfield Press.

Their family grave is one of the most visited in Glasnevin, but their names are rarely spoken there. Instead, people come in droves to see the memorial to Cecil's son-in-law, Brendan Behan. Cecil's daughter, Beatrice, would marry the writer in 1955. It was a small affair in Donnybrook church that eventually made its way into the city. Beatrice recalled a fiddler outside the Lincoln Inn playing traditional airs, and Behan following him into the street with a request: 'Play The Coolin. I'll buy you a jar if you play The Coolin.' He did, and 'Brendan's tenor voice soared above the violin music and the noise of the traffic. Girls in nearby offices opened the windows and leaned out.'[1] It's a nice image to picture walking by the pub today, which is more associated with the romance of James Joyce and Nora Barnacle, who worked in the neighbouring Finn's Hotel, and who first encountered Joyce strolling on Nassau Street. Bloomsday Lager, Joyce's Stout and Nora's Red Ale all appear on tap at the Lincoln Inn.

Not far away, the lasting legacy of the Ffrench Salkeld family to a Dublin pub interior is found at Duke Street's Davy Byrne's. A series of murals painted by Cecil, with the assistance of daughter Beatrice, remain a striking feature of the pub and one of the great artworks of the pub landscape in Dublin.

In his youth, Cecil's star burned brightly. In the Germany of the early 1920s, he exhibited at the first Internationale Kunstausstellung in Dusseldorf, alongside talents like Matisse and Boccioni.[2] A champion of modernism in Ireland, he was a founder (along with the writer Liam O'Flaherty) of the Radical Club in the Dublin of 1925, which sought:

> ... to provide a centre of intercourse for Irish intellectual workers; to encourage all forms of progressive cultural activity in Ireland; to fight for the freedom of cultural expression in Ireland; to promote solidarity among artists, writers, scientists, and all people engaged in intellectual pursuits in Ireland.[3]

By the 1950s, things were different, and Beatrice recalled that 'Cecil was a great man for the bed and spent as much time in it as he could. He was one of the first drop-outs, and he dropped out in comfort.'[4] To many, it seemed a sad waste of a brilliant talent, one that still shone on occasion in broadcasting and his more limited

The most famous pub lunch in Irish literary history is commemorated outside Davy Byrne's.

output. Ffrench Salkeld was happiest painting in his red fez, a budgie fluttering around the top floor of the family house. A visitor remembered that 'under the iron bed in the corner, with no attempt at concealment, was a crate of drink that could float the Asgard'.[5]

The murals date from the previous decade, and the taking over of the pub by the Doran family in 1942. Wisely, they would keep the name Davy Byrne's, commemorating its place in Joyce's *Ulysses*, in which it is described as a 'Moral pub'. Davy Byrne, a former barman would remember, was 'very strict, very fair. You could argue with him. He once told me he could paper the walls with the cheques he accepted that bounced on him.'[6]

The Dorans would bring an Art Deco touch to the interior. Seeking permission to amend the premises, the new owners spoke of 'a continental brasserie' as their aim. This was not something everyone welcomed. To one contemporary writer, the pub had become 'a super-lounge', and was best avoided, for 'The Palace is the Davy Byrne's de nous jour.'[7] To others, the move towards a more cosmopolitan interior, influenced by Parisian trends, represented an assault on tradition:

> Lounge bars, catering for the rising number of women drinkers, have sprung up all over the city. Even as I write, the builders' men are pulling down Davy Byrne's pub in Duke Street, and plans have been prepared to make it into a bar suitable for men and women frequenting the dance halls nearby. Tradition, the new owner appears to feel, does not pay in these modern days.[8]

CHAPTER 14. MURALS IN THE MORAL PUB

A young artist herself, Beatrice worked with her father on the Davy Byrne's murals, and she would later care for their maintenance, feeling a great pride in the upkeep of Cecil's work. In her memoir, she recalled with some sadness the relationship her father had with alcohol:

> If I was influenced as an artist by my father I was embarrassed by his drinking. Once when he was commissioned to paint a series of murals in Jammet's restaurant he asked me to help him. I had already worked as his assistant when he painted the murals in Davy Byrne's pub, where a school friend and I had helped him rough in the backgrounds. But when I arrived at Jammet's he was too drunk even to climb the ladder. I walked out of the restaurant, mortified, and he lost the commission.[9]

Entitled *The Triumph of Bacchus*, the name of the mural at Davy Byrne's is a tip of the hat towards the painter Diego Velázquez, whose 1629 work of the same name is popularly known as 'Los borrachos' ('The Drinkers'). The paintings became a defining feature of the establishment, with J. P. Donleavy remembering that the 'exotic Bacchanalian murals ... seemed to glow in the subdued lighting and under which the habitues sat on soft crimson banquettes'.[10]

Donleavy, a young American student benefiting from the GI Bill, which allowed soldiers to remain in Europe and secure an education, was wide-eyed at Dublin publand in the immediate post-war period. He had never known Davy Byrne's any other way, but was transfixed by its differences from other such spaces, and the so-called 'Gilded Cage', as the rear space of the public house became known. It was 'reserved for drinkers of spirits and champagne' and was 'further insulated from questionable accostings or any temporary rubbing of elbows with beer imbibers, by being separately entered from a side lane off Duke Street, thereby keeping discreet those elite comings and goings'.[11]

**One of the impressive murals in Davy Byrne's.**

While now more a restaurant than a public house, Davy Byrne's is a welcoming space, where stout or champagne drinkers alike can appreciate the work of Ffrench Salkeld and his talented daughter. Joining the murals are a variety of interesting artworks, including sculptures by Edward Delaney and John Behan (no relation to Cecil's son-in-law). Leopold Bloom perhaps wouldn't recognise the interior, but the gorgonzola sandwich remains, devoured by huge crowds each year on 16 June. As the writer Desmond Fennell traversed Dublin one Bloomsday, he viewed it all as a day of pilgrimage:

> In Dublin today they look across the Bay from the Tower, or buy lemon soap in Sweny's, or eat pork kidneys for breakfast in certain restaurants. In Davy Byrne's, they drink the saint's particular wine, and eat bread with his particular cheese, doing this in commemoration of him.[12]

# CHAPTER 15.
# THE HORSESHOE BAR

When Ernest Hemingway was asked to pen an introduction for the memoir of Jimmie Charters, the legendary barman of 1920s Paris who served (and banned) the great and the good, he couldn't help but joke that 'you should expect to be able to go into a saloon or bar and pay for your drinks without appearing in the bartenders' memoirs and I was shocked and grieved to hear that Jimmie Charters was writing his'.[1] To Hemingway, nothing appeared to be sacred or secret anymore.

Charters fell into a very small group of barmen who themselves became a part of the broader story of a literary moment. Memoirs from those who worked behind the counter of Dublin's public houses are rare, but one memorable exception came from Sean Boyd, who presided over the Shelbourne Hotel's Horseshoe Bar for decades. Born in Belfast in 1943, Boyd worked his way up to the bar of the most prestigious hotel in the city. To him, it was a profession, and 'being a good barman is rather like being a good priest. The greatest similarity between the two callings is the need to keep the secrets of the confessional.'[2]

Beginning life in 1824, the Shelbourne Hotel has a history that pre-dates its current form. Founded by Tipperary businessman Martin Burke, it was a bold undertaking in a city still reeling from the Act of Union of 1801, which had stripped the Irish capital of its parliament and reduced its social standing significantly as a result. In the 1860s, the architect John McCurdy would dramatically remodel a terrace of Georgian houses, creating the Shelbourne Hotel exterior we know in what has been described as 'High Victorian style'.[3] The hotel survived the drama of Easter 1916, when the neighbouring park (St Stephen's Green) was seized by the Irish Citizen Army. A machine gun on the roof of the hotel helped to clear them, and 'its overhead rattling fire made the chandeliers tremble: on every floor of the hotel it became harder to sing, talk, even to think'.[4] Constance Markievicz, who surely knew the hotel in her debutante days as a Gore-Booth, is today commemorated in a mural by artist Paul Slater in the members-only 1824 Bar. All is forgiven, with even a suite named in her honour.

When war came to Dublin again in Civil War days, the management of the Shelbourne worried what it might bring. In a rushed correspondence between the manager and partners based abroad, we read of a 'bedroom window and sittingroom window ... shattered by bullets last night, also rooms 75 and 27. All shops shut, but so far we have supplies. The fate of the Four Courts is tragic.'[5]

Beyond its physical opulence, the cultural history of the Shelbourne Hotel is itself significant. It was there, in 1876, that Bram Stoker first met Sir Henry Irving, considered the greatest actor of his generation. Stoker, then Dublin theatre reviewer, escorted Irving back to the hotel after a performance, in awe of the adoring crowd who accompanied Irving on his way: 'Up Grafton Street we swept, the ordinary passengers in the street falling of necessity back into doorways and side streets; round into St Stephen's Green, where the shouting crowd stopped before the hotel.'[6] That was a time before the Horseshoe Bar, but the two men wined and dined in the hotel, a meeting that would change Stoker's life and see him moving to London to manage Irving's Lyceum Theatre.

The Horseshoe Bar arrived only in 1957, the work of architect Sam Stephenson and Aidan Prior, then manager of the Brown Thomas interiors department. Stephenson's name instantly recalls his brutalist contributions to the architectural realm, in particular the former Central Bank on Dame Street and the Civic Offices of Wood Quay. Here is something entirely different in scale, and a room Boyd described as 'an environment similar to that of a gentleman's club ... The horseshoe-shaped bar was installed to add to the slightly decadent atmosphere, its pediment was crowned with a panel of engravings of *A Rake's Progress* by William Hogarth.'[7] An unexpected connection between William Hogarth and the hotel comes in the form of Paul Hogarth, a direct descendant and talented illustrator, who stayed in the hotel for no less than six months when creating the graphics for *Brendan Behan's Island*, an uneven and anecdotal book from near the end of Behan's life. In more promising times for Behan, the Shelbourne had been the location for a meeting with Iain Hamilton, editorial director of Hutchinson publishers. Hamilton worried about the image he presented: 'A bloody Presbyterian Scots chancer on the make, too neatly dressed, with a moustache a little too British military for comfort ...'[8] The meeting went well – but the Horseshoe was then in a state of construction. It is fitting that Behan is one of the characters commemorated in the Slater mural in the 1824 Bar.

A 'rake', should the reader be wondering, is described in the *Oxford English Dictionary* as 'a fashionable or wealthy man of dissolute or promiscuous habits'. These were plentiful in Dublin, but Hogarth's work depicts the fall of Tom Rakewell, heir to a wealthy merchant, who squanders the family fortune in London, before being imprisoned. He is 'a young bourgeois, first seen as a trembling youth with a fresh face haloed in curls, attractive, open,

The renowned Horseshoe Bar, presided over for many years by Sean Boyd. (With thanks to Karen Glackin and the Shelbourne Hotel)

innocent – and weak'.[9] By the end, he is drowning in debt and sin. A fitting enough character to watch over the Celtic Tiger days of the Horseshoe Bar.

Formerly the Reading and Writing Room, complete with a curving staircase, the redesigned room successfully turned a large and open space into one that feels much more enclosed, lowering ceilings and allowing no natural light to enter the space.

For Boyd, who witnessed the great change the Celtic Tiger years brought, the regulars of the Horseshoe Bar could be divided into a before and after cast. He remembered how:

> As the change to the new, moneyed class of the Celtic Tiger began to happen the old order drifted away from the Horseshoe Bar. One day, I heard one of them say, 'what's that dreadful smell?', and, answering his own question, said, 'ah, it's new money.'[10]

From the old money stock, there were few as interesting as Garech Browne (son of Guinness heiress Oonagh Guinness), who had moved to Dublin to be near to the literary and cultural world that so interested him. Browne would create Claddagh Records, bringing traditional music (like *The Liffey Banks* from Tommie Potts) and poetry (such as *Almost Everything* by Patrick Kavanagh) to the public. Between the Horseshoe Bar and its near-neighbour O'Donoghue's on Merrion Row, Browne was quite content living between two worlds. There was Lord Kilbracken, remembered by Boyd as 'an ace fighter pilot and much decorated in the Second World War. He returned his medals to the Queen after the events on Bloody Sunday.'[11] Many of the regulars of the bar, Boyd felt, 'were seen as English in Ireland and Irish in England'.[12]

The name and equine theme also cemented a relationship between the bar and the racing and horse show crowds. The Duchess of Westminster, owner of the beloved Arkle, was a regular presence.[13] Arkle himself had achieved such a level of cult fandom in Ireland following the defeat of Mill House in the 1964 Cheltenham Gold Cup that he probably would have been served on the premises.

And what of the later regulars? 'On an average night,' regular Eamon Dunphy wrote, 'there might be in one corner a politician, in another a slot machine baron from London.'[14] In some ways, the bar became a victim of its own reputation for a period, Dunphy lamenting that:

> A tolerable atmosphere in which eccentricity was, like privacy, respected, dissolved as those who wanted to sample what they had been led to believe was high society, invaded this lovely but, alas, rather small room.[15]

Proving the thesis, Boyd recalled of Dunphy how 'I was aware of the fact that people used to come to the bar just to look at him. He once said that this phenomenon gave him a perfect understanding of how the animals in the zoo felt.'[16]

Alas, all animals die in time, even a Celtic Tiger. The old quip of the Horseshoe being the bar 'where women with a past look for men with no future' still does the rounds, but the bar is – space permitting – a democratic space. A confident stride through the front door is all that separates a Dubliner from the hotel that has survived insurrection and changing fashions.

## CHAPTER 16.

# A BIRD NEVER FLEW ON ONE WING

All across the city the universe of John Gilroy is visible on public house exteriors.

**T**here is little dispute that the artist most present in the public houses of the capital is John Gilroy. Born in Newcastle-upon-Tyne in 1898, the in-house artist at advertising firm S. H. Benson worked with brands as diverse as Bovril and Macleans toothpaste before landing on the Guinness brief. Over a period of thirty-five years, Gilroy would produce more than a hundred press and poster advertisements for the stout. As Jim Davies notes in his history of Guinness advertising:

> Among them are two of the most enduring advertising images ever created: a workman casually carrying a huge girder on his shoulder for the 'Guinness for Strength' campaign, and the impudent sea lion making off with the zoo-keeper's pint in the inaugural 'My Goodness, My Guinness' poster.[1]

Gilroy, always modest about his own work, would talk of how 'posters are a kind of aesthetic meal-in-a-minute. The man in the street is usually in a hurry to catch a bus or avoid being caught by one, and has no time for lengthy contemplation.'[2] We see Gilroy's creations dotted all across Dublin publand, sometimes even outlasting the public house itself. Maye's pub on the corner of Frederick Street North is now a Centra, but Gilroy's worker is still there, affixing a clock surrounded by happy zoo animals. Gilroy's work proved transferable across cultures and continents; from Lagos to Kilburn, there is hardly an Irish pub on the planet where you won't encounter his distinctive work, and it has been parodied, reimagined and bootlegged.

In Dublin's public houses, the artist Harry Kernoff's work is frequently present as well. Reflecting his own taste (The Palace, Davy Byrne's, Peter's Pub and Neary's come to mind instantly), the artist sold his work in pubs, depicted public houses and their characters, and sometimes gifted work to friends on the other side of the bar. On occasion, a work might be produced to settle a tab. No other artist has so captured the Dublin pub and its place in cultural and literary history.

Born into a Jewish family in London in the opening year of the twentieth century, Kernoff was the son of a cabinet maker, and would learn skills from his father that transferred into his ability to make striking woodcuts. Settling in what was then Dublin's Jewish district, known as Little Jerusalem, the Kernoff family became a part of the small but influential Jewish community here. One resident recalled Clanbrassil Street as 'the kosher street'. As Ray Rivlin recalled in her history of the community, those who visited the street in the early twentieth century 'were transported to scenes more in keeping with nineteenth-century Russia than twentieth-century Ireland'.[3]

Harry Kernoff worked from a studio on Stamer Street, today marked by a plaque, a part of the landscape of remembrance of Jewish Dublin in the area. Though he was an accomplished landscape painter, what has held his place in the memory of the city are the depictions of the denizens of the city, many of whom visited his studio to sit for paintings.

'Artistic cliques do not interest him,' one profile noted, 'but the people with whom he comes in daily contact do.'[4] There are rabbis, firefighters, journalists, stage managers, street characters. There could be no greater example of the later than The Toucher

Doyle, who was said to have obtained such an illustrious nickname when he 'touched' King Edward VII for a fiver at the Leopardstown races. 'Touching' was considered different from begging – this was a promised loan, but likely never to be seen again. 'He touched me for 10 bob while I was painting him,' remembered Kernoff, 'but it was done with real artistry'.[5] We see The Toucher Doyle – holding a pint he presumably didn't pay for – in *A Bird Never Flew on One Wing*, one of Kernoff's most instantly recognisable works, which has been ever-present in The Palace in one form or another since Kernoff first produced it. It shows two men clutching pints, while behind them is a background of pub names that includes the familiar and the long lost. Like many Kernoff works, variations of *A Bird Never Flew on One Wing* are plentiful, but the original painting took pride of place in M. O'Brien's pub near Leeson Street for several decades. O'Brien's, auctioneer David Britton has noted, 'wasn't, in fact, listed as one of the 50 pub names in the painting, which prompted the owner to bring the picture to Kernoff's studio in Stamer Street and Kernoff added it in.'[6]

While not impressed by Kernoff's 'watercolour efforts at Irish scenery', a 1951 reviewer felt his strength lay in capturing the character of the capital:

> ... most people collected around his etchings and portraits. Here Harry Kernoff is supreme. No other Irish artist knows his Dublin 'character' or can portray him as completely as Harry ... What O'Casey did in turning the dramatic spotlight on Dublin 'local colour', Harry Kernoff is equally proficient in doing with an etching pen.[7]

Politically radical, Kernoff produced mastheads for newspapers on the socialist and communist left, including *Republican Congress*, the paper founded following the 1930s leftwards split from the IRA spearheaded by Frank Ryan and Peadar O'Donnell. His heroic depictions of James Connolly and Roger Casement made it to the front of the newspaper.

In the back bar of The Palace, we can still find a Kernoff woodcut depicting David Fitzgerald, an anti-treaty veteran of the Civil War who had remained active on the left, even visiting the Soviet Union with the artist as part of an Irish left-wing delegation. The work, depicting Fitzgerald in his IRA uniform, is displayed on the wall alongside more of Kernoff's work showing everyday life, from a market day in rural Ireland to a currach on the water.

A particularly beloved work hangs in the National Gallery, showing a view of Davy Byrne's from The Bailey across the street. The work is brilliant for its playfulness – Kernoff, instantly recognisable in his distinctive hat, places himself in the piece, visible in a mirror. Amidst the bottles of stout, wine and spirits, are two theatre handbills – *Look at the Heffernans!* at the Abbey, *Romeo and Juliet* at the Gate. Comedy and tragedy, together as always. In other works we see Kernoff alongside friends in public houses, including Davy Byrne himself.

Some of the Dublin pub views Kernoff gives us are still instantly recognisable, such as that of The International on the corner of Wicklow Street. Others, as in those he made of The Bailey and Davy Byrne's, show interiors that have since been radically transformed. One of Kernoff's favourite haunts that has changed little is the beautiful Neary's (still carrying the name of Thomas Neary, who acquired it in 1887) on Chatham Row. Neary's, Pat Dargan noted in his 2018 guide to Dublin pubs, 'is one of the few remaining Dublin pubs where the custom of white-uniformed barmen survives. Here the bar staff wear white shirts, black bow ties and black trousers.'[8] This touch of formality remains, as do the Kernoff works that dot the pub proudly. Neary's was a calmer institution than some he frequented, and Kernoff enjoyed quietly working there in the evening.[9] At nearby Peter's Pub, a woodcut of Roger Casement can still be found, alongside one depicting the poet James Clarence Mangan.

A brisk walk from The Palace to Davy Byrne's, McDaid's, Peter's and Neary's will reveal original works still hanging in each.

A flyer for a Harry Kernoff exhibition showing James Clarence Mangan. A woodcut of Mangan by Kernoff hangs in Peter's Pub. (With thanks to the Capuchin Archives)

# EXHIBITION OF NEW WORK
## BY HARRY KERNOFF, R.H.A.
### AT ACADEMY SMALL GALLERY
### 15 ELY PLACE, DUBLIN (SIDE DOOR)
### OPEN: NOV. 12TH – NOV. 24TH, 1951
### HOURS: 10.30 A.M. – 6 P.M.    FREE

# PERSONALITIES
## Harry Kernoff

Harry A. Kernoff, R.H.A., was born London in 1900 of a Russian-Jewish father and a Spanish-Jewish mother. He is a painter of portraits, landscapes and murals, a master of the woodcut and a charming illustrator of books. He came to Dublin when he was fourteen and studied at the Metropolitan School of Art. He won the coveted Taylor Scholarship at twenty-three, and since then has held fifteen one-man shows in Dublin, and others in London, Paris, Amsterdam, Chicago and New York. His pictures hang in foreign galleries. In height he is about five foot nothing, and lacks only a fair sized mushroom to sit upon to look the spit and image of a leprachaun. His hobby seems to be the telling of 'shaggy dog' stories. 'Almost drawing-room,' he titters by way of introduction to each and every one of them. You will always know him by the mysterious pouch he carries: something more than a handbag and less than a briefcase. If you catch him in an unguarded moment—which his difficult—you will discover that this pouch contains, not the tools of his trade, but an exhaustive file of Dublin street songs, which, if Mr. Kernoff takes to you, he may sing in an atrociously bad tenor voice. In conversation he can be witty in the extreme—generally at his own expense; he never, of his own accord, talks shop, and never never makes a really unkind comment on a colleague.

'At any rate he can draw' is about the most he will say. Those who can't draw he doesn't mention. Force Mr. Kernoff to his own subject and the story is likely to come in a series of axioms. Beauty is the artist's conception of nature in a rhythmic form, emphasising his viewpoint with controlled emotion and with perfect balance, like the wavering of a compass needle . . . Continual experiment is the only way to progress in artistic expression . . . Memory work is of paramount importance . . . Just as a man is perhaps a symbol of a greater thing, so a picture should symbolise humanity . . . Design is the fundamental necessity in any work of art.

. . . A picture should express a mood, and these are infinite in range . . . Genius is a perfect harmony of the emotions and mind . . . The painter must have faith in himself, or else inhibit himself by listening to everybody and not to himself . . . The greater the number of individuals a picture appeals to, the greater the picture . . . More nonsense is written about painting than about any other subject . . . Art criticism in Ireland? You ask is it bad? But there isn't any.

Beginning in a period of extreme orthodoxy, Kernoff was first looked upon as an amiable eccentric, and, as art critic Edward Sheehy has remarked in his penetrating preface to one of the artist's books of woodcuts, the fact that Kernoff's work is now taken for granted is due, not, as is generally the case where the pioneer is overtaken by the general practice, but to his persistence and continuous development along the line of his original innovation. Kernoff's individuality as a painter cannot for a moment be doubted, and his innovations are largely due to the emphasis he places on form ("design is the fundamental necessity in any work of art"). As Sheehy remarks: 'Clarity of vision,

**HARRY KERNOFF**
in his studio

the refusal to poeticise, a sanity expressed through a careful and untemperamental craftsmanship, these are the predominant qualities of Kernoff's work.' And if he has limitations, and if his work appears hard, it is because of these. He is an Academician without being academic. He is an experimentor in many directions, without ever letting the experiment run away with him. He is as sincere and earnest an artist as one could wish to meet, and yet is capable of the most elaborate jokes, even on the R.H.A. Remember his 'Composition In Space-Time'? But lately elected a full member of the Academy, he foisted this fantastic piece on the selection board. He had the satisfaction of seeing it hang to puzzle the pundits of the Dublin art world. Since then Kernoff has done a woodcut of this picture which is reproduced with this article. While the meaning may be vague, there can be no doubt as to the excellence of the composition. Even when joking Kernoff's deep sense of design evidently does not desert him. As I have pointed out, Kernoff's experiments have led him in many directions. Several of his admirers have deplored this, and some have fallen away, coming, I suppose, to regard him as a sort of jack of all trades. However, when one remembers Kernoff's passionate belief that a picture should express a mood and that these are infinite in range, one knows that he is happy in the knowledge that he eludes a label. As he told the Dublin Rotary Club some time ago: If the painter decides to become a recipe-artist, he is destroying his own creative power; and though he may become well-to-do materially, he will, inevitably, be finished aesthetically. Mr. Kernoff despises those who would place artists in different compartments of the mind, holding that such people are lazy thinkers. That some people should prefer his Dublin street scenes to his woodcuts, makes little or no difference to him. He is catholic in his tastes and gets as much aesthetic kick from one type of work as from another. He is perfectly satisfied if in each new work he propogates his own point of view, his own emotional reaction to the environment, person or persons responsible for the mood which resulted in the work. In spite of this militant independence of spirit. Mr. Kernoff is an intensely sociable being, and likes to please as many people as he can. Artistic cliques do not interest him, but the people with whom he comes in daily contact do. While, as he says himself, a creative man can paint to please himself aesthetically, he also wants other people to get some pleasure from the beauty and manifestations of nature which he notes. No man can live in a vacuum and be sane. We humans are all gregarious and shall remain so to the end. Visit Kernoff's studio off the South Circular Road, Dublin, and you will realise that while you may be in the presence of a lonely man, you are also talking with one who has stretched a friendly hand in, perhaps, too many directions.

—Nimrod.

This is the first in a series of profiles in which NIMROD will deal with leading artistic, theatrical and sporting personalities.

Tommy Smith, late proprietor of Grogan's, recalled Kernoff's name amongst the McDaid's set, who were 'a mixed bunch comprising republicans recently released from jail, soldiers just back from the war, American GI's on scholarships to Trinity, writers, artists and a great mix of Dublin's working class'.[10] Kernoff felt the pub a natural environment in which to display art, laying out ten good reasons in a letter sent to the newspapers in the early 1960s:

> 1. They decorate the place. 2: They create conversation and discussion. 3: They are aesthetically educational. 4: They're an investment and appreciate in value as time passes. 5: They can be changed about. 6: They act as a perpetual exhibitional venue for artists. 7: They raise the status of art and artists generally. 8: Better for the artist, than for him to wait for the odd patron in his studio. 9: Better than murals which gather dirt and date. 10: Create aesthetic appreciation by being visible at all times, Sunday too. Which is better than the odd limited exhibition.[11]

The painter Michael Kane, in his memoir *Blind Dogs*, remembers Kernoff as 'a cheery little man who one sometimes encountered hurrying across Stephen's Green, with his briefcase, on his way to meet a client'. But what Kane recalls as important is the vision of the work — it is 'sunny-day socialism all the way, and if the ordinary people were not at the hustings, they were cavorting at the seaside or enjoying a day in the country'.[12]

Kernoff, the great artist of the Dublin public house, died on a day when they were closed. On Christmas Day 1974, news of his death made its way across the city he had captured over so many decades. Obituaries were kind and plentiful; he was, the *Evening Herald* told readers, 'as much a part of Dublin as the Coombe or the Daisy Market'.[13] Perhaps the finest tribute to him in the public houses of the city is to leave the work where it is, so that The Toucher Doyle and James Clarence Mangan may continue to gaze down on a new generation of Dublin drinkers.

A profile of Harry Kernoff. In it, we see an image of him working on a painting which shows the Davy Byrne's set. (With thanks to the Capuchin Archives)

CHAPTER 17.

CHAPELIZOD AND BEYOND

As the month of November was just beginning, the Halloween decorations were still up in the public houses of Chapelizod when I visited the area for this book. It all seemed fitting enough, as this Liffeyside village attracts more attention than most at that time of year. Chapelizod was immortalised in the work of Joseph Sheridan Le Fanu, the influential writer of fantastic fiction and ghost stories in Dublin's Victorian age. In *The House by the Churchyard*, his 1863 novel set there, Chapelizod itself emerges as something of a character:

> In those days, Chapelizod was about the gayest and prettiest of the outpost villages in which the old Dublin took a complacent pride. The poplars which stood, in military rows, here and there, just showed a glimpse of formality among the orchards and old timber that lined the banks of the river and the valley of the Liffey, with a lively sort of richness. The broad old street looked hospitable and merry, with steep roofs and many coloured hall-doors. The jolly old inn, just beyond the turnpike at the sweep of the road, leading over the buttressed bridge by the mill, was the first to welcome the excursionist from Dublin under the sign of the Phoenix.[1]

The interim period has been one of mixed fortunes for Chapelizod. A visitor today will notice the surprising number of vacant and decaying buildings in the village and its environs, but equally the very strong sense of revival and recent renewal. Busy cafés and modern apartment buildings have brought new life to the old place, which was never quite intended for twenty-first-century traffic. On a Sunday morning, we move slowly enough through the bustling and vibrant village to catch a good glimpse of the titular house by the churchyard itself, still standing with the help of support beams.

Le Fanu's Chapelizod was shaped by his childhood, and the fact that his father, an Anglican clergyman, had been chaplain of the Royal Hibernian Military School in the neighbouring Phoenix Park. It was a well of inspiration he returned to often, and before *The House by the Churchyard* he wrote a series of ghost stories about the village for the *Dublin University Magazine*. 'Take my word for it,' he told his readers, 'there is no such thing as an ancient village, especially if it has seen better days, unillustrated by its legends of terror.'[2] In his world – fusing fact, fiction and folklore – publicans and public houses would frequently feature. James Joyce was also drawn to the work and characters of Le Fanu's Chapelizod, with *The House by the Churchyard* looming large in *Finnegans Wake*.[3] In *Dubliners*, he sets the story 'A Painful Case' in the village, telling us that our protagonist, Mr James Duffy, lived in Chapelizod 'because he wished to live as far as possible from the city of which he was a citizen and because he found all the other suburbs of Dublin mean, modern and pretentious'.[4]

Deciding to end at the Mullingar House, scene of the aforementioned *Wake*, I begin my visit to the public houses of Chapelizod and its environs (in this case, the Strawberry Beds) at the furthest point, The Wren's Nest. On the way back, we intended to visit the Strawberry Hall and The Villager. For the historian who cannot drive, I recommend a civil servant complete with driving licence. Thankfully, my wife's interest in the Irish supernatural means Chapelizod wasn't a hard sell.

Situated on the northern banks of the Liffey between Chapelizod and Lucan, the Strawberry Beds feels at once familiar and at a remove from Dublin. Getting there requires passing underneath the recently conserved Farmleigh Bridge, known to generations as the Guinness Bridge. Most likely constructed by the Engineering Department of the Guinness Brewery in the 1880s, this bridge serviced Farmleigh House, which was home to Edward Cecil Guinness, 1st Earl of Iveagh. On one side, the bridge sits within South Dublin County Council's jurisdiction and suburban Palmerstown. It was Fingal County Council, local authority on the northern side of the Liffey, that paid for its conservation, though there are no plans to reopen the bridge. It is still a reminder of the wealth and influence of the city's most significant brewing family.

The Strawberry Beds, a nineteenth-century guidebook to Dublin noted, offers:

> for several miles a series of most delightful views. The banks upon which the fruit is cultivated, rise almost perpendicularly to the right. To the left is the river, with its opposite side clothed in masses of the darkest green, or spreading with meadows as rich and luxuriant as any in the Green Isle. The neatly thatched cottages, with their pretty gardens, and roses or woodbine twining round their doorways, are kept by persons who live chiefly by the sale of strawberries and cream during the months of June and July.[5]

A jaunt to the Strawberry Beds was a summer day well spent for generations of Dubliners seeking something removed from the life of the city. In the days of revolution, and with men on the run in a romantic state of mind for the land they were fighting for, Harry Boland would ask 'was there anything as enjoyable as getting on an outside car on a bank holiday with a few friends and driving to the Strawberry Beds or some such place, singing the good old Dublin songs'.[6]

Plenty of good old Dublin songs can he heard in The Wren's Nest, which feels almost like a country pub when it eventually appears in sight. In his 1950s *Irish Press* column, in a piece entitled 'Up the Ballad Singers!', Brendan Behan would recount hearing a song 'from an old County Dublin man in the Wran's Nest, out in the Strawberry Beds'.[7] The pub also appears on the front of the Dubliners LP *At Home with the Dubliners*, released in 1969. There, we see the band posing before a raging fire. In that same year, Luke Kelly listed it as one of his favourite pubs in an interview with *New Spotlight*, telling them, 'I'm not happy with the way they are changing all the auld pubs around, all this carpet and these fancy seats.'[8]

There's just one problem. On entering the pub, I can't see the fireplace from the familiar vinyl record, and I wonder if I've got this one wrong. Una behind the bar, quick as a flash, produces a series of keys that open a door into a small side room. Amidst ageing posters of Parnellite MPs and historical images of the Strawberry Beds, there it is. The Dubliners are just part of the musical heritage of this tiny room, where, a framed music sheet tells us, Thomas Walsh first performed his composition 'Inisheer' in 1970. While its name may not be familiar, it is a piece of music anyone who spends time around traditional music sessions has heard before, consciously or otherwise. Walsh has said of 'Inisheer':

> I went [to Inisheer, in the Aran Islands] for three days and came home three weeks later, due to a lack of money. I composed 'Inisheer' the next day while I was walking in the Phoenix Park dreaming of what I had left behind, and the peace and tranquillity it gave me.[9]

Una's impromptu tour is offered up with her none the wiser why I am there that day, suggesting this kind of generosity of time and spirit is dished out to all curious visitors. While the early history of the pub is unclear, she proudly points to a pitch pine beam bearing the date 1588. The pub, she states with considerable pride, is at least as old as Trinity College Dublin.

An accordion of remembrance in The Wren's Nest.

Georgie Johnston's Accordion

The Wren's Nest is a small space, split into the bar and the room in which The Dubliners posed, now known as the Tap Room. Despite its scale, it is clearly a space of importance in an area that feels a little remote. On a Sunday afternoon, a group of around ten ladies are enjoying tea and coffee. They began meeting here during the pandemic, enjoying hot drinks outside. Now, they continue the custom weekly, bringing cakes and biscuits and discussing matters as diverse as *Small Things Like These*, Halloween and the surprisingly decent weather. As you might find in a pub in rural Ireland, it feels like a community hub.

The walls of The Wren's Nest contain a variety of interesting historical titbits. We find words from 'A Short Description of the Strawberry Beds', a poem from the 1880s that presents the area to the visitor:

> Mr. Ennis keeps the Wren's Nest,
> A little farther than the rest,
> And has charming shady bowers
> Where you might spend some happy hours.

On the other side of The Wren's Nest, accordions belonging to former regulars take pride of place, a reminder of the musical heritage of the bar. We learn that Georgie Johnston, a bus conductor,

The Strawberry Hall.

was known as 'smiley', such was the joy he brought to working his route on the bus. Framed pictures on the wall of a public house are one thing, but accordions have a great commanding presence. They rest there like regimental standards, with a new generation of musicians playing below them.

The isolation of The Wren's Nest geographically (reviews online are only in the handful, thankfully) means a car is pretty much essential to visit it from the city. On the day we visit we meet Michael, a Canadian who is zigzagging Dublin's public houses with the warm affection of a nineteenth-century guidebook writer. From The Glen of Aherlow to The Gravediggers, he has been to them all. I'm impressed he had made the marathon journey from his B&B in Clontarf to see the pubs of this less-explored part of the county. Loading him into the back of the car, we make for the nearby Strawberry Hall, where he is also headed. It too gained mention in the poem that honoured Mr Ennis and The Wren's Nest:

> Mrs. Williams keeps the Strawberry Hall,
> Never pass without a call.
> She is a cheerful kindly woman,

Pride of place for the drum of the Straw Hall House Band.

and will be glad to see you coming,
Her place was lately renovated,
and you will be highly accommodated.

If traditional music has shaped the identity of the last public house, sport is king at the pub affectionately known as 'The Straw Hall'. In the side room, the old sign of the Jackie Jameson Bar in Dalymount Park honours the player Bohemian FC supporters still call 'The Great Man'. Needless to say, Jameson was a rare example of a broadly adored player in the League of Ireland's story. In *Ballyfermot Memories*, a local oral history, a Pat's fan reflected on how 'Jackie had a great step over and many times Jackie bamboozled opposing defenders with his skill, for a man so tall he had exceptional skills on the ground. His close control was excellent and his vision with his back to goal was second to none.'[10]

From the car park opposite the public house, you can see across into Palmerstown, where St Patrick's Athletic and Shamrock Rovers compete for local southside loyalties. At the Straw Hall, however, images of Bohemian's red-and-black-shirted players leave you in no doubt where the loyalties rest here. You're on the northside, just about.

A historic image of The Anglers Rest, with thanks to the family of signwriter Kevin Freeney, whose work is explored later in this collection.

Many of the sporting heroics honoured here happened in the neighbouring Phoenix Park – motor racing, horse racing, athletics and association football. Some games are played much closer to home, the pub boasting a bagatelle – a billiards-like indoor table game that was at the height of its popularity in the Victorian age, but which has its origins in seventeenth-century France. It's a reminder that public houses were also places of recreation, like the game of rings that can still be played in the back bar of The Gravediggers. The humble dartboard ultimately won the day across the city.

The Strawberry Hall is best known for its extravagant annual Christmas lights show, a tradition the pub began back in the 1960s.[11] Great as that is, the sporting miscellanea that hold the wall for the other eleven months of the year are its own kind of treasure trove. The Strawhall House Band drum wrestles back some space for music, recalling to me the public houses of villages and towns like Daingean Uí Chúis, in Kerry, where drums take pride of place, marking traditions like the Stephen's Day 'Wran', as the day of revelry in honour of the wren bird is known.

We journey on, passing The Anglers Rest, which features in the music video for The Dubliners' 'Seven Drunken Nights', quickly made for *Top of the Pops*. Filmmaker Peter Whitehead followed the band along the bumpy roads of the Strawberry Beds, not long after

Photographer Colm Keating captured Frank Harte enjoying (and sharing) a drink. (Courtesy of Colm Keating)

his *Charlie Is My Darling* film on the Rolling Stones. These days, it's a popular wedding venue at the weekend, and a happy couple taking pictures outside don't need to know such trivia.

Making for Chapelizod village, we stop at The Villager. Once The Tap, this premises was owned by the Harte family, and was the childhood home of the legendary Dublin song collector Frank Harte. In the pub, the 'Frank Harte Musical Snug' marks the connection. In recent years, Harte's legacy has been championed by a new generation of traditional and folk musicians. Time and again in interviews, members of Lankum have quoted Harte's words: 'Those in power write the history and those who suffer write the songs.'[12] In a collection of Dublin street songs, Harte made an emotional argument for why there was an obligation to try to capture the oral tradition:

The thought of a song dying with its singer, or lying in a book or a tape on a shelf gathering dust, fills me with horror. If a song is lost, it means the loss of a story that will never again be told, a story told possibly hundreds of years ago that I could have heard again today. A story that could give me an insight into the feelings of the people of that particular time as no history book can.[13]

Harte remembered the 1960s as 'a time when publicans, instead of throwing us out of the pub for singing and playing music, realised they could increase their turnover by promoting Irish music and song and encouraging that aspect of Irish culture which they had previously looked upon solely as a nuisance'.[14] Profitability was of little concern to Harte when it came to the tradition, and as singing went in and out of fashion in Dublin public houses, Harte remained a constant presence on the scene. Since his passing in 2005, he has been honoured with the annual Frank Harte Festival.

Nearby, the Mullingar House marks the end of the journey. While Davy Byrne's on Duke Street is the public house most associated with Joyce today, the Mullingar House is surely the most important watering hole connected to the writer. If *Ulysses* is the story of a day traversing Dublin, *Finnegans Wake* is likely the dream of a Chapelizod publican, playing out entirely on this premises. His name? Humphrey Chimpden Earwicker. Repeatedly, his initials come to the fore in the novel. There is a nod to that in the wording of the plaque over the door: HOME OF ALL CHARACTERS AND ELEMENTS IN JAMES JOYCE'S NOVEL FINNEGANS WAKE.

It was a book that came to dominate the life of the writer. He told one interviewer that:

> Since 1922 my book has become more real to me than reality, and everything has led to it; all other things have been insurmountable difficulties, even the smallest realities such as, for instance, having

A postcard depicting a jaunt to the Strawberry Beds. (Courtesy of the National Library of Ireland)

**Here Comes Everybody at the Mullingar House.**

to shave in the morning. There are, so to say, no individual people in the book – it is as in a dream, the style gliding and unreal as the way it is in dream.[15]

Chapelizod was an obsession to Joyce, who was drawn to it for reasons personal and literary. His father had worked for a period for the Dublin and Chapelizod Distillery Company, 'the still that was mill' in *Finnegans Wake*. Peter Chrisp, in his fascinating blog dedicated to all things Joyce, presents a letter penned by Joyce's father and discovered among his son's papers years later. In it, John Joyce recalls his friendship with the owner of the pub, and the culture of competition between pubs then:

> Broadbent and I were very great friends. He had the Mullingar Hotel there, and a fine decent fellow he was. We used to have great times there. There was a bowling green at the back of his hotel and I was considered a celebrated bowler ... On one occasion Dollymount challenged us to a game. We won and we stood them food and drink after it. This was followed by a splendid musical evening as we had a lot of musical fellows down with us ... We beat Dollymount and I made a big score; and by God I was carried around the place and such a time we had.[16]

The Mullingar House is a different pub today, a busy carvery feeding a packed backroom and televised football from the neighbouring island holding the attention of the front bar. Joyce, the eternal modernist and the writer of the everyman and everyday, would undoubtedly have preferred that to a place frozen in time.

# CHAPTER 18.
## ONE OF DUBLIN'S PRINCES

A carriage turns on College Green during the inaugural Bloomsday celebrations, as captured by photographer Elinor Wiltshire. (Courtesy of the National Library of Ireland)

**W**riting in his memoir, the poet John Montague recalled how McDaid's on Harry Street had been 'the bohemian shark tank of a decade', but that all things must pass.[1] In the immediate aftermath of the Second World War, McDaid's claim to the crown of Dublin's literary public houses was undeniable, at least amongst the young, who viewed it as a break from the more formal Palace set. Perhaps under the weight of the gathering of personalities around it, things would widen out again.

As well as its champions, McDaid's had its detractors. Privately, novelist John McGahern would comment that the 'McDaid world is such a jungle that it's impossible'.[2] To him, some writers were 'McDaid's writers', a labelling not meant as a compliment.[3] Perhaps McDaid's simultaneously benefited and suffered from the scale of Dublin; the critic John Jordan would wryly assert that:

Dublin's literary jungle is probably no better or worse ultimately than that of any other city. The aggravating hazard, however, lies in the fact that the jungle is miniature, and the beasts keep on running into each other.[4]

One of those who emerges clearest now from the McDaid's moment is John Ryan, thanks to his classic memoir *Remembering How We Stood*, published in 1975. He was the proprietor of The Bailey bar and restaurant on Duke Street, and a plaque honours him on the front of the premises today, alongside another marking its surprising connection to the world of *Ulysses*. McDaid's barman Paddy O'Brien, later destined for Grogan's on South William Street, would tell Kevin C. Kearns that 'John was a founder member of McDaid's. He's the man who made it a literary pub. He had this thing called *Envoy* going and he'd come over to McDaid's and have a drink. And then, bit by bit, it all came into a circle.'[5] 'If barman was a university subject,' *Sunday World*'s Pub Spy quipped on visiting Grogan's in 1978, 'Paddy O'Brien would be dripping with doctorates.'[6]

Educated at Clongowes Wood College and the son of the founder of the successful Monument Creameries business, Ryan was upwardly mobile in a literary world where many (s)tumbled downwards. Ryan, J. P. Donleavy remembered, 'sailed the most treacherous of these bohemian seas with the same skill he used as a mariner when navigating his yacht around the unpredictable and hostile waters of this island'.[7] His *Envoy* magazine was viewed in the city as a worthy successor to *The Bell*, the earlier publication of Seán Ó Faoláin and Peadar O'Donnell. Ó Faoláin encouraged would-be contributors to 'write about your gateway, your well-field, your street-corner, your girl, your boat-slip, pubs, books, pictures, dogs, horses, river, tractor, anything at all that has a hold on you'.[8] They did all of this, along with rallying against literary censorship and breaking new ground in poetry. *Envoy* featured many of the same writers, but also heralded the arrival of new talent like James Plunkett, Thomas Kinsella and Val Mulkerns.

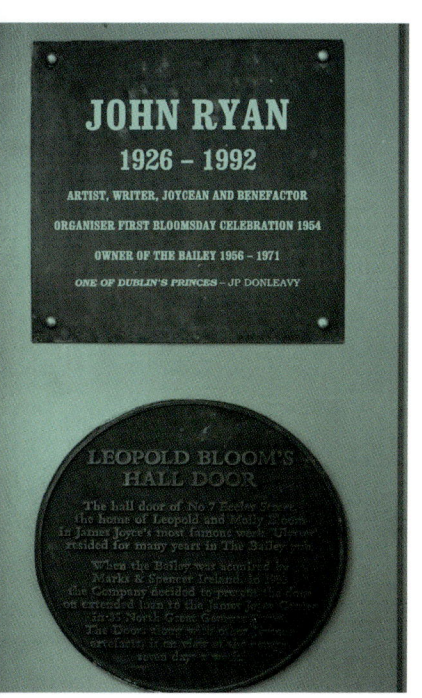

The words of J. P. Donleavy honour John Ryan outside of The Bailey.

John Ryan's acquisition of The Bailey in 1956 marked a curious sort of rebirth for what had been a pub, before becoming 'more of a restaurant in its pre-Ryan incarnation'.[9] In an earlier life, the Duke Street spot had been popular with Irish Parliamentary Party types, including Charles Stewart Parnell, and later became a favourite drinking den of Arthur Griffith and others around the Gaelic Revival.[10] It was a place where one literary regular recalled 'poetry spoken of with the assured carelessness with which a carpenter talks of his planks and of the chairs and tables and oddments he will make of them'.[11] All of that seemed like the distant past, but Ryan wished to bring it back. 'When I took over as licensee,' he recalled, 'I set about restoring the original atmosphere as much as possible, and it again became a meeting-place for actors, painters and writers.'[12]

Around the same time as Ryan's *Remembering How We Stood*, Anthony Cronin's memoir, *Dead as Doornails: A Chronicle of Life*, appeared. Both books are vital reads to understand this literary era, but while Ryan's is often a pleasant jaunt through the bohemian Dublin of the day, Cronin's can strike a more sombre note. Exploring his friendships with Brendan Behan, Patrick Kavanagh and Myles na gCopaleen in detail, all three emerge as brilliant but deeply troubled souls. We first encounter Kavanagh as the king of Baggotonia, as Baggot Street came to be known:

> Seldom can there have been such a small area so patrolled by genius: every gurrier in Kilmartin's the bookies, every dart-playing docker in Tommy Ryan's, every gin-drinking landlady or middle-class soak in the Waterloo Lounge was known to him.[13]

His last encounter with the poet occurred in Sheehan's of Chatham Street in 1966, Kavanagh being banned from McDaid's (as was Cronin) at the time. Both Cronin and Ryan chronicle a day to which Kavanagh was centrally important in their respective memoirs: Bloomsday, 1954.

That day carried significant importance to Dublin's literati, as it marked the fiftieth anniversary of the day on which *Ulysses* is set. 'When the hundredth anniversary of Bloomsday comes around,' the *Irish Times* editorial noted that day, 'Leopold Bloom either may be forgotten, or may stand in stony effigy as high as Nelson stands today.'[14] Little could they have known that, by then, Horatio Nelson's pillar would be gone, and a statue of James Joyce would be staring at its replacement.

The idea to emulate the route of *Ulysses*, beginning by the Martello Tower at the Forty Foot and traversing into the city, was the brainchild of Myles na gCopaleen. To him, Joyce's works were 'a garden in which some of us may play'.[15] Cronin remembered Myles approaching him with the idea in a pub. 'It would be necessary to go somewhere else,' Cronin recalled Myles telling him, 'for there were too many dangerous people – chancers, and intriguers and go-betweens and Johnny-come-latelys of all descriptions – in the pub we were in.'[16]

That the day descended into a drinking session early on is well documented. If there is an overlooked figure in the story of that first Bloomsday, it is the photographer Elinor Wiltshire, one of the great chroniclers of a changing Dublin, who this day found herself capturing the ceremonies. Her patience clearly knew no bounds. Images from outside Goggins in Monkstown reveal a party that is still broadly held together – shots later in the day show members of the party being helped back into the carriages, and Myles na gCopaleen with his head in his hands. Kavanagh's biographer, Antoinette Quinn, would later write that 'they made several stops along the route at public houses not known for their Joycean associations'.[17] It all culminated in The Bailey, Cronin recalling that 'the jealousies among the mountaineers of the morning seemed to have been forgotten'.[18]

A sketch of Myles by John Ryan. (Courtesy of the National Library of Ireland)

Ryan cemented the connection between The Bailey and *Ulysses* a few years after acquiring the premises, by displaying what was undoubtedly one of the most peculiar pub artifacts in Dublin's history. It was a time of great transformation for the inner city, with Kavanagh lamenting how:

> The children take delight in levelling the city,
> Violently tear down the walls,
> Screeching from the steps of a ruin
> Where a broken milk bottle rolls.[19]

John Ryan and Donagh MacDonagh attend the unveiling of Leopold Bloom's door at The Bailey. (Courtesy of the National Library of Ireland)

With the demolition of houses on Eccles Street – including the address of Leopold Bloom in the novel, 7 Eccles Street – Ryan secured the door and would display it proudly in The Bailey, where it remained from 1967 until 1995, when it was loaned permanently to the James Joyce Centre on North Great George's Street. At its unveiling, Kavanagh drew comparison to the address of Sherlock Holmes, telling the crowd how 'this door is as famous to the mythology of Dublin as 221b Baker Street is to London'.[20]

The Bailey was to prove important to the memory of Kavanagh too. It was there that he encountered the young troubadour Luke Kelly, who would later introduce a song before a televised performance:

> On the one occasion that I dared actually to speak to the man … we were in a pub, we won't name the pub, but it was in The Bailey anyway. And he was singing in his own peculiar manner and so was I, in my own peculiar manner. And he said, 'I've got a song for you! You should sing Raglan Road.'[21]

This curious figure of a sailor with a sextant in hand has been on quite the journey across the city, beginning life outside a Capel Street opticians. Today, he stands over The Bailey in a modern reproduction of the original. (Courtesy of Dublin City Library and Archives)

Deeply loyal to those he called friends, Ryan was later the driving force behind the successful campaign for a memorial bench to Patrick Kavanagh along the canal, near to the

Elinor Wiltshire captured this scene of a carriage at Smith's pub in Ringsend during the inaugural Bloomsday celebrations. (Courtesy of the National Library of Ireland)

Baggotonia beat he knew so well. Not to be confused with John Coll's later statue, this simpler nearby bench was unveiled on St Patrick's Day, 1968. Ryan recalled that it was designed by the artist Michael Farrell, 'basing his scheme on a rough sketch I had done on a drip-mat at the bar on The Bailey'.[22]

Today, The Bailey is not unlike how Ryan first found it, thought of more as a restaurant than a public house. While Davy Byrne's will forever be part of the story of *Ulysses* itself, John Ryan's former establishment will always remain a key part of the story of Bloomsday.

# CHAPTER 19.
# AT THE SIGN OF THE ZODIAC

**S**tanding on Harry Street opposite McDaid's, Bruxelles boasts a beautiful Victorian exterior, including its striking turret. Bruxelles is perhaps best known for what stands outside it: Paul Daly's 2005 statue of Phil Lynott, frontman of Thin Lizzy. Before it became known as Bruxelles (a name chosen to honour Ireland's accession to the European Economic Community, forerunner of the EU), it was called At the Sign of the Zodiac, one of the most peculiar pub names in the history of the city. A journey inside to its bar reveals reminders of its former incarnation. In 1947, newspaper advertisements told the public that 'the newest and quaintest cocktail bar in Dublin is now open. Come and see for yourself the unusual murals showing the ancient signs of the Zodiac, and try the exotic cocktails and long drinks'.[1]

There was nothing particularly new about a bar offering cocktails in 1940s Dublin. In earlier decades, they were sometimes referred to as 'American drinks'. At the Mayson Hotel in Dublin's docklands, advertisements for McDonnell's, which occupied the site over a century ago, adorn the walls and reveal a surprising array of drinks. A punter could enjoy a 'Tom and Jerry', a 'Morning Glory' or even a 'Zenith Gun-Running Cocktail', a curious name for a drink in the Ireland of 1914, when plenty of guns were being landed off the coast of Howth and Larne.[2] Even earlier, in 1912, the *Evening Herald* informed their readers that more than ninety cocktails could be tried at Jury's.[3]

**Looking closely around Bruxelles today, astrological signs are still visible.**

In Ireland, as in America itself, cocktails were generally marketed to women. As America moved towards prohibition and the temperance movement sought to gain its own strength again in Ireland, cocktails were denounced as particularly harmful, as women were enjoying them in social settings beyond a licensed premises. Mallory O'Meara, in her entertaining history *Girly Drinks*, documents a publishing history going back to the 1860s in the United States, as women put out works like *Mrs. Beeton's Book of Household Management*, providing cocktail recipes amongst other things. Despite being a time when women's drinking culture 'continued to be mostly private', the cocktail was reshaping the relationship between some women (especially in the middle and upper classes) and alcohol.[4]

The cocktail bar is 'not a stationary thing', one temperance advocate argued later, in the 1940s, 'but roves from place to place; from dancehall to tennis club and from wedding party to business deal'.[5] Young women were 'cultivating the cocktail habit, imagining that it charmed away the possible evil consequences of strong drink. Gin was gin, whether it was taken in the "Lady in Pink" or the "Lady in Green"'.[6] Many ignored such criticisms; the All-Ireland Cocktail Competition attracted considerable attention, when Dublin hotels shone brightly. The 1949 tournament was won by the Metropole Hotel for the Metropolitan Moon.

As for Bruxelles, the symbols of the zodiac – or astrological star signs, as we more commonly know them now – are still visible in the upstairs bar. The 1930s had witnessed the rise of the newspaper astrology columns internationally, and it was reported that 'jewellers are producing rings and brooches wrought in silver and enamel, each taking one of the signs of the zodiac as its theme. To give a friend such a trinket, chosen according to the month of her birth, is supposed to bring luck and avert evil.'[7]

The name of Bruxelles' downstairs lounge, the Zodiac Bar, is a nod towards this earlier time and cocktail heritage. It was to the Zodiac Bar that Richard Harris frequently retreated while in Dublin

Celebrating Irish membership of the European Economic Community, the flags of member states welcome the visitor to Bruxelles.

performing the lead role in *The Ginger Man*, a stage adaptation of J. P. Donleavy's novel that was predictably condemned from the pulpit and quickly withdrawn.[8]

A visitor going down the stairs of the pub will notice the real pride the establishment feels in its connection to Phil Lynott, whose fondness for the pub has been documented by biographers and friends.[9] Jim Fitzpatrick, the artist whose work is inseparable from the memory of Phil and the band, has recalled how Grafton Street was the great promenade to his friend:

> Above all he loved the vibe of 70s Dublin and he loved the vibe of Grafton street and the young people, all decked out in their colourful best and he milked it. Not for ego, simply for the people, the vibe from being home in Dublin and to be so beautifully acknowledged, I believe, gave him strength and renewed his prodigious energy. Dublin was home, he loved it and it loved him back tenfold and still does to this day.[10]

# CHAPTER 20.
# ELIZABETH TAYLOR AND AFTER

Cusack's on the North Strand has a strong nautical theme, a reminder it was once popular with the men who worked Liffeyside. Framed images recall local history, from the bombing of the area during the Second World War to the contributions of local men and women during the War of Independence. Scanning the walls for one particular newspaper, I eventually ask the barman, 'is this the pub where Elizabeth Taylor went to the jacks?' It is, he tells me, though a previous owner kept the framed memento. In 1965, with her partner Richard Burton filming *The Spy Who Came in From the Cold* in Dublin, Elizabeth Taylor learned that public houses were not always the most accommodating places for women. To be on the premises at all was something of an achievement. At Cusack's, the absence of a ladies' bathroom said everything, but Taylor was permitted to use the gents.

For ten weeks, Burton and Taylor lodged in the Gresham Hotel. A suite is today named in Taylor's honour, but she was perhaps not a dream guest. The director Franco Zeffirelli recalled:

> Liz had somehow acquired a bush baby (a small African primate), which had not taken to its luxurious imprisonment and had set about rearranging the decor. It had knocked over vases and lights, ripped the curtains and had, by the time I arrived, taken refuge near the ceiling of the bathroom, where it was clinging, wide-eyed with fear, to one of the water pipes.[1]

Burton may not have noticed the out-of-control 'bush baby', spending much of his time away from the cameras frequenting the public houses of the capital. Taylor visited some too, including Bartley Dunne's and – perhaps more surprisingly – the Comet Bar in Santry.

Women had been drinking in public houses for decades before all of this, but it certainly depended on the environment. Public houses in market areas – as discussed in the chapter exploring early houses – had female customers who would drink on an equal basis to men. But to panicked moralists, the presence of women in such environments was something to be discouraged. A 1908 report in a nationalist newspaper writes of the kind of women one would encounter in a Dublin pub:

> Poorly dressed, some with infants in arms, others with children clinging to their skirts, some old, some young, some timid and shrinking, others brazen and unashamed. One or two bear on their faces the bruises resulting from recent conflicts, all those slatternly in the highest degree. The drunken mirth of the younger women in this section is more pathetic than even the faces of the hungry children, who ill-clad and shivering linger round the door waiting for their mothers.[2]

Cusack's on a quiet Sunday morning.

Previous page: Dwyer's of Moore Street was a popular public house with market traders, including women. As this 1950s image shows, there was no question around serving a woman a pint on the premises! (Fáilte Ireland Photographic Collection. Courtesy of Dublin City Library and Archive)

Such classist commentary was not entirely unique to Ireland. In London, the 1903 text *Life and Labour of the People in London* similarly suggests the kind of women one encountered in a public house were exclusively working class, from 'the factory girl who drinks once in a way, the prostitute who drinks in the course of business and very seldom gets drunk, the laundry-woman who drinks by reason of the thirsty nature of her trade'.[3] For one Dublin newspaper, 'established to advance the interests of labour', it was a sad day when a woman felt comfortable even being seen walking into or out of a licensed premises:

> We recollect when a woman going into a public house to drink would be 'the talk of the parish'. We recollect when a woman in Dublin would look half a dozen ways at once, to see that no one saw her enter a public house, and if she did enter one with her husband, sent him out first on leaving, to look up and down, and see that no one was coming who would know her.[4]

Some of these voices were broadly in favour of temperance, and didn't think much higher of a man darkening the door of a pub, 'Ireland Sober' being 'Ireland Free'. For others, the issue was a gendered one. Men drank in public houses because they enjoyed it, but women were always there as a result of their economic circumstance and tragedy. The pub, to these writers, was no place for them.

Almost fifteen years on from Taylor's symbolic trip to the toilet, a journalist from the *Irish Press* discovered in 1979 that some things hadn't changed much in the area. As Isabel Conway went from pub to pub in Dublin's north inner city with friends, the Five Lamps was the first stop:

> 'We don't serve ladies' announced the barman when we asked for two pints of stout and a pint of lager. 'We had your sort, them women's libbers in here before, and we told them the same thing.'[5]

From there, they moved on to another establishment, near Connolly Station. Here, like Elizabeth Taylor, they were told it was an issue of plumbing:

> The elderly barman was spiking bar receipts on one of those old-fashioned filing nails, so we made ourselves comfortable. But before we had time to give our order he whispered apologetically, 'sorry, no ladies.' 'We don't have proper accommodation for you', he explained. 'The Corporation would be after me if I served you. You see we don't have any ladies' lavatory.' We could always nip across to the [Connolly] station for accommodation, we suggested, but the barman had his orders and they did not include accommodating ladies.[6]

Was there any obligation on such establishments to provide facilities for women? Investigating the issue, a reporter noted in 1974 that outdated legislation remained in place, written in a time the public house was a space women did not inhabit:

In time, social attitudes to women in public houses changed so significantly that images aimed at international tourist audiences showed the new diversity in traditional bars like Doheny and Nesbitt's. (Fáilte Ireland Tourism Photographic Collection. Courtesy of Dublin City Library and Archive)

Strictly speaking, pubs aren't legally required to provide female lavatories at all. Legislation was framed at a time when women just didn't feature on the drinking scene. They are supposed to provide toilet and washing facilities for staff and make arrangements for male patrons. The Sale of Intoxicating Liquor Act does allow Inspectors to 'require an updating of standards', which evidently can be interpreted to make sure that a 'ladies' is provided.[7]

By 1979, such public houses were thankfully becoming outliers. The playwright and publican John B. Keane insisted that he could no longer understand how any publican 'can refuse a woman a pint in this day and age', as 'some of my best customers are women pint drinkers and they are better behaved, better disposed and of nicer mien and manner than the men'.[8] In the District Court, some women began objecting to the renewal of licences for public houses that refused to serve them. The bars included Fagan's of Drumcondra and the Brian Boru on Botanic Road, with Justice Donnelly outlining their argument:

> As far as all of them are concerned, there is still a demand for their men only section and they have no plans to serve women in the men's bar in the future. The reason: customers like to have a pint in their working clothes and don't want to feel discomfited by too plush surroundings or lots of women around![9]

Objecting to the renewal of a licence was one form of action women could take, but there were others. A particularly famous example of protest took place at Neary's in July 1974, in a story that has morphed into several variations. In a 2006 feature on veteran feminist Nell McCafferty, it was claimed 'she liberated women pint-drinkers in Dublin by ordering 40 brandies in Neary's pub and refusing to pay until they gave her a pint'.[10] In the newspaper report on the day after the incident, things played out a little differently:

> Last night, Pint Commandoes of the Women's Liberation Movement stood up in a protest round with the staff of a Dublin bar when they were refused pints.
> 
> The 18-strong group stepped up to the bar in Neary's of Chatham Street and were told by the head barman that they 'did not serve pints to ladies.' It was a rule of the house, he said. The women protested that it was dearer to drink by the half pint and were told they would not be served any drink in the establishment. A man in the bar bought one of the women a pint of Smithwicks and was told that he would not be served any more drink either ...
> 
> Miss McCafferty asked the customers to refuse to drink until she had got a pint. The barmen were asking customers if their pints were for women or men. 'No more drinking until we get a pint', chanted the Pint Squad. Then Miss McCafferty sang a verse

of the ballad: 'There's nothing so lonesome, so morbid or drear as to stand in the bar of the pub with no beer.'

The barman called in the Gardaí, who quietly got both sides to negotiate and in a few minutes the head barman announced that he would negotiate with management to ensure that women were served pints in the future. The Libbers cheered, but they had to leave without their pints.[11]

By the late 1980s, only a handful of public houses were still clinging to the division of men and women between bar and lounge. Kevin C. Kearns suggested Stoneybatter's Walsh's as 'probably the last truly segregated pub in Dublin', with head barman Tom Ryan refusing to sit women at the bar as late as 1988, insisting 'it's a male preserve. Men prefer to be on their own. I know this from experience. Women just wouldn't fit in.'[12] Even later, in 1989, the *Sunday Press* visited Fagan's of Drumcondra, 'the bar of which we were reliably informed was still staunchly men-only'.[13] The journalist engaged with customers on the subject, leading to one particularly memorable exchange:

> Suggesting to another staunch proponent of the male-only bar that this form of discrimination was comparable to the racial sort in Africa left the man gazing at me somewhat bewildered: 'But there's no discrimination here', he said, 'black women aren't allowed in here either.'[14]

Where did the story end? On that, credit is due to Kathleen Maher, described as a 'committed community activist', who led a fifteen-month campaign to have women served in the Shamrock Lodge in Finglas in 1991. Objecting to the licensing of the premises, a judge only agreed to renew it on the basis that the pub serve men and women on an equal basis. Photographed in the press enjoying a pint of plain outside the pub, she told the journalist 'a pint never tasted so good'.[15]

# CHAPTER 21.
# 'A MOST UNUSUAL PUB'

Bartley Dunne's from *In Touch* magazine. (Irish Queer Archive, with thanks to Tonie Walsh)

In May 1975, London's *Gay News* listed a number of Dublin public houses in their guide to the city. These were described not as 'gay bars', but rather as pubs where gay people socialised and which could appeal to a gay visitor. When an Irish newspaper brought this to the attention of the respective publicans, the response was everywhere the same. One insisted 'we are not a gay pub. There is no evidence that a significant number of our patrons are homosexuals.' At another, the owner told the paper 'I strongly object to this being printed ... we would prefer that they did not come in.'[1]

The sensationalist coverage of the list in the Irish press led the Irish Gay Rights Movement to retort:

> Yet again, must we ask for mature reporting on a subject that touches on more than 200,00 [sic] Irish lives, is this too much to expect? The facts about homosexuality may be less sensational than fiction, yet all the elements of human life are there.[2]

Two of the public houses referenced in *Gay News* were Rice's and Bartley Dunne's, two institutions that have become inseparable in the telling of the story of gay Dublin. As Anthony Redmond noted in a reflective piece for *Gay Community News* (*GCN*), accompanied by a picture of the bulldozer that brought down Bartley Dunne's:

> Now, BDs was never an overtly gay pub in the sense in which The George, The Loft or The Parliament Inn are. The clientele was always mixed and, for me, the ambiguous atmosphere was part of the magnetic appeal. One never quite knew with certainty the sexual orientation of the person sitting next to you. There was an exciting sense of discovery, like exploring a cave or visiting a strange country. There was an air of magic and wonder about it.[3]

Many iconic public houses internationally which are today gay bars began their lives similarly to Rice's and Bartley Dunne's. In London, the Admiral Duncan was earlier most famous as the pub where Dylan Thomas left the handwritten manuscript of *Under Milk Wood* on a drinking session in 1953. Its bohemian atmosphere meant it was a space viewed as more tolerant, gradually becoming what it is today. In Ireland, the criminalisation of homosexuality until 1993 meant that long after gay bars were an accepted part of most European cities, a semi-secretive code remained here.

Bartley Dunne's and Rice's were bound by more than clientele, with Rice's standing on the corner of Stephen's Green and South King Street (the entrance to the present-day shopping centre) and Bartley Dunne's a short stroll away on Lower Stephen Street, at the site currently home to the Grafton Hotel. As a nod to the life of the earlier site, the Grafton's bar is called Bartley's. Bartley Dunne's influence spreads far beyond that today, with a bar on New York's West 54th Street carrying the name Bartley Dunne's, and styling itself as 'a most unusual pub'.[4] That claim too is a nod towards the Dublin pub's own advertisements:

Rice's, like Bartley Dunne's, was considered a 'gay-friendly' bar in the Dublin of its time. Its location is now occupied by a shopping centre. (Fáilte Ireland Tourism Photographic Collection, Dublin City Library and Archive)

Unusual in character. Continental in atmosphere. A breath of Paris. Bistro Parisienne, Left Bank mood. French, Danish, English Cheese. Exquisite soups, French rolls. Austrian Salami. Irish, English and Continental Beers Stocked. Specialist in Wines and Spirits of the World.[5]

While Rice's was a traditional public house interior, with a front bar and lounge, Bartley Dunne's had a unique ambience, with David Norris recalling:

> It was an Aladdin's cave to me, its wicker-clad Chianti bottles stiff with dribbled candlewax, tea chests covered in red and white chequered cloths, heavy scarlet velvet drapes and an immense collection of multicoloured liqueurs glinting away in their bottles.[6]

What were these multicoloured liquors? An advertisement for the pub in a literary journal in 1959 promised the visitor:

> Polish Vodka – 140% proof spirit
> Hungarian Slivovitz
> Greek Oyso
> Italian Strega
> Japanese Hakutsuru Sake
> Danish Akvavit
> Polish Wishiowka
> Bulls Blood of Eger
> Barack Palinka
> Mexican Tequila[7]

The embryonic scene that emerged in Dublin, Paul Candon noted in a history for *GCN*, 'seems to have been largely concentrated around the more bohemian set in the city', pointing to Micheál Mac Liammóir and Hilton Edwards as being 'the city's most obvious and publicly accepted homosexual couple at the time'.[8] Edwards and Mac Liammóir, creative partners who had driven the golden age of Dublin's Gate Theatre, have been described as 'Ireland's only visible gay couple'.[9] There was considerable irony in the life of Mac Liammóir, real name Alfred Willmore, who had no Irish stock. He had invented a biography and origin story, but was comfortably himself with Edwards in the public gaze. The front bar of Rice's was a regular haunt for the pair, as was Davy Byrne's of Duke Street.

Though the pub is unnamed in the report, a *Sunday Independent* 1974 feature on visiting a 'gay pub' is most likely an account of Bartley Dunne's, based on its physical descriptions of the space:

> The atmosphere was of cigarette smoke and subdued red lighting. Dimly lit alcoves gave the impression of clandestine rendezvous. The place was crowded, and it seemed as if

Bartley Dunne's in New York pays homage to a legendary Dublin institution. (With thanks to all at Bartley Dunne's)

everybody looked around to inspect me as I came in. I sat on a stool by the counter, opened my newspaper – *The Guardian* – and tried to look liberal-intellectual with the help of a Johnnie Walker on ice ... Records were continually playing and, no doubt, it was an accident that 'Come on Baby, Light My Fire' was about ten decibels too high.[10]

The piece struck a new note of empathy in press coverage of such places, a customer telling the writer that 'there is no such thing as the typical homosexual. We are just ordinary human beings like everybody else.'[11] Coverage of the social lives of gay people in Dublin, even when well-intended, sometimes fell short of this understanding. A later feature on the Flikkers Disco in Dublin's Hirschfeld Centre even noted that 'though homosexuals have a reputation for voracious sexual appetite, there is little evidence of it here'.[12]

Bartley Dunne's and Rice's were spaces in which, for gay clientele, trust and discretion were everything. In his history of Irish LGBT life since 1974, Páraic Kerrigan points to the visit of Rock Hudson, then one of Hollywood's biggest stars, to both establishments when visiting Dublin for work in 1968. To Kerrigan, the privacy of Hudson's visits to both 'shows the underground and hidden nature of Ireland's gay scene'.[13] Actors, politicians, broadcasters, school teachers, artists and labourers all held to the abiding principle of privacy.

At the same time that Bartley Dunne's and Rice's were thriving as 'gay-friendly' spaces, Dublin witnessed the emergence of social spaces that were unapologetically and proudly connected to the gay and lesbian movements. Venues such as the Phoenix Club at Parnell Square and the later Hirschfeld Centre on Fownes Street in Temple Bar defied decriminalisation and transformed the social lives of young gay, lesbian and bisexual people especially. The Hirschfeld Centre, named in honour of the pioneering sexologist Dr Magnus Hirschfeld, displayed the pink triangle over its entrance with pride. This centre was a place of leisure, but it also had organisational importance, with David Norris recalling that 'not only did we have offices for our political campaigns, but we were also able to house telephone helplines and counselling rooms, and a restaurant where people could meet for lunch'.[14] Its thriving disco – Flikkers – is an important part of the story of Dublin's electronic music heritage, as a nightclub where 'records are imported directly from London and, as a rule, are played months before they hit the radio and charts'.[15]

The centre was an alcohol-free space, but as LGBT representation became more present in the life of the city, this also impacted on public houses. The Viking, opening in 1979 at 75 Dame Street (now Brogan's) would be described in a courtroom setting as 'effectively a gay pub',[16] and is remembered as the first public house in Dublin where no effort was made to hide its gay identity and clientele behind the banner of 'cosmopolitanism'. Under the stewardship of Noel Palmer, The Viking not only became an important social space in its own right, but paved the way for Palmer to acquire The Parliament Inn (now the Turk's Head) in the late 1980s. A larger space, The Parliament Inn also catered to what was a diverse clientele, *GCN* in 1994 describing how:

The ground floor bar, christened 'The Works', was popular with an older clientele. The middle bar, entitled 'Limelight' was favoured by a younger crowd, and on Thursdays and Sundays, by Transvestites. The top bar, closed over a year, was aptly named 'Rafters', and housed 'Damsels', the night-out for lesbians.[17]

The Hirschfeld Centre, The Viking and The Parliament Inn all serve to demonstrate the more open nature of Irish society as time progressed, but the early 1980s brought intense scrutiny of Dublin's gay community, pushing some back into the shadows. The brutal murder of Charles Self, an openly gay man who frequented Bartley Dunne's, in 1982 led to much investigation of the gay community by the authorities. Edmund Lynch, a gay rights activist, would later recall how Gardaí 'decided to make Pearse Street garda station their headquarters, and then started to bring in gay men for questioning … This made hundreds of people frightened, humiliated and in fear of their lives.'[18]

One bar in Dublin that remains open for business and serves as an important part of the story is Bridie's Bar, a part of The George a passer-by could easily overlook, as it is now subsumed within a much larger premises and nightclub space. Affectionately known as 'Jurassic' by a younger generation, its name is a nod towards a much-missed former staff member who was part of the community built around The George. Reflecting on him, a staff member told *GCN* that 'he would have been a huge character on the scene. Apparently, his wake and funeral party lasted about a week.'[19] There are other spaces that also form part of the story; Street 66 (an example of a name change seemingly nobody in the city observes, still being known popularly as The Front Lounge) gained mention in a 1995 *GCN* feature as 'a pub not often included in gay listings, but which really should be'.[20] For women especially, The Front Lounge was just as important a place as The Viking in the story of these public houses.

## CHAPTER 22.

# THE BALLAD BOOM AND AFTER

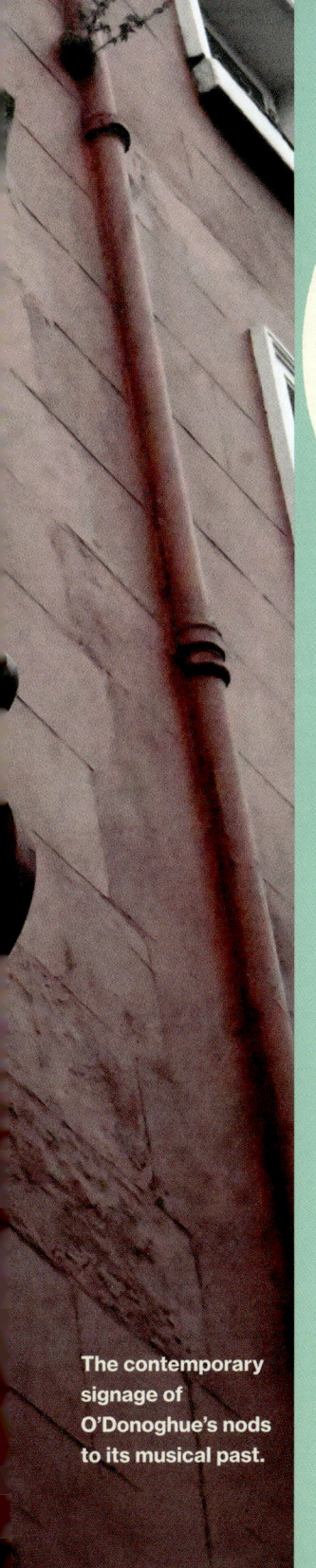

The contemporary signage of O'Donoghue's nods to its musical past.

**W**hen Paddy and Maureen O'Donoghue decided it was time to retire in the late 1970s, they did so quietly. A handwritten letter was dispatched to Ronnie Drew at his Greystones home, telling him 'we are retiring from business on the 7th October, a date we would like to keep to ourselves otherwise the souvenir hunters will claim all our precious memories from the back room'.[1]

Thankfully, the back bar of O'Donoghue's on Merrion Row is still something of a time capsule, and the wall of memories remains. Like actors on the wall of the Trocadero restaurant, here are the black-and-white publicity shots of Irish folk and traditional musicians and singers. From a time before the smoking ban, tobacco has weathered labels, but many of these faces need no introduction in the world of such music: Frank Harte, Christy Moore, Seosamh Ó hÉanaí, Séamus Ennis, Margaret Barry and Dominic Behan are all there, amongst others.

In popular memory, O'Donoghue's means The Dubliners and The Dubliners mean O'Donoghue's. A plaque on the exterior commemorates the group, who became so synonymous with the public house as to film *O'Donoghue's Opera*, a 1965 mock opera that begins in the back room, and centres on the ballad 'The Night Before Larry Was Stretched', with Ronnie Drew playing the role of our doomed protagonist. On entering the premises, one of the first things a visitor encounters are portraits of the members of the group by the musician's corner, while tour posters attest to their international popularity.

One would be forgiven for presuming it was always thus, and that The Dubliners are so associated with the pub *because* it was a traditional music haunt. Yet before their moment arrived, O'Donoghue's was a different pub entirely, popular with students from the nearby universities and more a place of chatter than *ceol*. It was, in the words of the artist Michael Kane (author of one of the finest Dublin memoirs), 'a talking pub, the back lounge a leisurely, quiet refuge to dispute the great questions of the day and complain about the state of art administration, "the market", and of course books and the theatre'.² It was Kane who introduced Ronnie Drew to the pub. The rest, as they say, is history, as 'those of us who saw pubs as places of quiet thought and talk were forced to find another bolthole and chose the easiest alternative as soon as the guitars were unpacked in Paddy's lounge'.³ Some made for the neighbouring pubs, but a new crowd descended on O'Donoughe's.

O'Donoghue's was not the very beginning of traditional and folk music in the public house. In his memoir, the writer Benedict Kiely remembered Margaret Barry, the great travelling singer who traversed Ireland as a street singer, performing in the Brazen Head in the 1950s. She lodged there with the Sligo musician Michael Gorman when in the capital, and her distinctive voice could be heard often in the bar, with Kiely introducing her to his friend Brendan Behan. This led, Kiely said, to 'my feeling like some minor God of the Sea, ruler of vast sluice-gates who had, suddenly and for the first time, sent two lively tides racing together'.⁴ In the great tradition of the travelling singer at the market or fair, Barry was also to be found on occasion at Hanlon's Corner, as the busy cattle market

'I like this pub and it hasn't changed over the years,' said Ronnie Drew in 1990. This image from the 1980s shows a still immediately recognisable O'Donoghue's. (Fáilte Ireland Tourism Photographic Collection, Dublin City Library and Archive)

Across Dublin, different clubs and nights emerged serving all kinds of traditional music circles. Liam Weldon was the backbone of several singing clubs, and a regular face at the historic Brazen Head. (Courtesy of Colm Keating)

and drovers were winding up their working day. 'Now women weren't served but these buskers were known and they were brought into the pub and given bottles of stout,' jarvey Tommy O'Neill recalled to Kevin C. Kearns in his oral history of Dublin pubs.[5]

Also predating O'Donoghue's were the pub sessions of the Irish diaspora in Britain, with the Devonshire Arms in London's Kentish Town often cited as the beginning of this tradition in the 1940s, before spreading into every significant centre of Irish migration. A young Luke Kelly would have an epiphany in Birmingham, hearing 'The Auld Triangle' at a folk night, and later joining the left-wing Clarion Singers Club. A young political radical, it was the English folk club tradition that first opened Luke's eyes to the intersections of politics and folk music, remarking that 'there's a new spirit among young people, a social and political awareness that I think is directly related to the ballads … I think things are going to happen in Ireland again.'[6] In Des Geraghty's biography (and memoir) of Luke, we read of him arriving home in Ireland in 1962, 'with a banjo case full of Communist literature, which fell out when he opened it to take out the banjo'.[7] By a strange turn of events, England's radical folk music tradition would inspire something similar here.

What O'Donoghue's did represent was a new epoch of sorts. The band that would become The Dubliners began performing together there, and were adamant that they could and would make a living from their art. Luke had returned from migration, while Ronnie would recall the telephone exchange he had worked at, staying there a year before he 'realised that this pension everyone was so keen on would not be collected for about forty years, and this great security business they were on about was becoming a bit of a pain in the arse, so I decided to part company with the Telephone Exchange'.[8]

One of those who encountered the Ronnie Drew Ballad Group on Merrion Row was Peggy Jordan, the daughter of a revolutionary and committee member of the United Arts Club, whose Kenilworth Square home was famous for the quality of its social gatherings. An obituary noted how 'she sought to fill their home with an eclectic spectrum of people, preferably able to sing or play a musical instrument'.[9] In a scene where musicians were often paid in pints of stout, Jordan firmly believed in the importance of helping them to support themselves. Later, it was commented that 'people thought this was a dirty thing, turning the traditional music into a business'.[10] Yet Jordan put real value on the work, which was just one part of her contribution to the emerging scene at the time.

Paddy and Maureen ran the pub on their own terms. In September 1971, readers of the *Sunday Independent* were told:

> Not only headmasters resent long hair at this time of year. It worries certain licensed vintners, too. At the famous singing pub of Paddy O'Donoghue, in Dublin's Merrion Row, customers with long hair have been barred for four years – ever since, according to Mr. O'Donoghue, those sound traditional singers from the Oireachtas 'had the mickey taken out of them by long-hairs' and moved to another pub across the road.[11]

There were exceptions to the rule, and some imaginative interpretation. When the journalist quizzed Paddy on Luke Kelly, he was informed the ballad-singer's hair was 'fuzzy, not long'. By then, the public house had achieved international recognition, described in the report as 'a club as much as a tourist attraction'. By the time Senator Ted Kennedy had visited, 'with a motorcycle corps and a fleet of Embassy cars waiting outside, everybody knew about O'Donoghue's'.[12] By the end of the same decade, the pub was famous enough for *Magill* magazine to tell their readers it was a venue where 'every Irish traditional musician with any self-respect and many more with none, have featured ... in the last 15 years'.[13]

Not everyone in the O'Donoghue's milieu achieved commercial success, or even wanted it, but respect and recognition was important. The Connemara singer Seosamh Ó hÉanaí (also known as Joe Heaney), a former building site labourer, ensured the place of sean-nós traditional singing in the pub alongside the so-called 'ballad boom'. Before Ó hÉanaí departed for New York in 1967, the *Evening Press* reported a large crowd in O'Donoghue's to 'wish Seosamh bon voyage. He is going to a job in New York as a hotel doorman. And he will sing there in the evenings. Needless to say, the hotel owner is Irish.'[14] That moment in time has made its way into song. Andy Irvine's musical tribute to O'Donoghue's alludes to musicians plying their trade in the front bar, while 'Joe Heaney sings in the cold night air, in the laneway after closing.' It captures the diversity of talent and the inter-generational nature of the emerging session culture.

O'Donoghue's had a formative influence on a young generation, like Irvine, who would establish their own folk music clubs across the city. When Dónal Lunny and Irvine (both founding members of Planxty later) founded the Mug's Gig club at Slattery's on Capel Street, their first invited guest was Ronnie Drew of The Dubliners. In its own way, this was an acknowledgement of the importance of the scene that had emerged before them. Even earlier, the much-respected Tradition Club had been established in the same venue (initially known as the Listener's Club) with Kevin Conneff of The Chieftains recalling how 'the whole thing was run very idealistically. On a bad night we would have to dip into our own pockets to try and make the musicians' fee a little bit more respectable than the takings would allow.'[15]

O'Donoghue's broke the mould of where folk music could be heard in Dublin. In his memoir, Brian Warfield of The Wolfe Tones recounted the band's early Dublin shows happening in hotels like the

Young singers like Maeve Mulvaney were to be found in Howth's Abbey Tavern, a pub which would even produce numerous traditional music LPs from its House Band. (Fáilte Ireland Tourism Photographic Collection, Dublin City Library and Archive)

Four Courts Hotel on Inns Quay, or in dance halls that had served the showband scene. Times and tastes were now changing, and 'as the popularity of our ballad sessions grew, every venue and pub wanted to be part of this new craze that was spreading like wildfire'.[16]

Beyond O'Donoghue's, some of the public houses that were most engaged with the folk music revival were on the outskirts of the city. At Howth, the Abbey Tavern's enthusiasm for this burgeoning scene was matched only by The Embankment in Tallaght. Singer Johnny McEvoy praised both as 'pioneers. They were providing their customers with ballads at a time when most people didn't want to hear them. Now there are singing pubs mushrooming all over the place.'[17] The Abbey Tavern even predated the O'Donoghue's scene, with the Abbey Tavern Singers group formed in 1962. For owner Minnie Scott-Lennon, the idea of an in-house performing group was something she hoped would attract visitors to the pub. It was a far more successful enterprise than that; in America, the group's 'We're Off to Dublin in the Green' was released on VIP Records, a subsidiary of Motown Records. The group broke the American Hot 100 in 1966, and entered the Canadian Hit Parade.

The Abbey Tavern. (Fáilte Ireland Tourism Photographic Collection, Dublin City Library and Archive)

It's unsurprising that Bord Fáilte photographed an Abbey Tavern session for their promotional materials, such was the level of recognition for the pub.

The Embankment, under the stewardship of the charismatic manager Mick McCarthy, was a pub that benefited enormously from being in the right place at the right time. As Dublin grew westwards, and town planners encouraged the authorities to build larger suburbs, Tallaght would become one of the largest suburban communities in Europe. A bricklayer by trade, who boasted of being at the Battle of Cable Street where Oswald Mosley's Blackshirts were confronted by Irish and Jewish migrants in London, McCarthy would be recalled as 'a publican, trade unionist, father-figure of the Irish ballad-singing world and all-round pinch of salt of the earth'.[18] McCarthy searched the city for talent, approaching The Wolfe Tones in the Four Courts Hotel and telling them he owned 'a bit of a kip at the foothills of the Dublin mountains called The Embankment'.[19]

The Dubliners were frequent visitors to The Embankment, while McCarthy also championed theatre and performance. Micheál Mac Liammóir would bring his one-man show about Oscar Wilde to suburbia, as 'McCarthy persuaded Mac Liammóir to venture out of the city by reminding him that in his day Oscar had taken his show to America's Wild West.'[20] Popular footage of

Luke Kelly singing 'Scorn Not His Simplicity' comes from The Embankment, while the 1967 LP *Live At The Embankment* gives a sense of the diversity of folk and traditional talent who performed there.

While The Embankment is no more, and the site on Blessington Road awaits redevelopment, both the Abbey Tavern and O'Donoghue's remain musical pubs. After Paddy and Maureen O'Donoghue, Dessie Hynes of Longford acquired the famous Merrion Row bar. At fourteen, he 'threw his schoolbag into the Shannon' and began working in his uncle's pub, suggesting that there was to be no other life for him. When interviewed in 2007, at the age of seventy-eight, Dessie was asked of future plans, replying that he'd 'love to be a stockbroker or get a job at the front of the Shelbourne talking to Americans'.[21] There are plenty of Americans in O'Donoghue's now, and plenty of locals too. Some of them even have long hair.

The legacy of The Dubliners is too great to be subsumed within the story of pub balladry. Luke Kelly would attempt to distance the band from this image in an interview with *Spotlight* magazine, insisting 'we have an image of being devil-may-care, unpredictable, hard-drinking artisans. We're not really. Of course, we drink, but it's not our complete way of life … Singing in pubs is not our real forte. We're gradually getting away from it. A two-hour concert is what we relish. No noisy drinkers or interruptions from popping corks or clanging trays.'[22]

Today, traditional and folk music is in a very healthy state across the city, both in public houses and on stage. McNeill's former music shop on Capel Street is now a public house, trading under the same name, which hosts excellent traditional music sessions. On the exterior of new arrival Piper's Corner, opened by uilleann piper

A leading light of traditional music in Dublin today, the front of Piper's Corner honours Séamus Ennis.

The Cobblestone, by Mack Signs.

Seán Potts and publican Eamonn Briody in 2017, an image of the great piper Ennis adorns the front of the premises, which prides itself on the quality of its sessions. The Cobblestone in Smithfield has become synonymous with the current moment, hosting the important singing session 'The Night Before Larry Was Stretched' in its back bar every month and featuring prominently in the award-winning documentary *North Circular*. In 2011, Neil Hegarty wrote in his guide to Dublin that the pub had become 'the most famous of Dublin's music pubs', but that 'I have heard it may be demolished and rebuilt.'[23] The Cobblestone finds itself in the curious position of being a beloved public house in a building it doesn't actually own, and hundreds took to the streets in October 2021 when a planned hotel redevelopment of the site became public news. Pubs come and go, but The Cobblestone came to represent a much broader question of hotels and their place in the city. On Francis Street, a hotel that replaced the Tivoli Theatre includes historic pictures of the theatre within its own walls, like a ghost lingering around, reminding us of a city that once housed more places of recreation. The Cobblestone, unusually in the current moment perhaps, won the day.

## CHAPTER 23.
# FROM SINGING PUBS TO KARAOKE

Lalor's is now The Landmark.

**P**erhaps nowhere in Dublin has publand been transformed as rapidly in recent times as in the Liberties. This reflects broader changes in the area, where an overconcentration of aparthotels, student accommodation blocks and built-to-rent apartments which can never be purchased outright has created a general feeling of transience over community. As the city centre becomes more expensive real estate, there are no prizes for guessing who is moved to the peripheries.

A feature of inner-city working-class public houses is karaoke. Though these pubs are ever-shrinking in number, a walk around the Liberties and its immediate neighbouring environment still reveals a healthy culture of social singalong. At public houses like Tom Kennedy's, The Harold House and The Liberty Belle, karaoke is often an intergenerational ritual. People — and their mammies — come ready to sing.

If there is a forerunner to the karaoke of today, it is found in the so-called 'singing pubs' of the mid-twentieth century. The very words may bring to mind O'Donoghue's, The Cobblestone or other pubs explored elsewhere in this volume. Yet the pubs that marketed themselves as such in the 1950s predated any ballad boom, and generally catered to a different kind of song. In a room that often centred around the presence of a piano, patrons were encouraged to sing along. In 1954, Cork's *Irish Examiner* explained the phenomenon of these Dublin pub to their readership in their Dublin correspondent's page:

> There are a few 'singing pubs' left in this city. These are establishments where the licensee is permitted to allow music to be played and his customers to sing while they are having alcoholic refreshment. Singing or the playing of music is an offence in public houses which are not licensed for this purpose. Generally speaking, the police do not look with favour on the granting of such licenses [*sic*].[1]

It may seem extraordinary to us today that singing a song in a public house could be a matter of law above the taste of the owner. In Dublin today there are several notable pubs where singing is not allowed; not even the funeral of Luke Kelly could shift policy at The Gravediggers.[2] The Grogan's ban is even immortalised in the poetry of Críostóir Ó Floinn, who reminded patrons to 'remember though no songs allowed, in Grogan's just like old McDaid's'.[3] In both institutions and others like them, such rules stand testament to the ambience the owners wish to create in their establishment. It was a different thing entirely when the law kept public houses silent. On occasion, it could make curious decisions. Downey's public house in Dún Laoghaire applied for a licence in June 1954, to only be granted a licence for piano playing but not for singing. Perhaps the judge was worried what chorus might be struck up, as the pub was best known for a fourteen-year picket on its premises by a trade union, in opposition to what they viewed as the unfair dismissal of a member of staff.[4] The last thing Downey's needed was a contentious song.

'Singing Pubs', one observer in the early 1960s insisted, were 'one of the last outposts of the common man'.[5] Equally, they belonged to the common woman. While much coverage earlier went on the arrival of the lounge and the cocktail as things that were bringing women into what were predominantly viewed as male spaces, these public houses were also more egalitarian spaces.

Geographer and social historian Kevin C. Kearns maps these institutions in his oral history of Dublin pubs. Lalor's on the corner of Wexford Street and Kevin Street (now The Landmark) began the tradition in 1938, with Ted McGovern (a barman who would go on to take over the establishment) telling Kevin it was quickly decided to convert a former private quarters 'into a formal singing lounge holding about 130 people'. To sing in Lalor's was to partake in an occasion:

> Lalor's was the first singing house in Dublin which became world famous. Anybody who was here in Dublin, it was a must to go to Lalor's. We got people from all areas and from all walks of life. From plumbers to foreign dignitaries and professional people – the lot. And everybody was dressed up as if they were going to the cinema or a hotel.[6]

On occasion, these public houses competed against one another. In October 1959, the press reported that Mrs Rose Murphy, representing Downey's of Crumlin, emerged victorious in a 'Singing Pub Competition' in the concourse of Busáras. Other competitors came from a variety of inner-city pubs, and the City of Dublin Working Men's Club on Wellington Quay.[7]

Naturally, if something is competitive, it requires rules. The 'Singing Pub' operated on the principle of 'One Song One Voice', with an MC guiding proceedings. Tom Corkery, in his guide to Dublin, noted:

> The master of ceremonies will open proceedings with the command: 'ORDER NOW PLEASE!' As of this moment, a decorous and seemly hush should fall upon the house. The voice of a good singing-house MC can be heard over the combined noises of two hundred customers talking simultaneously, fifty customers shouting orders at ten waiters, and ten waiters relaying the orders to five barmen.[8]

Corkery penned those words in 1980, perhaps unaware that even then there were significant changes afoot that would alter the nature of public house singing forever.

Karaoke was born in Japan in the early 1970s, but the exact circumstances remain in dispute. To quote one history of popular culture there, it began 'as part of all-male team building among corporate employees, who were generally expected to get drunk together after work rather than go home'.[9] In Kobe, nightclub musician Daisuke Inoue is credited with the invention of the humble karaoke machine, though he never made his millions from it. He is philosophical about it all, telling one newspaper how 'at the time, I thought that patents were only for unbelievable inventions that produced something from nothing. The first karaoke machine just brought together some electronic components that already existed.'[10]

The arrival of karaoke in Dublin public houses in the late 1980s is initially reported with some bemusement, and in light of Channel 4's *Kazuko's Karaoke Klub* television programme, which arrived in Dublin to scout out potential talent at The Lower Deck. The presenter of that programme told the *Evening Herald*:

> It's not a relaxing hobby in Japan. It's a highly pressurised thing. It's self-promotion, and that's terribly important to the Japanese.

After five o'clock, they go to the pub – but always with guests or clients. They can't relax, so for the businessman, karaoke is part of work.[11]

The new technology offered financial opportunities, with karaoke sales and rental outlet The Singing Machine reportedly making £250,000 from providing the equipment to just fifteen city-centre public houses throughout 1990 and 1991.[12] Not everyone was as enthusiastic, with the *Evening Press* warning readers that 'concern is mounting that the traditional Dublin pub is under threat from a karaoke invasion that is sweeping across the country'.[13] With tongue firmly in cheek, the paper informed readers how 'anti-karaoke activists fear that the traditional Dublin Bar Stool Philosopher will become extinct – to be replaced by the Bar Room Elvis'.[14]

For something that arrived only in the late 1980s, the importance of karaoke in inner-city and suburban Dublin public houses has already made its way into the literature and drama of the city. Maria Pramaggiore, an authority on twentieth-century Irish cinema, has written of the symbolic importance of a pregnant Sharon Curley performing Madonna's 'Papa Don't Preach' in the big-screen adaptation of Roddy Doyle's *The Snapper*: 'As the whole of Dublin's Barrytown jeers at Sharon, the public nature of her problematic pregnancy is clearly evident. As a spectacularly pregnant woman channelling Madonna, Sharon is a figure of exotic fascination.'[15]

Today, karaoke exists outside the surroundings of a public house in Dublin. On Parnell Street and Capel Street, several Asian restaurants offer private karaoke rooms, an experience not unlike the one you could have in Tokyo or New York City's Chinatown. These are great experiences on their own terms, but there is a great democracy in the open floor of public house karaoke. New faces are welcome, but the best old songs are already claimed.

# CHAPTER 24.
# VIENNA IN TRINITY COLLEGE DUBLIN

**W**hen flames took hold of the Dining Hall of Trinity College Dublin in July 1984, 'a human chain was formed as almost all the valuable paintings, silver, antiques and furniture inside were saved'.[1] And indeed, stepping off Parliament Square and into the Dining Hall today, the eighteenth-century building still reveals many gems of the past to the visitor, including a table from Daly's Club on College Green, once described as 'the chief resort of the aristocracy and Members of Parliament'.[2] A portrait of Queen Elizabeth I, founder of the college, is displayed within the building, though most wall space is occupied by former administrators and academics. If there's a drink of choice here, it's coffee. Amidst subscription copies of *The Economist*, *The Phoenix*, the *London Review of Books* and every other publication worth its salt, the sound of busy coffee machines reminds the visitor that this place is – for most – a respite from the working day.

A rare view inside the Vienna-inspired bar of Trinity College Dublin. (Courtesy of Oliver Deane)

It is perhaps one of the last buildings in Dublin in which you'd expect to find a pub. But tucked away in the corner of the Senior Common Room is a hidden secret, something that few graduates of the university have seen for themselves – a replica of the famous American Bar (or Kärntner Bar) in Vienna, which has been described as 'one of Vienna's architectural jewels'.[3]

The American Bar was the work of celebrated architect Alfred Loos, a pioneering figure of modern architecture whose legacy to that city includes beautiful public housing and the commercial Looshaus at Michaelerplatz. The bar feels larger than its 290 square feet, through the use of wall mirrors that create what *Vanity Fair* described as 'a glimmering spaciousness'.[4] With its mahogany, marble and onyx, there is an elegance and timelessness to the bar, which offered American cocktails to drinkers in a setting far removed from the celebrated beer halls of its hometown. Putting the bar in context, Mary Costello tells us:

> These establishments, which began to appear in Europe from the 1890s, generally took the form of a standing bar, and served 'American' or 'mixed' drinks to an all-male clientele. The introduction of bars to Vienna provided an alternative space to the ubiquitous coffeehouse for intellectual and cultural exchange.[5]

The refusal to admit women to the American Bar was quickly abandoned; gender equality came sooner there than on the Dublin campus. In the early 1960s, *Trinity News* told its readers that 'The time would seem ripe for rethinking about the position of women in College and the function of the Major Societies.'[6] Only in 1968 were female academics admitted to Fellowship, making them eligible for full membership of the Senior Common Room.[7] If the Loos Bar, as it became known, had opened twenty years earlier, they wouldn't have been allowed to avail of it.

Following the 1984 blaze, de Blacam and Meagher Architects were tasked with the restoration and redesign of the Senior Common

Room. Responding to the desire of some staff for a bar, the architects were given free reign on its design, and Shane de Blacam told the *Dublin Inquirer* that, when he visited the American Bar, he had been impressed by 'the miracle of the mirrors' created there by Loos.[8] Though the materials used were considerably more modest, the aesthetic and feeling of the celebrated bar were successfully created in miniature. Wood panelling and mirrors are important in this 1985 space, but so too are other little details that show how committed de Blacam and Meagher were to the task. The artist Alice Hanratty reproduced the portrait of Peter Altenberg by Gustav Jagerpacher that hangs in the original bar, though here Altenberg faces away from the bar.[9] The choice of honouring Altenberg for the original bar was an inspired one, linking the premises to one of the most celebrated of the Jung-Wien (Young Vienna) writers. The motto of Altenberg's journal insisted that 'art is art and life is life, but to live life artistically: that is the art of life'.[10]

If you'd like a glimpse inside this very special bar, you don't have to obtain a professorship in Trinity College Dublin. As part of the Open House Dublin festival, an annual celebration of the built heritage of the city from the Irish Architecture Foundation, the bar allows the curious to visit, but tickets are in short supply and demand is high.

More democratic is 'The Pav', as the Pavilion Bar is known to students at the university. Overlooking the cricket pitches of Trinity, the bar is housed within an 1885 pavilion designed by Thomas Drew, who went on to design the beautiful Graduates Memorial Building, the neo-Gothic building that houses some of the most historic student societies on campus. Past members of the Hist (the College Historical Society) include Samuel Beckett, of whom *Trinity News* wrote in 1956:

> Characteristically shy and quiet, he had, however, a fondness for Beamish – in fact, since he left there is none to be had in Dublin. Food was not so important to him, and his mother used to pay periodic visits to College to try to force him to eat.[11]

# CHAPTER 25.
# A REMINDER OF THE TOWERS

Ballymun was to be a 'New Town' initiative, close to the city but self-reliant. Little in the line of what was promised to residents of this bold new departure in public housing was delivered, however, with Ballymun leaving a community of some two thousand new residents with little in the line of social provisions. As geographer Joseph Brady notes, 'it would have beggared belief that any planner could fail to understand the need to provide for the population who were being located to this new world'.[2]

What it did have was a public house, and a significant one. In scale, The Towers was perhaps the nearest thing in Ireland to the so-called 'estate pubs' that dot the landscape of working-class public housing in Britain. These post-war pubs came to serve newly built estates across Britain, and in some cases became the subject of ridicule and stereotype, with a warning to 'never drink in a flat-roofed pub'.[3] In some cases, public houses were actually built on new estates by local authorities, conscious of the importance of places of recreation in different spheres of life.

The Towers was significantly bigger than many of these pubs, reflecting the scale of the Ballymun project more broadly. An advertisement for the pub when later listed for sale described it as an 'extensive two-storey licensed premises which extends to approximately 1,150 m² (12,470 ft²). The accommodation comprises ground floor public bar, lounge bar and stores with a further lounge bar and nightclub and store on the first floor.'[4]

Ballymun's superpub was managed by the Belton Group, founded by Patrick Belton (who one contemporary nicknamed 'two-gun Pat, the Drumcondra Financier'). Belton was a former revolutionary turned property developer, and his legacy to Dublin's northside would include Collins Avenue, Griffith Avenue and – displaying little modesty – Belton Park.[5] He had opened his first public house on Collins Avenue, and his son and namesake continued the family tradition. Significantly, they came to dominate the suburban pub landscape, chasing newer markets instead of competing for the city centre. The group purchased

Crumlin's Submarine Bar in 1959, for example, expanding the premises to four times its original size.[6]

The Towers pub opened in 1970 as the Seven Towers initially, drawing on its neighbouring structures for inspiration. The press reported that 'one wall is dominated by a Muriel Brandt montage of the signatories of the 1916 proclamation and the places where they fought in Easter Week ... Liberty Hall, the GPO, Boland's Mills'.[7] More than a montage, this was a mural by one of Ireland's leading artists in the field.

Born in Belfast in 1909, Brandt was a graduate of the Royal College of Art in London, where she studied at the mural decoration department. A distinguished artist, her work included the 1949 postage stamp marking the formal declaration of Ireland as a republic, and she frequently exhibited work at the RHA.

Apart from the signatories gazing down on the customers, Aslan frontman Christy Dignam would recall another nationalist dimension of the pub, then common across Ireland. Having sung there with an earlier band, Electron, he recounted:

> We finished the set after what seemed like an eternity. But I'd got through it and the ordeal was over. Except it wasn't. The organisers came up and told us that we had to finish up with 'Amhrán na bhFiann' ('The Soldier's Song'), the national anthem ... It was sung by the rebels holding the General Post Office against the British, and was a favourite in the republican internment camps that followed ... And of course, we didn't know it.[8]

The great optimism of the 1960s around the Ballymun project soon faded. In the early 1980s the journalist Gene Kerrigan penned an in-depth piece in *Magill* magazine that championed the good while also highlighting the bad, noting how 'an Irish school was founded, again on the initiative of tenants themselves and teachers with commitment to the area, and is today widely-known for its academic standards. It is non-denominational, co-educational and effectively managed by the parents – and there's a waiting list.' Such victories were achieved by local people for themselves, but Kerrigan also described how:

> Parents on the fifth, tenth or fifteenth floor found out the hard way that these structures were no place for raising children. Some let the kids go down to the handful of swings, the glass and the traffic, more kept the kids with them in the flat and reached for the Valium. Perversely, housing policy was such that this estate unfit for children was swamped by them.[9]

In the end, the towers that opened in the Golden Jubilee of the Easter Rising would not stand to see its centenary. Beginning with the demolition of Pearse Tower in 2004, the towers were gradually removed, with the final resident reminding the press that, despite the issues, 'all of our neighbours were fantastic. There was a great community spirit. We all helped each other out.'[10]

Today, Muriel Brandt's mural is displayed in Ballymun Civic Centre, which has been a driving force of the rejuvenation of the area. And Ballymun's stories are told on stage in the neighbouring Axis Theatre. Almost sixty years on from the birth of this so-called New Town, it finally has the civic amenities required. Alas, it awaits another good-sized pub.

# CHAPTER 26.
# CODDLE, SANDWICHES AND TAYTO CRISPS

Muriel Brandt's mural from The Towers survives in the Ballymun Civic Centre today. Along with the seven signatories of the Proclamation, it also shows how the Rising was experienced by the civilian population.

**I**n the end, The Towers public house outlasted the structures it was named after. The Ballymun towers were built in the 1960s and named in honour of the signatories of the 1916 proclamation, harking back to a heroic past while also representing modernity and the arrival of a new way of living on our shores. When the first of the towers was completed, the *Irish Independent* told readers:

> Sunshine and symmetry in Ballymun ... these towers epitomise the achievements of modern construction techniques. All in all, there will be seven of these blocks at Ballymun, each of which provides 30 three-room flats, 30 two-room flats and 30 one-room flats.[1]

**No genuine Irishmen could relax in comfort and feel at home in a pub unless he was sitting in deep gloom on a hard seat with a very sad expression on his face, listening to the drone of bluebottle squadrons carrying out a raid on the yellow sandwich cheese.**[1]

**S**o wrote Myles na gCopaleen in 1940, in an article observing (and sometimes lamenting) the rapidly changing nature of the pub trade in the capital. Much of the change observed was in the appearance of the pub; gone were 'liberal lashings of sawdust and mobbing-rags to prevent the customers from perishing in their own spilling and spewing'.[2] The lounge bar had arrived, and a pint of plain was no longer your only man.

Beyond the passing mention of yellow sandwich cheese, food doesn't feature. It would be more than two decades before the term 'pub grub' was widely used, describing the offerings of Dublin public houses. 'We call it pub grub,' the advertisement for the Dolphin Inn on Essex Street told readers in 1969, 'our customers call it marvellous. Soups, cold joints, hot pies ...'[3] Food made its way into the public houses of Ireland more slowly than it did in Britain, but there too there was disagreement on whether it was an important part of the trade, or should even be encouraged. 'You get food in a café, you get beer in the pub' was the response of one York publican to the question in the 1940s.[4] When Roy Bulson penned his *Irish Pubs of Character* in 1969, a guide to the city for visitors keen to sample its famous watering holes, the food scene was still small enough that the food listing for Glasnevin's Brian Boru House was a pretty good reflection of the offering in a Dublin public house: crisps and nuts, coffee, Irish coffee.[5]

Peanuts, pork scratchings and pickled eggs became standard fare in Britain, but it would be decades before pubs specialising in restaurant-quality food came to the fore. Brian J. Murphy, in an essay examining the history of food in the public house in Ireland, timelines the emergence of so-called gastropubs in Britain for useful comparison. The Eagle in London's Farringdon is, Murphy tells us, generally agreed to be the first gastropub, opening its doors in 1991 and 'reputed to have come up with the concept of providing restaurant-standard food in a pub setting'.[6]

Before the gastropub, a humble opaque bag of potato crisps was the lofty heights of pub grub for many. Tayto, established by Joe 'Spud' Murphy in 1954 and beginning life in a small premises on O'Rahilly Parade off Moore Street, lay claim to inventing the first cheese-and-onion-flavoured crisp.[7] In that same decade, Donal O'Neill launched Manhattan as a popcorn brand, but it would move into the pub crisp market later. Pub crisps feature in several memoirs and even novels, where writers recall being 'treated to endless bottles of red lemonade and packets of Tayto crisps', or how children 'would be left sitting outside the pub drinking from a bottle of red lemonade and eating Tayto crisps bought by tipsy fathers to appease us young ones'.[8] More than a way of keeping children content, there is much to be said for a bag of crisps among friends. Food writer Ali Dunworth tells us that 'in proper pub crisp etiquette, it's polite to open the bag right side up, then tear along the seam on the side, allowing the pocket to open flat for easy sharing'.[9]

A primary argument against offering a significant food menu for many publicans was the absence of physical space, but a number of public houses took advantage of the scale of a premises to offer

A 1977 view of the upstairs of The Lord Edward. (Fáilte Ireland Tourism Photographic Collection, Dublin City Library and Archive)

food totally separate from the main environment. The Lord Edward at Christ Church is a highly regarded public house in the city today, with its downstairs bar and upstairs lounge maintaining completely different atmospheres (televised horse racing downstairs, the occasional ballad by the fire or poetry recital upstairs). Historically, The Lord Edward was the trading name of the seafood restaurant on the third floor of the premises, but it has been adopted by the pub in recent decades.

The roots of The Lord Edward restaurant are to be found in the Red Bank Restaurant on D'Olier Street, named not for a former financial institution but for a famed type of oyster hailing from Clare. When Red Bank ceased trading in 1967, Tom Cunniam of 1 Werburgh Street – the Cunniam Tavern – took the opportunity of establishing a seafood restaurant above his public house. The standard of food in the restaurant was high; while acknowledging that 'when it came to gastronomic delights, Ireland in the seventies

CHAPTER 26. CODDLE, SANDWICHES AND TAYTO CRISPS

was something of a backwater', food writer Lucinda O'Sullivan listed The Lord Edward as a notable exception.¹⁰ In the former living quarters of the Cunniam family, the restaurant over the pub quickly gained a reputation for the diversity of its menu. A later review noted:

> The array of fish on offer is large: turbot, sole, salmon, crab, lobster, shrimps, eel (off the night we were there) sea trout and prawns. All these fish are offered in a variety of sauces, all of which you could find in the *Larousse Gastronomique*.¹¹

Richard Kearney, in a personal reflective piece on his friendship with Seamus Heaney, recalled days of good eating and drinking, and how 'for its black sole and Riesling, the Lord Edward, with its bay window belled by Christchurch Cathedral, and reverentially unswept for at least forty years, was our favourite by far'.¹²

Some of the most unusual food offerings in a Dublin pub today can be found at John Kavanagh's on Prospect Square in Glasnevin, known popularly as The Gravediggers. Beside what was once the primary entrance to Prospect Cemetery, founded by Daniel O'Connell in 1832, the public house dates from 1833. Although it is often described as a Victorian pub, a promotional leaflet for the pub boasted of predating her reign, and how 'this isn't a wealthy Victorian bar of stained glass and gilt mirrors'.¹³ Kavanagh's has history in abundance – once-popular bar games are

A handbill promoting John Kavanagh's public house to visitors of the neighbouring cemetery. It lists the food offerings of the pub. (With thanks to all at John Kavanagh's)

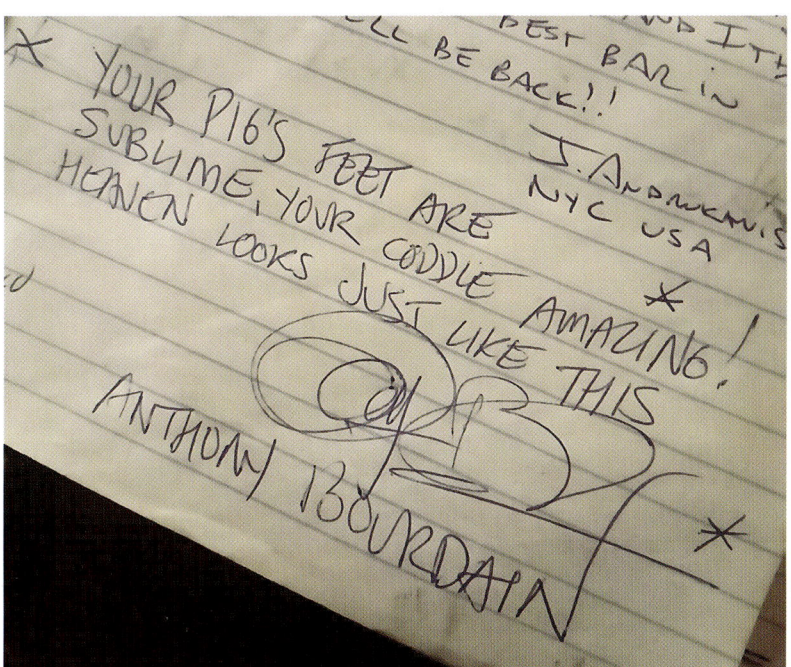

The guest book of John Kavanagh's includes many notable international visitors. Anthony Bourdain's comments are a source of considerable pride for all at the pub. (With thanks to all at John Kavanagh's)

mounted to the wall, as are relics of the neighbouring cemetery and posters from films that have featured the bar – but the pub isn't constrained by the past. Chef Ciaran Kavanagh, who represents the seventh generation of his family to work on the premises, finds inspiration in all kinds of things for the food he offers, including history, but also his own travels and taste. The words 'Irish' and 'tapas' can co-exist, with surprising results. When author, chef and broadcaster Anthony Bourdain visited on Bloomsday 2012, he signed the guestbook:

> Your pig's feet are sublime, your coddle amazing. Heaven looks just like this.

The Gravediggers prides itself on coddle, a hearty stew on which there is little agreement, and which gains mention in *Finnegans Wake*. It was a hard dish to sell in the beginning, Ciaran told one visiting television presenter, 'because everyone says their mother makes the best one'.[14]

Suitably hungover after a night in The Gravediggers, Bourdain also enjoyed a fry at Slattery's early house on Capel Street, something alluded to outside of the pub today. Some of Bourdain's stops from his Dublin visit are gone (such as Roma II, a chipper on Wexford Street, and the South City Markets branch of Lolly and Cooks, from which he had a sausage roll), but that his visit is still commemorated at the public houses he visited is something he would take pride in: 'There are few places I'm more comfortable than a really good Irish pub.' He also described Dublin stout in a way only a chef could:

> This divine brew is so tasty, creamy, so near chocolatey in its rich, satisfying, buzz-giving qualities, that the difference between the stuff here, and the indifferently poured swill you get where you come from, is like night and day. One is beer, the other, angels sing celestial trombones.[15]

If the gastropub represented a moment of real transition, as restaurant-quality food and alcohol came to share the public house, another development has been the emergence of more traditional restaurants within former strictly pub settings. Spitalfields, located on the Coombe in the heart of the Liberties, may still have the architectural feel of a public house, but it is primarily a restaurant, as the prominently displayed Bib Gourmand from the *Michelin Guide* team can attest to. On Stoneybatter's Manor Street, L. Mulligan Grocer still has some of the trappings of the public house (including excellent traditional music sessions in its front bar and a solid offering of local beers), but the strong seasonal menu drawing primarily from Irish producers is what brings most visitors. Today, the Bar of the Year Awards include two categories focused on pub food, a reminder that there is more than one way to operate a licensed premises.

# BUYING WINKLES (*extract*)
## Paula Meehan

She'd be sitting outside the Rosebowl Bar
on an orange-crate, a pram loaded
with pails of winkles before her.
When the bar doors swung open they'd leak
the smell of men together with drink
and I'd see light in golden mirrors.
I envied each soul in the hot interior.

From *The Man who was Marked by Winter*
(Gallery Press, 1991)

# CHAPTER 27.
# CON HOULIHAN'S DUBLIN

The magnificant and little-changed interior of Mulligan's. (Courtesy of photographer Andy Sheridan)

Underpinning all of this endeavour and excitement are the ever-faithful who have followed the Saints through thin and thinner. I have been privileged to drink with them and exchange songs with them and lament with them and rejoice with them.[1]

The Camac terrace was one of Con Houlihan's happy places, even when there was little to cheer about on the pitch for St Patrick's Athletic in Inchicore. Before 'Friday night lights', it was a ritual of Sunday afternoons. What ultimately drew him to the football club were the people around it. The club had been founded by railway workers, and had gone on a journey around Dublin before settling back in Richmond Park. Con admired the devotion of the faithful: 'for a long time its members and its followers were like one of the lost tribes of Israel'.[2]

Born in Kerry's Castleisland in 1925, Houlihan became not only Ireland's most recognisable sports journalist but its most unique, peppering accounts of sporting matches with literary references and philosophical insights. It is unlikely anyone else could have penned the words 'sometimes, when I am in Inchicore I think of a novel by the great Belgian Georges Simenon, *The Man Who Watched Trains Go By*'.[3] In a different lifetime, Con may have remained within a world that was focused on literature. His MA thesis was on the 'social and literary background of the eighteenth-century English poet, William Cowper'. In one interview, he rattled off names like Thomas Hardy, Edward Thomas (a somewhat forgotten World War I poet) and Ernest Hemingway, advising that 'any young aspiring writer should read him'.[4] He brought these passions into his sports writing. One could come away with little clue of how a game had played out in the middle of the field, but with a new appreciation for *A Farewell to Arms*.

In the beginning, there was *The Kerryman*, where 'Con wrote in pencil on large sheets of white butter paper with one paragraph per page.'[5] In 1973, Dublin won out, beginning Con's long association with the *Press* group of newspapers, before its sad demise brought him to other pastures. By the time he arrived in Dublin as a jobbing journalist, Houlihan was forty-seven. He would write until his dying day, with his final column – in celebration of Katie Taylor – appearing in the press posthumously.

Houlihan loved sport in the broadest sense. For him, Kerry's strong and enduring rugby connections were a source of great pride. Historian Richard McElligott, an authority on the GAA in Kerry, has suggested that the popularity of rugby in the country 'was greatly facilitated by the characteristics it shared with caid [a name given to traditional Irish mob football games]. Both involved scrimmages of men attempting to gain possession before passing to the fleeter-footed players hovering on the wings, who ran with the ball in hand.'[6] The jersey of Castleisland's rugby club was placed on Con's coffin. Just as the people of Inchicore attracted Con to the Camac, he viewed rugby as a game of the people.

But it was Gaelic games that would inspire what was undoubtedly Houlihan's most recalled line of an Irish match report. Of the 1978 All-Ireland Football Final, he described Dublin goalkeeper Paddy Cullen running back towards his goal after Kerryman Mikey Sheehy's attempted lob as 'like a woman who smells a cake burning. The ball won the race and it curled inside the near post as Paddy crashed into the outside of the net and lay against it like a fireman who had returned to find his station ablaze.'[7]

It seems right then to begin an examination of the public houses Houlihan frequented by a sporting ground, and the Camac. The demographics of Inchicore have shifted considerably since Con stood on the terrace. In September 2024, *Time Out* magazine named Inchicore as 'one of the 38 coolest neighbourhoods in the world'.[8] If you lived in Notre-Dame-du-Mont in Marseille, your rent may have doubled instantly on news you lived in the world's coolest neighbourhood. For Inchicore, twenty-fifth place sufficed to cause considerable excitement in the national press. The rousing rendition of 'Inchicore is full of smack' (to the tune of 'When the Saints Go Marching In') from an away end these days can only suggest the opposition supporters are not keen readers of the property supplements.

As Inchicore has changed, the types of pubs and the offerings of what were once more traditional public houses have diversified. That, of course, is no bad thing. Con had his matchday pubs, which included the Richmond House, a pub that has a greater physical presence on Emmet Road than the football stadium behind it. On its exterior, it lists 1868 as the year of establishment. Hidden behind a row of red-brick terraced houses, a visitor on a passing bus could miss the existence of a football stadium. Like Dalymount Park on the northside, the stadium lures 'groundhopper' tourists in search of what they view as an authentic window into the football stadiums of yore. Within the Richmond House, a plaque honours

Ronnie Drew attends a book launch of his friend Con Houlihan in Mulligan's. (Sportsfile)

Michael Hartnett, who Con described as 'the celebrated poet from Newcastle West'. Positioned beside where the poet liked to sit, it mentions both his birthplace and his adopted home:

> Bury my sins on Tom White's Hill
> Lay them all down and say no more
> All the rest leave to Newcastle West
> But bury my heart in Inchicore.

Hartnett's *Inchicore Haiku* was partly penned there. It stands as a reminder of a time before *Time Out* magazine had heard of the district:

> In the Richmond House
> the floorboards ooze ancient tears
> of unemployment.

There was also the Horse and Jockey, now a curious ruin on a transformed Emmet Road, where the faithful recall Houlihan dissecting what had just played out on the neighbouring pitch. As the name would suggest, there was at least one other sport keenly observed there. Horse racing was a sport Houlihan respected, recalling that his 'neighbours knew horses not as names in the newspapers and the form-books – they knew them as creatures of flesh and blood and minds and spirits'.[9]

On the return leg to the city, there was always time for the Royal Oak. A walk down Kilmainham Lane, past the historic Kilmainham Mill and onwards towards the Liberties, even now has the feeling of being outside the capital. Con wrote of how:

> It is like a piece of the country in the heart of the city. It has green spaces and hedges and trees and there you can hear the birds sing. There, too, you will find a little pub which from the outside looks like a private house.
>
> This is the Old Royal Oak – and long may it last.[10]

Richmond Park and its surrounding public houses were a part of Con Houlihan's Dublin, but there were other stadiums for other codes. Baggot Street, in near proximity to Lansdowne Road, brings memorials to Con at The Waterloo and Searson's, both frequented on the walk towards the city centre following rugby matches. Still, the epicentre of his city was Burgh Quay, home of the *Evening Press* newspaper. A short walk from the site of the *Press* offices will bring you to memorials to Con in The Palace, Chaplin's, Mulligan's, O'Neill's of Suffolk Street and The Bank on College Green. Con's association with The Palace ran deep enough for him to be included in the four bronze plaques outside the establishment, sharing ground with Behan, Kavanagh and Myles na gCopaleen. Like Wellington's testimonial in the Phoenix Park, it was made all the more impressive by the fact that Con was still alive at the time of its unveiling. Similarly, a plaque inside Mulligan's on Poolbeg Street was unveiled in his own lifetime. It includes a homage from publican, writer and sportsman John B. Keane:

> When he entered the sporting scene, the cobwebs of bias and bigotry were blown away by the pure breath of his vision and honesty. I played rugby against him, but drank porter with him. We were useful enough players, but we excelled at the other.

For Con, public houses were places of work as well as leisure. Reports and columns could be finished there, before someone would be dispatched from the offices of the *Irish Press* to collect them. It was a practice that had begun earlier in his journalistic career at *The Kerryman* in Tralee, recalling how:

> ... sometimes I had perforce to write my mortal words in The Brogue Inn, then the epicentre of our capital town; I had my table in front of a blazing fire of logs, winter or summer – when we had summer.

> At an appointed time a runner would come from *The Kerryman* – and usually he was so breathless that liquid sustenance was essential.
>
> Such runners were a throwback to more colourful days; they were known as printers' devils.[11]

Houlihan's day typically began even before that of the milkmen of the capital. He was a familiar presence in the early houses of the city, enjoying the company of the workers who visited them around Dublin's dockside and markets areas. When interviewed over a drink by the journalist Harry McGee for the *Sunday Press*, he explained his early starting routine:

> You rise at 4am. It is a country habit. And even before you set pen to paper, your words have already been set out, line by line, page by page, in your mind. In effect, you are always writing ... through every waking hour, in idle moments between conversations, among the cygnets and waterhens and mallards of Portobello.[12]

Many of the public houses Con frequented around Burgh Quay are no more, either levelled in the name of progress or completely unrecognisable. The Scotch House is gone, replaced by 'a contemporary and prominent seven-storey modern office building' which carries the name Scotch House.[13] It had a long-standing connection to journalists, including those who were nominally employed in doing other things. Myles na gCopaleen spent enough time there to refer to the establishment in the *Irish Times* as his 'office'; J. P. Donleavy remembered him 'reflectively sipping his whiskey matriculated in the interior of The Scotch House on the Quays'.[14] In his other life, as Custom House civil servant Brian O'Nolan, the pub was sufficiently close to nip out to during the working day, but sufficiently distant (and on the other side of the river) to avoid the eyes of those to whom he reported. Another Houlihan favourite, The White Horse, is now a Starbucks, explored

Mulligan's on Poolbeg Street. (Courtesy of photographer Andy Sheridan)

elsewhere in this book. Benedict Kiely evoked it as a pub that was popular with *Press* journalists, but which also had 'the people form the Dublin docks, genuine dockers and local residents for whom the nearest next town was Liverpool'.[15]

A copy of the final edition of the *Press* can be found today at Mulligan's, signed by Con. This pub was his first port of call on returning from the Italia '90 World Cup, a national celebration he joked that he had missed out on, being in Italy at the time.[16] Mulligan's association with the *Press* was so strong that the journalist Declan Lynch has recalled how 'I wrote articles for that paper for quite a while without ever entering the actual premises on Burgh Quay, because it never seemed that necessary while Mulligan's was there.'[17]

A statue of Houlihan stands in the entrance hallway of one of Dublin's most interesting public houses, architecturally speaking:

The Bank on College Green. This bar opened in 2003, and the statue is perhaps best understood as an appreciation of Con from Charlie Chawke, owner of the bar and a number of others in the city. A friend of Houlihan's, Chawke was just the kind of bar owner Houlihan respected, having worked his way up from working behind the counter of Davy Byrne's at the age of sixteen.

The bust of Con's head, behind the bar in The Palace, has an interesting lore. Liam Aherne, who had taken over The Palace from his father Bill, 'had originally seen it in the office of the then Tánaiste Dick Spring. He "borrowed" it from Dick and it's been in The Palace Bar ever since.'[18] In truth, it's a perfect copy. Houlihan had been a great supporter of Dan Spring, father to the later Labour leader, and would describe himself as a socialist until his dying day, with the Starry Plough taking its place beside the Castleisland rugby jersey on his coffin. Some would describe Houlihan's politics as anti-nationalist, a claim he would reject, seeing himself as within a certain Irish tradition: 'As soon I was able to wield a brush and white wash "Up James Connolly" on an innocent wall, I became a bucket-carrying member of the Irish Labour Party.'[19] The origin of the much-loved bust is a reminder of Houlihan's political leanings, and his connection to the Springs.

Further from the Burgh Quay beat, Houlihan also counted Doheny & Nesbitt as part of his beat, a pub that now recalls what is jokingly called the 'Doheny & Nesbitt School of Economics', synonymous more with the Irish parliament than the *Irish Press*. Con remembered in 1990 that 'I was a regular in Doheny & Nesbitt long before it became fashionable. Away back in the sixties it was about as trendy as The White Horse is now; in simple language, it was very much a working-class pub and none the worse for that.'[20] He delighted in the success of Ned Doheny and Tom Nesbitt, two returning barmen who had emigrated from Tipperary to New York City and returned to put their names over the door of such an establishment. A bust of Con gazes down on visitors to the bar today.

Hugh Hanratty's statue of Con takes pride of place inside the doorway of The Bank. A copy of the *Evening Press* sits in Con's pocket.

The end for the *Press* group came in 1995. It was a sudden shock to the city, and left many journalists seeking work. Despite the fact that Con had a degree of independence, which would see his name appearing in other publications on occasion, and was very likely to be headhunted quickly, he waded in behind the *Press* workforce. The writer Frank Kilfeather remembered how 'the sight of Con Houlihan, the *Evening Press* columnist, standing on O'Connell Bridge with a can in his hand collecting money for the workers' fund was heartbreaking'.[21]

For many years, Con lived in Portobello, which gave him a variety of locals, especially after the death of the *Press*. At the Lower Deck, a framed image of Houlihan takes pride of place, while he is fondly recalled in The Harold House, a pub that was happy to serve up his favourite drink – the curious mix of brandy and milk. In a fine tribute, Sean Creedon (a member of the Soccer Writers' Association) noted that 'Tom Ryan Jr, son of the late Tom Ryan of The Harold House pub on Clanbrassil Street, used to say that his father would make sure a member of staff rushed out to get a carton

A plaque outside The Palace on Fleet Street.

of milk whenever they saw Con approaching.'²² Readers can try it at their own peril, but the drink is unlikely to make an appearance in any of the city's cocktail bars.

Con Houlihan died in August 2012. A few months later, St Patrick's Athletic would lose an FAI Cup final in Lansdowne Road, but the long-standing cup final curse was finally broken two years after that, delivering the first win since 1961. Con was remembered in plaques, busts, statues and framed newspaper articles in pub snugs, but a flag in Lansdowne Road honoured him in a way he may have appreciated even more. It quoted words he was proud to have once found scrawled on a pub wall:

> St Patrick's Athletic have survived many crises. At times, it seemed they might cease trading. In this context, I got the highest tribute of my life. One Sunday long ago I saw it inscribed on the back of a toilet door in Inchicore: 'Con Houlihan says that Pat's will never die.'²³

# CHAPTER 28.
# THE RELICS OF THE IRISH HOUSE

If the Americans had such a specimen, they would jack up the house and roll it along to another site. Here we have no other use for a ninety-four-year-old landmark of a public house when it gets in the way of site clearance than to knock it down.[1]

Whatever about the belief of the *Irish Examiner* that the Americans would have saved it, The Irish House was a great loss for Dublin. Torn down as part of the redevelopment of Wood Quay and the eventual construction of the Civic Offices, the building was a riot of colour and packed with nationalistic design and Celtic Revival influences. Located on the corner of Winetavern Street and Wood Quay, the pub was one of the most photographed in the city, appearing in places as diverse as Sybil Connolly fashion shoots and Bord Fáilte images of Ireland. Opened in 1870, it was torn down in the name of progress in 1968.

A rapidly changing Liffeyside and Wood Quay amidst the redevelopment of the site for the Civic Offices. (Courtesy of the National Library of Ireland)

While pubs around the city have tended to honour Ireland's revolutionary past, the exterior of The Irish House (O'Meara's) paid homage instead to the constitutional nationalist tradition. Here was Henry Grattan addressing the College Green Parliament and Daniel O'Connell clutching the unachieved dream, Repeal of the Act of Union. The work of stuccodores Burnett and Comerford, the building's façade also featured harps, wolfhounds, round towers, Celtic crosses and the forlorn figure of the Maid of Erin, clutching a stringless harp. The building, constructed for use as a public house in 1870, has been described as one that 'vividly reflected the Romantic Movement that swept across Europe in the latter part of the nineteenth century'.[2] C. P. Curran, an authority on Dublin decorative plasterwork, would describe the building as having 'its whole frontal all-glowing in colours like a Byzantine casket'.[3]

We get a glimpse of The Irish House in Joseph Strick's ambitious 1967 big-screen take on *Ulysses*. Strick made no attempt to hide 1960s Dublin from the cameras, and the city itself emerges as one of the stars of the film. We see Liberty Hall, Desmond Rea O'Kelly's sixteen-storey building by the Liffey, and modern cars and fashions. Strick originally intended to make the film more than eighteen hours in length, though financial constraints thankfully prevented this. Instead of The Citizen chasing Leopold Bloom from Barney Kiernan's, the scene was filmed at The Irish House.

In 2012, I got a chance to see some of the figures from The Irish House when they went on display in the offices of the Dublin Civic Trust, then on Castle Street. Where possible, pieces of history were saved from the front of the building at the eleventh hour, with plaster casts of stucco panels also taken. Lord Moyne, vice-chairman of the Guinness Brewery, 'negotiated and financed a project to salvage the building's exterior'.[4] Here were Grattan, O'Connell and the weeping Maid of Erin all on display once more. As Peter Walsh noted in an essay on the building,

The Irish House on Wood Quay. (Courtesy of the National Library of Ireland)

guardianship of the pieces passed in 2003 to the Dublin Civic Trust, 'which carries the mantle and keeps alive the remit of the shamefully mothballed Dublin Civic Museum'.[5]

And there was more to The Irish House than just the figures that adorned the pub exterior, with the *Evening Herald* pondering on its interior:

> Features of this historic public house, once standard in most old Irish pubs, will soon disappear along with the building. The homely potbellied stove is unlikely to grace the centre of modern, carpeted lounge bars. The rich, dull shine of the brass taps and counter pumps will never be seen again – unless it is in some pub museum. And where will the fine old clock set in its great oaken harp end up?[6]

Those wishing to enjoy a pint around constitutional nationalist heroes these days may have to make for Kilkenny, where the Home Rule Club can still be found, initially established in 1894. On its

These images show details of the figures that once adorned The Irish House. A beautiful publication exploring the public house is available from Dublin Civic Trust, who generously provided these images.

walls you'll find former Irish Parliamentary Party MPs, including John Redmond, the leader who came closest to the dream of the men who adorned The Irish House. On Belfast's Falls Road, the Clonard Ancient Order of Hibernians (AOH) Social Club proudly honours local politician Wee Joe Devlin on its walls. Once the assistant manager of the famed Belfast boozer Kelly's Cellars, Devlin's main claim to fame is surviving the Sinn Féin wave in the 1918 General Election, being returned as one of Ireland's few surviving Home Rule MPs.[7] It may seem curious now, but when all of Ireland voted for Sinn Féin, the Falls Road said no.

# CHAPTER 29.
# SIGNS OF THE TIMES

Designer Niall Sweeney's iconic sign for Pantibar on Capel Street.

**B**efore setting foot inside any establishment, our eyes are drawn to a number of things. The physical building itself can be interesting. In Rathmines, Rody Boland's is a peculiarity, as the pub has two fronts. Behind a rather nondescript modern front and beyond an outdoor terrace is a second pub frontage, physically transported from Nenagh, where the pub was first opened in 1873. Complete with hand-painted signage, the rural pub front belies the fact that this is one of the area's largest establishments. In the relocation of Boland's, the *Nenagh Guardian* reported in 1994, the owners tried to preserve as much of the premises as possible. This meant 'not alone using the counter, bar fitting and snug in Rathmines, but the original pub front is also being used as an inside door'.[1]

Rody Boland's began life in Nenagh, before transportation to Rathmines.

In recent times, the return to fashion of hand-painted signage has been a noticeable and welcome feature of Dublin publand. This is part of a broader move towards traditional signage on businesses in the city. In an interview with online food and travel magazine TheTaste.ie, signwriter Vanessa Power shared her own belief that 'it shows they take pride in their business, that they appreciate things that are crafted, that take time to complete. It says that they take care and put time and value into the products they're selling.'[2] At the same time as our main thoroughfares have sometimes felt cluttered with temporary printed signage, a walk down other streets can reveal this revived and now thriving trade.

Dubbed a 'Gentleman of Letters', Kevin Freeney (1919–1986) is now recalled as the most celebrated sign painter in the history of the city. A 1978 *In Dublin* magazine feature acknowledged his leading status in the industry:

The sign for Cleary's on Amiens Street is the work of sign writer Colm O'Connor.

Kevin Freeney is probably the most active signwriter in Dublin today and certainly one of the best. His father was a signwriter before him and his own sons and nephews are in the business. Kevin is a very versatile signwriter who works in many media and in different styles … He has painted signs for several well-known Dublin businesses – pubs like Bowe's in Fleet Street, Mulligan's in Poolbeg Street and recently Peter's Pub in South William Street.[3]

The neon signs of the 1930s and the more recent plastic illuminated signs, *In Dublin* told its readers, 'are all the rage [but] have not ousted the traditional hand-painted sign. Too many neon and plastic signs are having a brutalising effect on the city. They obscure the character of buildings and shopfronts and upset the coherence of the streetscape.'[4]

One business owner told the *Irish Times* of how Freeney 'comes along with a case full of different brushes and colours and you'd be mesmerised watching him doing the whole thing'.[5] Today, Freeney's Graphics continues this legacy.

By its nature, hand-painted signage must be refreshed with the passing of time, and the removal of layers can reveal previous incarnations of the premises. In 2022, the name 'Bowe's' was revealed beneath the signage of Grogan's on 15 South William Street, linking the pub to James Bowe, who also maintained a premises on Stephen Street (now the Hairy Lemon) and Fleet Street, the latter still trading as Bowe's. While a pub on the site of Grogan's was widely believed to have begun trading in 1899, a year that appears on the Castle Street side of the building housing the premises, advertisements for Bowe's at 15 William Street, 'widely known for the best drinks – Three Star special malt', appear in the *Evening Herald* seven years earlier.[6] The revealing of a sign untangled aspects of the history of the site.

Mack Signs produced this mirror for a Belfast public house, but first placed it on the streets of Dublin. (With thanks to Mack Signs)

The signage for O'Regan's on South Great George's Street by the artist Eoin Byrne is an example of a new and unique approach to a time-honoured tradition.

In Smithfield, Mack Signs (a firm led by Cormac Dillon) uncovered the signage of Gerry Power's Place when painting a new sign for The Cobblestone. The new sign includes the name of the proprietor family (Mulligan), along with traditional music instruments. As branding, it instantly connects the establishment in the mind with traditional music, capturing its self-declaration of being 'A drinking pub with a music problem.'

Beyond painting public house signage, Mack Signs have also painted advertising mirrors, harking back to the once-standard Victorian practice. The resurrection of historic distillery names –

including D. W. D., Dunville's and Roe's – has led to a plethora of 'new' advertising joining old mirrors in public houses, with the lines blurred somewhat. Using the same traditional skills utilised in painting signage, Mack Signs painted a mirror complete with gold-leaf detail for Power's, which is now on display in a Belfast pub, but which was first positioned on the streets of Dublin. Over several days people stopped to photograph the mirror and themselves in it, a reminder that something once commonplace is now an unusual piece of craftsmanship for many.

Walking across Dublin, we encounter other beautiful works of craft that may not fit within our vision of what is traditional but which have become a part of the streetscape. The designer Niall Sweeney and Rory O'Neill have a friendship and working relationship stretching back decades in Dublin, collaborating on events like Alternative Miss Ireland and clubnight Powderbubble. O'Neill's PantiBar is marked by a distinctive 3.5-metre PANTIBAR sign, first unveiled in March 2015. It is not a neon sign, as reported in the press, but traditionally backlit, with Sweeney noting:

> Dublin has a great history of fantastic street signage (painted masonry, illuminated, intricately gilded glass, mosaic …) – one strand of which is variations on the theme of neon, some surviving examples of which are internationally celebrated. Any current 'old favourite' was once a contemporary upstart. They speak of their time (they never looked back). They cause the working faces of their buildings to come alive in the present. Their considered crafting, quality and vision transcends the ages, approaching the sublime – no matter how simple or how complex their construction or message. They are part of the cultural, social and economic fabric of the city we live in.[7]

In 2016, An Bord Pleanála ruled that 'exceptional circumstances' applied to the signage and that 'the sign is integral to the social, historical and cultural significance of the current use of the

The signage of newcomer disndat includes a nod to the nearby 'Why Go Bald?' signage on Dame Lane. The original has been a feature of the locality since the 1960s.

premises'. Lisa Godson, lecturer in design history and material culture, was one of those who successfully preserved the 'Why Go Bald?' sign on Dame Lane in 2001. In the *Irish Times*, she made a compelling case for the PantiBar sign, referencing Broadway and Berlin:

> The palette is 1920s German modern, the bulb reference signalling carnivalesque, burlesque entertainments. While it isn't part of a 'Great White Way', it heralds probably the most interesting and diverse street in Dublin, where pet shops sit beside the suppliers of martial arts equipment, sex shops beside Karaoke bars beside hardware stores. While a frequent complaint about Grafton Street is that it could be any British high street, Capel Street is gloriously itself. In fact, the Pantibar sign replaced a standard Carlsberg one.[8]

# CHAPTER 30.
# ART AND TRADITION IN THE CASTLE LOUNGE

**GROGANS**

JOINTLY OWNED
BY
PADDY KENNEDY
&
TOM SMITH
SINCE 1973

**K**evin Monaghan's name may not be as familiar as that of J. P. Donleavy, author of *The Ginger Man*, but the same circumstances had brought him to Dublin. Both were veterans of the Second World War who had availed of the GI Bill, which accommodated American soldiers staying in Europe to study. In theory, they were meant to attend universities and learn about the world before coming home and settling into a normal, picket-fence life. Many threw themselves into all the continent of Europe had to offer, and some never left. Tommy Smith of Grogan's would recall Monaghan to Kevin C. Kearns as:

> ... an aesthetic eccentric, a dandy dresser, you know, impeccable and whirly whiskers which he'd be waving away. One of the pleasures of going into McDaid's was seeing him leaning against the bar. He was a friend of J. D. Salinger's, Kevin had served with him in the war.[1]

When asked in 1985 what Normandy and war was like, Monaghan declared that, 'after all that time, I still think army life stinks. The military mind is nothing more than a decline of physical faculties.'[2] Monaghan was part of the McDaid's set who followed barman Paddy O'Brien and made the move to Grogan's in the early 1970s. For Monaghan, loyalties and custom were divided primarily

**Paddy Kennedy and Tommy Smith were co-proprietors of Grogan's on South William Street.**

A historic advertisment for Grogan's from the 1970s.

between the South William Street pub and The Dawson Lounge on Dawson Street, Dublin's smallest (in size but certainly not character) public house.

In November 1989, Monaghan was commemorated with the unveiling of a painting in his honour by Owen Walsh. From Westport, Walsh was a graduate of the National College of Art, and an artist who had exhibited widely and travelled far in pursuit of learning this trade. After studying at the Círculo de Bellas Artes in Madrid, he went to Venice and Ravenna in Italy to learn mosaics.[3] Art critic Brian Fallon would note that 'his style was romantic and moody, using primary colours a good deal, with no kow-towing to fashion'.[4] Walsh and Monaghan, who had seen the continent of Europe in very different circumstances, became and remained great friends. The portrait of Monaghan came with a brilliant stipulation. As Deirdre Kelly (historian and friend of Monaghan) told the *Evening Herald*:

> He was a great character, and we want to ensure that Dubliners will remember him for many years to come. For this reason, we have decided that the lovely portrait of him done by Owen Walsh should

A mural by Owen Walsh in The Star Bar, Baggot Street.

hang in his two favourite pubs – the Dawson Lounge and Grogan's. The painting will hang in each for a year before being rotated.[5]

Walsh himself was also something of a character, described by one journalist as a 'swaggering hell-raiser who devours whole afternoons in the pursuit of pleasure'.[6] True to what was planned, a crowd would make their way behind Walsh's portrait of his friend as it switched homes between Grogan's and The Dawson Lounge, normally in a horse-drawn cart. This ritual, ever jovial, continued for many years. The work of Walsh is still visible in another Dublin pub today, with his mural in the Star Bar, formerly Larry Murphy's, on Baggot Street. Painted on a Good Friday in the 1960s, the mural depicts rugby players in battle, alongside an audience of drinkers. Presumed lost, it was rediscovered during renovations in 2022.

In the absence of a television, the walls themselves are the primary visual draw on entering the Grogan's premises, hosting a constant art show from which the pub itself takes no commission. Tommy Smith recalled his unending opposition to a television in the pub, remembering a rare break from tradition:

> There was one exception, when a film of the people who fought in the Spanish Civil War featured a regular called Bob Doyle, a republican who drank here. On that occasion we brought in a telly, but it didn't work. It was a good omen.[7]

Some artworks in Grogan's hid and hide in plain sight. Many would have missed the 'small secular shrine' to the memory of Gainor Crist, another beneficiary of the GI Bill and a close friend of J. P. Donleavy, who influenced *The Ginger Man* more than any other person, living or dead. It nestled behind the bar over decades. In *J. P. Donleavy's Ireland*, he included an image of Crist at the side gate of Trinity College Dublin, clutching an electric fire he was on the way to the pawnshop to trade in:

> This saintly expedient gentleman on this day had resolutely made the decision that money for a few pints and a ball of malt in the pub would keep him as comfortably warm as any electric fire. And as he said, the steam from his piss could prove it.[8]

Nothing could quite prove Grogan's claim to be the inheritor of the spirit of post-war McDaid's quite like artist Desmond McNamara's tiny memorial to Crist, no longer on the premises and latterly loaned to the Little Museum of Dublin. An outsider, Crist was 'able to do nearly the impossible, that of running up credit in an Irish public house'.[9]

The poet Paddy Finnegan is visible in 'The Night People' stained-glass window. A familiar face selling poetry and the *Big Issue* on the streets of Dublin, Paddy even wrote a poem on being banned from McDaid's.

Gone is the Gainor Crist shrine, and Monaghan's portrait resides on another continent entirely, at home in the United States. Still, Grogan's has art to impress any visitor, in the form of Katharine Lamb's two stained-glass works. Entitled 'The Day People' and 'The Night People', they date from the 1990s and honour two distinct sets of regulars and staff. Lamb was a recent graduate of the National College of Art and Design when she began these distinctive works:

> When I was studying in NCAD as a student, that's where we used to go to drink, seemingly all the time. Myself and [artist] Rachel Ballagh were very close friends at the time, and we'd sit perched up at the bar, just by the hatch that goes up and down … I was studying for about three years, and when I graduated with a degree in art design, I thought I'd like to do a piece sort of emulating Harry

Clarke's techniques ... I said to Tommy, can I make some stained glass for the pub?[10]

Smith, a collector of art and champion of young talent, was firmly taken with the idea when Katharine explained that the work would honour the customers of the bar. Looking in both windows, there are a variety of interesting characters who were well known in Dublin more broadly. I spotted the actor Donal McCann, sitting at the circular table visible in 'The Day People' window, nearest the South William Street entrance of the pub. Lamb's parents were both actors in their working lives, with her mother starring alongside McCann. She explained to me how his inclusion in the work came to be drawn not from a photograph in the pub, but from a theatrical image:

> That image of McCann came from a production of *Juno and the Paycock*. My mother played his wife, and he was Captain Boyle. So Tommy asked him because he was kind of a bit contrary, you know. Tommy asked him and he gave his permission to be put in the window, he said he did want to be in it, but to just do my thing and there was no need to meet me. So, it's kind of a nod to my mother as well.[11]

There are distinct differences in the two windows, in terms of not only the people they depict, but how they were created. 'The Day People' came first, before 'The Night People' nearest the toilets. Lamb explained:

> The first one is all hand painted. Large sections of it have two layers of glass surrounded by lead. That's flashed glass, which is clear glass with the layer of colour on it. Then that's acid etched away.
>
> I was interested in how you did things technically, and then I was interested in how to break the rules with that, which I didn't do in this job. But I think I was setting myself a technical work as well ... The first window is all etched glass, and the second one I screen printed the glass.

Detail from a stained-glass window in Grogan's showing Thérèse Cronin.

> I photocopied the drawings. I did them on large A3 pages, and then I sat in the studio with a candle on my desk and projected the slide onto the wall at a distance.[12]

New aspects of these windows reveal themselves to me all the time, as I learn a little more about just who is depicted within them. In 'The Night People' we see reminders of how small Dublin truly is. There is Rachel Ballagh, Lamb's friend and artist who helped her in capturing the regulars to be included in the works. We see the artist Corban Walker, subject of an artwork by Ballagh that was shortlisted for the Zurich Portrait Prize. Seán Kearney, the recently departed barman of five decades' service, is unmissable. City councillor Gerard Mannix Flynn, poet Paddy Finnegan and Tommy Smith's son and current co-proprietor, Donal Smith, are all visible too. Both windows depict many female regulars, with Thérèse Cronin (recalled by writer Brighid McLaughlin, who is also in the work, as 'intelligent, brilliant and absolutely inspiring'[13]) perhaps the most visible presence in 'The Day People'.

Each year, Grogan's hosts an annual Christmas Art Show, now overseen by a team that includes the artist Orla Mellon. She explained to me how:

> In the weeks leading up to the show, Grogan's puts out a message on social media, inviting anyone who wants to exhibit their artwork to bring it in. The ethos of the show is inclusivity — everyone is welcome. What makes it even more special is that when a piece sells, Grogan's gives 100 per cent of the sales back to the artist. In a city where galleries often take up to 50 per cent commission, this generosity is truly rare.
>
> On the morning of the show, the team gathers to bring it all together. It's usually myself, Donal and Daniel Smith, Karl (the bar manager), artist Ausrine Kuze, and Brian MacMahon — the artist who first started the tradition. We begin by unwrapping the bubble-wrapped artworks and carefully organising them. We start

with the largest pieces, then arrange the smaller ones around them, making sure everything looks just right. The process takes about three hours – just in time for the bar to open.[14]

For Orla, Grogan's is a place of personal importance. Moving to Dublin from Scotland in 2011, she found it difficult to break into any kind of art scene in Dublin, with galleries that 'weren't exactly welcoming to an unfamiliar name'. All roads led to South William Street:

> Then, someone mentioned Grogan's bar. I had visited a few times for a pint, but I hadn't realised it was also a space for artists to showcase their work. Determined to take a chance, I brought two of my paintings – a fox and a pheasant – under my arm and walked into the bar. That's when I met Tommy Smith for the first time. I nervously asked if they might consider exhibiting my work, and to my surprise, Tommy didn't hesitate. He took a look at the painting and said, 'Yes, we'll find a spot for them, no problem.'
> 
> That moment was a huge boost for my confidence, and it marked the beginning of something special for me in Dublin.
> 
> Over the years, I built a wonderful relationship with Tommy. He was always so kind and welcoming, and every time I brought in new artwork, we'd sit together over cups of tea. He'd share stories of growing up in Cavan, while I'd recount tales from my own childhood in Tyrone. Those conversations were filled with warmth and humour, and they made me feel like I truly belonged. Tommy's passion for the arts shone through in everything he did. He had a deep appreciation for creativity and loved to support artists like me.

As a piece is sold, a new one will take its place over the subsequent year, ensuring that Grogan's serves as an art gallery throughout the seasons. Work from regulars like Tom Mathews ('although cartoonist Tom Mathews seems to have been around Dublin forever, he remains something of an enigma', said the *Irish Times*) share space with work from new and emerging figures.[15]

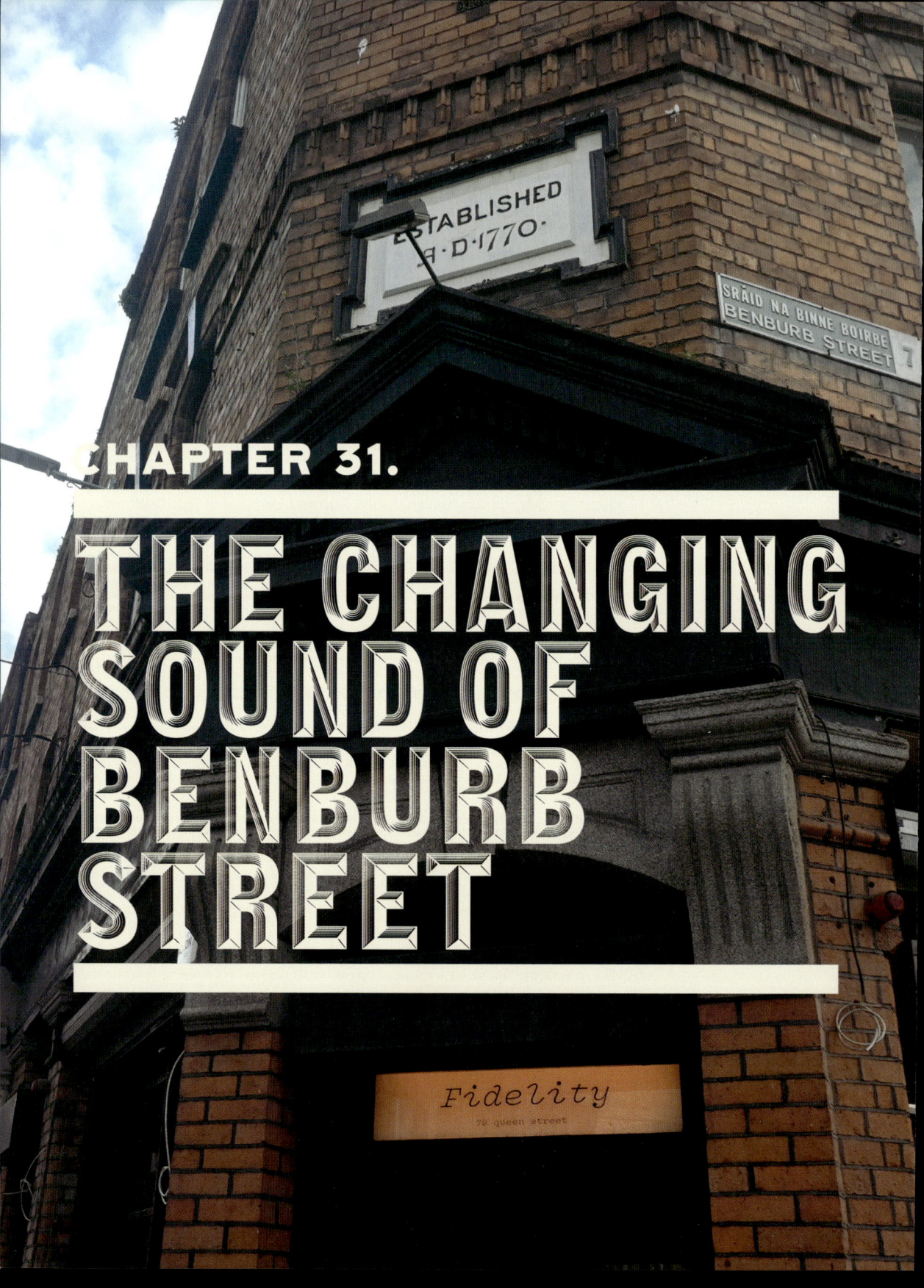

# CHAPTER 31.
# THE CHANGING SOUND OF BENBURB STREET

Fidelity sits at the intersection of Queen Street and Benburb Street. A sign above the pub lays claim to a 1770 origin for the pub site.

**F**idelity's postal address may be on Queen Street, but the public house also looks out on the adjacent Benburb Street, with the Luas passing right by those who drink outside on the rare days of sunshine the city is blessed with. Recent times haven't been kind to the public houses of Benburb Street, with H. Matthew's and the Museum Rest (once the Regal Bar) both forlorn and closed. When the front of the Museum Rest was given a coat of red paint, one reviewer described it as 'about the only concession to modernity. Within, the ambiance is unadulterated '70s.'[1]

Benburb Street takes its name from the 1646 Battle of Benburb in the Irish Confederate Wars, a rare Irish victory on the battlefield. Once upon a time, this was Barrack Street, a name that nodded to the neighbouring Royal Barracks. An unflattering account of the street from the 1830s paints a picture of a street populated by brothels, disease and dodgy boozers:

It is known to every officer whose regiment has been quartered in the Royal Barracks at Dublin that their vicinity has long been cursed with a line of brothels and low public houses called Barrack Street, and filled with the most abandoned crew of rogues and prostitutes which even all Dublin, with its unhappy pre-eminence in that species of population, can produce. The influence, in any neighbourhood, of such dens of filth and iniquity, wherein every kind of disease was engendered and propagated, and every description of crime contrived and encouraged, may readily be conceived.[2]

It was on Benburb Street that Dublin Corporation built its first exercise in public housing flats, with the Chief Medical Officer insisting that the city authority should itself rehouse the poor. Built in 1887 and into the following year, the scheme 'contained 144 small flats', but was 'built to such a low sanitary and constructional standard that they needed constant remedial work'.[3]

'All well and good', I hear you say, dear reader, 'but what has that got to do with Dublin pubs?' One of those lucky enough to live in those flats was my great-grandmother, a tiny woman with a large personality. Her husband went off to the First World War with the Royal Dublin Fusiliers, returning (physically at least) before dying in the nearby Richmond Hospital at the age of 41 in 1924. He was buried in an unmarked grave in Glasnevin Cemetery, a sad and not untypical end for a serviceman of the war.

Long before Fidelity, the corner of Benburb Street and Queen Street was occupied by a public house, which remains a formative memory of my own mother's childhood. She remembers seeing her grandmother drink bottles of Guinness amidst the men, and occasionally returning bottles from her nearby flat. Situated so close to the markets where many of them worked, women mingled with men in the pubs of Smithfield, Stoneybatter and the surrounding area. For a woman who had endured much hardship and raised children alone after the death of her husband, this pub was a place

**What remained of the Museum Rest pub in May 2025.**

of community and importance. 'There are some pubs where it's all widows,' Brendan Behan recalled, 'they sit talking about their late husbands all night until they start crying over them.'[4] First World War widows replaced the earlier Boer War widows Behan had entertained in his own drinking youth.

For many years, the tiled 'L' of Loughman's was still visible as you walked into the premises, a reminder of a woman and former regular I never met. The sound of horses en route to the Smithfield market has been replaced by the bell of passing trams, and Loughman's is unrecognisable. Still, it's a reminder of how some of the city's public houses have had multiple lives.

Many will remember Fidelity as Dice Bar, a self-styled dive bar that prided itself on the strength of its beer offering and its equally solid music offerings, in a time when vinyl decks were a more unusual feature in a pub than they are today. Like Anseo on

Camden Street – a pioneering pub in introducing a vinyl booth to drinking proceedings – Dice Bar was dark and always buzzy. When it closed its doors in 2020, it was perhaps the most high-profile victim of the pandemic in city-centre publand.

What has emerged in its place is a bar that prides itself in having 'a state-of-the-art sound system and comprehensive acoustic treatment to deliver an exceptional auditory experience'. This doesn't sound unlike an emerging international trend, and one that has its roots firmly in Tokyo. Music cafés, or *ongaku kissa*, first emerged there in the 1920s. The city is today dotted with audiophile bars, all priding themselves on the quality of their sound systems, though sometimes tucked into tiny spaces the casual visitor could easily stroll by. *Resident Advisor*, the go-to guide for electronic music fans internationally, has described how 'Tokyo is teeming with small, music-focused cafés, clubs and bars, tucked away in basements, back-alleys and high-rise buildings. A venue exists for just about every niche of music you can imagine.'[5]

Fidelity followed on from The Big Romance, with co-owner Stephen Manning telling me that while the Japanese listening bars did shape these establishments, they were also influenced by the changing landscape of Dublin clubland. Closing at a remarkable rate, the campaign group Give Us The Night noted in January 2025 that just eighty-three nightclubs remain open for business in the republic today, a staggering 83 per cent decline since 2000.[6] The founders of The Big Romance and Fidelity felt that there was a space in the market for those who wanted to hear music on a good sound system, even if this meant a physical move from the traditional setting:

> With a background in being club promoters, we are very much musically led. Myself and Dave Parle were initially influenced by hi-fi listening bars such as Brilliant Corners and Spiritland but more so the Japanese kissa culture. For our first venue, The Big Romance,

we wanted a deep listening space that had a purpose-built hi-fi sound system and could house our personal vinyl collection. It is a vinyl only space and while the original Japanese Jazz bar ideology focused on deep listening, we also have a dancing culture which happened organically. While the cultural landscape is changing and clubs have been rapidly closing in Ireland over the last few years, there is still a demand for people to listen to good music on a great sound system.[7]

On entering Fidelity, it is impossible not to notice the speakers, the work of Toby Hatchett, whose Hatchett Sound speakers can be found across the city, in venues like The Big Romance and Row Wines on Coppinger Row. Hatchett has emphasised how 'I design and produce unique and handcrafted work that marries sound and space.'[8] Big and bold, the sound system fills the room without overpowering it.

These hi-fi listening bars, as they emerge across continents, give us much to ponder. With their emphasis on physical vinyl records (who would dare plug a USB stick into such a sound system?) and the collective shared experience of listening to music, they stand in contrast to streaming platforms, where the emphasis is very much on the trending hit. For Manning, the return of vinyl is no surprise:

> I think vinyl resonates as a great high-end listening experience. As music formats such as CDs, digital and streaming have been introduced, often the sound and speakers have not progressed in the same way and developing a better audio experience is important to us.[9]

Mulligan's Pub, 1960s. (Dublin City Library and Archive)

# SELECT BIBLIOGRAPHY

## PRIMARY SOURCES AND ARCHIVES

1901/1911 Census Returns, National Archives of Ireland
Bureau of Military History Witness Statements, Military Archives
Capuchin Archives
Dáil Éireann Archives, www.oireachtas.ie
Department of Justice Files, National Archives of Ireland
Harry Kernoff Papers, National Library of Ireland
National Folklore Collection, University College Dublin
Property Losses (Ireland) Committee, 1916, National Archives of Ireland
Rebellion Papers, National Archives of Ireland
RTÉ Archives

## NEWSPAPERS, JOURNALS AND PERIODICALS

*An Phoblacht*
*Dublin Historical Record*
*Envoy*
*Evening Herald*
*Evening Press*
*Freeman's Journal*
*Gay Community News*
*History Ireland*
*Irish Arts Review*
*Irish Historical Studies*
*Irish Independent*
*Irish Press*
*Irish Times* (in particular, An Irishman's Diary)
*Magill*
*Martello*
*Saothar*
*Sunday World* (in particular, Roy Curtis)

*Sinn Féin*

*Sunday Independent*

*Sunday Press*

*The Bell*

*The Catholic Standard*

*The Dublin Magazine*

*The Dublin Temperance Gazette*

*The Irish Worker*

## SECONDARY SOURCES

Barry, Michael. *Victorian Dublin Revealed: The Remarkable Legacy of Nineteenth-Century Dublin* (Dublin, 2012)

Bennett, Douglas. *A Dublin Anthology* (Dublin, 1994)

Bohan, Eddie. *Thirst for Freedom: Alcohol and the Battle of Irish Independence* (Dublin, 2020)

Boran, Pat, Smyth, Gerard. *If Ever You Go: A Map of Dublin in Poetry and Song* (Dublin, 2014)

Bowen, Elizabeth. *The Shelbourne* (London, 1951)

Boyd, Sean. *Behind the Horseshoe Bar: At Dublin's Shelbourne Hotel* (Dublin, 2009)

Brannigan, John (ed.). *A Bit of a Writer: Brendan Behan's Collected Short Prose* (Dublin, 2023)

Bunbury, Turtle, Fennell, James. *The Irish Pub* (London, 2008)

Carden, Sheila (ed.). *The Streets of Dublin 1910–1911* (Dublin, 2013)

Casey, Eamonn. *The Dublin Pub Saunter* (Dublin, 1992)

Cashman, Dorothy, Mac Con Iomaire, Máirtín (eds). *Irish Food History: A Companion* (Dublin, 2024)

Colum, Mary. *Life and the Dream* (London, 1947)

Cronin, Anthony. *Dead as Doornails: A Chronicle of Life* (Dublin, 1976)

Cullen, L. M. *An Economic History of Ireland since 1660* (Bristol, 1972)

Dargan, Pat. *Dublin Pubs* (Dublin, 2018)

De Burca, Seamus. *The Soldier's Song: The Story of Peadar Kearney* (Dublin, 1958)

Devoy, John. *Recollections of an Irish Rebel* (New York, 1929)

Donleavy, J. P. *J. P. Donleavy's Ireland* (London, 1986)

Dooley, Terence. *The Greatest of the Fenians: John Devoy and Ireland* (Dublin, 2003)

Drew, Ronnie. *Ronnie* (Dublin, 2009)

Dunne, Declan. *Mulligan's: Grand Old Pub of Poolbeg Street* (Dublin, 2015)

Dunworth, Ali. *A Compendium of Irish Pints* (Dublin, 2024)

Fennell, Desmond. *Bloomsway: A Day in the Life of Dublin* (Dublin, 1990)

Ferriter, Diarmaid. *A Nation of Extremes: The Pioneers in Twentieth-Century Ireland* (Dublin, 1999)

Geraghty, Des. *Luke Kelly: A Memoir* (Dublin, 1994)

Gillespie, Elgy. *The Liberties of Dublin: Its History, People and Future* (Dublin, 1973)

Gray, Tony. *Mr Smyllie, Sir* (Dublin, 1994)

Honor, Tracy. *Mind You, I've Said Nothing!: Forays in the Irish Republic* (London, 1953)

Houlihan, Con. *Windfalls* (Dublin, 1996)

Jennings, Paul. *The Local: A History of the English Pub* (Cheltenham, 2021)

Kane, Michael. *Blind Dogs: A Personal History* (Dublin, 2023)

Kearns, Kevin C. *Dublin Pub Life & Lore: An Oral History* (Dublin, 1996)

Kearns, Kevin C. *Dublin Tenement Life* (Dublin, 1996)

Kelly, Bill. *Me Darlin' Dublin's Dead and Gone* (Dublin, 1987)

Kelly, Thomas. *The Streets of Dublin: 1910-1911* (Dublin, 2013)

Kenny, Colum. *The Enigma of Arthur Griffith* (Dublin, 2020)

Kerrigan, Gene. *Another Country: Growing Up in '50s Ireland* (Dublin, 1998)

Kerrigan, Páraic. *Reeling in the Queers* (Dublin, 2024)

Kiely, Benedict. *The Waves Behind Us: Further Memoirs* (Dublin, 2000)

Killeen, Terence. *Lee Miller in James Joyce's Dublin* (Dublin, 2014)

Le Fanu, Sheridan. *The Cock and Anchor: Being a Chronicle of Old Dublin City* (Dublin, 1845)

MacThomáis, Éamonn. *Me Jewel and Darlin' Dublin* (Dublin, 2024)

MacThomáis, Éamonn. *The Labour and The Royal* (Dublin, 1979)

Malone, Aubrey. *Historic Pubs of Dublin* (Dublin, 2001)

Martin, Kevin. *Have Ye No Homes to Go To?* (Cork, 2016)

Maxwell, Constantia. *Dublin Under the Georges* (Dublin, 1997)

Montague, John. *The Pear is Ripe: A Memoir* (Dublin, 2014)

Myler, Patrick. *Dan Donnelly 1788-1820: Pugilist, Publican, Playboy* (Dublin, 2010)

Murtagh, Tim. *Irish Artisans and Radical Politics, 1776-1820* (Liverpool, 2022)

Nic Shiubhlaigh, Máire. *The Splendid Years: Recollections of Máire Nic Shiubhlaigh as Told to Edward Kenny* (Dublin, 1955)

Norris, David. *A Kick Against the Pricks: The Autobiography* (Dublin, 2012)

O'Brien, Edna. *Country Girl: A Memoir* (London, 2012)

O'Leary, John. *Recollections of Fenians and Fenianism: Volume II* (London, 1896)

Prunty, Jacinta. *Dublin Slums 1800-1925: A Study in Urban Geography* (Dublin, 1998)

Quilligan, Colm. *Dublin Literary Pub Crawl: A Guide to the Literary Pubs of Dublin and the Writers They Served* (Dublin, 2008)

Quinn, John F. *Father Mathew's Crusade: Temperance in Nineteenth-Century Ireland and Irish America* (Massachusetts, 2022)

Ryan, David. *Blasphemers and Blackguards: The Irish Hellfire Clubs* (Dublin, 2012)

Ryan, John. *Remembering How We Stood* (Dublin, 2008)

Wade, Christine. *Filthy Queens: A History of Beer in Ireland* (Dublin, 2025)

Warfield, Brian. *The Ramblings of an Irish Ballad Singer* (Dublin, 2018)

Whelan, Fergus. *May Tyrants Tremble: The Life of William Drennan, 1754-1820* (Dublin, 2020)

## WEBSITES

Brand New Retro (www.brandnewretro.com)

>An invaluable archive of Irish pop culture history. Brian McMahon is dedicated to preserving and sharing magazines, zines and more besides.

Come Here To Me! (www.comeheretome.com)

>Before podcasts, there were blogs. Established in 2009, Come Here To Me! had plenty of public house history in its time.

Dictionary of Irish Biography (www.dib.ie)

>An important and ongoing project from the Royal Irish Academy, in which you'll find everyone from brewing titans to barman Paddy O'Brien.

The Dublin Publopedia (www.thedublinpublopedia.com)

>If they have not visited every pub in the city, they are certainly close to it. Enjoyable and humorous reviews by two admirers of Beamish and James Joyce in seemingly equal measure. 'It's a business doing pleasure with him' is a fine review of a barman.

Dublin By Pub (www.dublinbypub.ie)

>As well as maintaining the website, Dublin By Pub have a very active social media presence, becoming a great source for news (and gossip) from Dublin publand. An important archive.

Dying For a Pint (www.dyingforapint.blogspot.com)

>A very interesting project chronicling deaths in Irish public houses, touching on all from the revolutionary period to Dublin gangland.

Every Pub in Dublin (www.everypubindublin.blogspot.com/)

>Another attempt at visiting every watering hole in the city, this blog also has a great understanding of the history of the trade and the differences in types of public houses.

Publin (www.publin.ie)

>John Geraghty's celebration of the Dublin public house is also a podcast of the same name. Episode topics include Dublin dockers and the pub, unusual pub names and the missed theatre pub The Plough.

Substack: Lisa Grimm (www.weirdbeergirl.substack.com)

>A co-presenter of the excellent Beer Ladies Podcast, Grimm's insights on the brewing trade and Dublin public houses are always interesting, with plenty of history in there.

Mick's Bar at 49 Parnell Street. In 1964, the front section of this beautiful premises crashed into the street. (Fáilte Ireland Tourism Photographic Collection, courtesy of Dublin City Library and Archive)

# ACKNOWLEDGEMENTS

As always, my primary thanks are to my wife, Sarah Rochford. There was perhaps an ominous sense of doom when I told her I intended to write a book about Dublin public houses. In the end, she shepherded me across terrain as diverse as the Strawberry Beds and Howth Head in pursuit of telling this tale.

The recollections of a truly diverse collection of people informed this book, and some of them are quoted in the text. Orla Mellon, Dara Gannon, Jimmy Murphy, the Smith family and Eoin Kennedy at Grogan's, Katharine Lamb, Stephen Manning, Ciaran Kavanagh, Andy Sheridan (a pub authority as well as a pub photographer!), Willie Aherne, Cormac Dillon at Mack Signs and others were all more than generous with their time and in fielding questions.

Sincere thanks to Gerard Smyth and Paula Meehan for allowing me to reproduce their work, and to The Gallery Press. Likewise, the photographer Colm Keating added immensely to this work by allowing me to reproduce his images of the Brazen Head scene. Thanks to Brian McMahon (Brand New Retro) for pointing me in the right direction more than once. I am grateful to all who allowed me to reproduce their images in the book, including the family of Kevin Freeney.

Thank you to all listeners and patrons of the Three Castles Burning podcast. Thank you to my parents, Las and Maria Fallon, and to my brother, Luke Fallon, for their love and encouragement.

Of the existing body of work on the subject, it would be impossible to overstate the importance of Kevin C. Kearns and his pioneering oral history. Dublin owes a tremendous amount to Kevin for decades of work spotlighting its working-class history. I also want to acknowledge the great output of Roy Curtis, who knows and champions the pub trade today so well.

Thanks to a very wide range of historians including Padraig Óg Ó Ruairc (together we have explored the pubs of Daingean Uí Chúis on more than one occasion), Fergus Whelan, Lorcan Collins, Tommy Graham and Tim Murtagh, who are all generous with their knowledge and time. Beyond historians, there were good insights from many friends, particularly Rory Mulvaney. Thanks also to Dara Yeates, who has such a fantastic knowledge of the musical dimensions of this story.

Thanks to all at the National Library of Ireland, National Archives of Ireland, National Gallery of Ireland, Dublin City Library and Archive, Military Archives, Royal Irish Academy, Ann Marie Duffin at Fáilte Ireland and other institutions that were invaluable in the writing and illustrating of this book.

Thanks to all at the Castle Lounge, The Lord Edward (in particular Tommy O'Neill), Fallon's on the Coombe, The Cobblestone, The Harold House, John Kavanagh's, Bartley Dunne's (NYC) and The Palace. Thanks to Joe and all at Rascals and Heather and all at Beamish.

Thanks to editor Neil Burkey for bringing clarity to the manuscript, and asking great questions of it. It is a much stronger work for his excellent insights. The design work by Niall McCormack is excellent as ever, and it is an honour to have a book designed by one of the leading designers in his field.

It is always a privilege to work with the team at New Island Books, the inheritors of the flame of Raven Arts Press. My admiration for them, and what Dermot Bolger created, knows no bounds.

## INTRODUCTION

1   Douglas Bennett (ed.), *A Dublin Anthology* (Dublin, 1994), 5.
2   Stephen Gwynn, *Dublin Old and New* (London, 1938), 32.
3   Tony Farmar, *The Legendary Lofty Clattery Café: Bewley's of Ireland*, quoted in Bennett, *A Dublin Anthology*, 82.
4   Honor Tracy, *Mind You, I've Said Nothing!: Forays in the Irish Republic* (London, 1953), 57.
5   *Irish Times*, 23 January 2024.
6   Anthony Foley, 'The Irish Pub: Supporting Our Communities', a report for Drinks Industry Group of Ireland (August 2023).
7   Sheila Carden (ed.), *The Streets of Dublin 1910–1911* (Dublin, 2013), 23.
8   Seumas O'Sullivan, *Essays and Recollections* (Dublin, 1944), 105. For more on Griffith see Colum Kenny, *The Enigma of Arthur Griffith* (Dublin, 2020).
9   Máirtín Mac Con Iomaire, 'Gastro-Topography: Exploring Food-Related Placenames in Ireland', *Canadian Journal of Irish Studies* (Vol. 38, No. 1).
10  Peter Somerville-Large, *Dublin: The Fair City* (London, 1996), 92.
11  Kevin C. Kearns, *Dublin Pub Life & Lore* (Dublin, 1996), 10.
12  T. C. Barnard, *Cromwellian Ireland: English Government and Reform in Ireland, 1649–1660* (Oxford, 2000), 77.
13  Elgy Gillespie (ed.), *The Liberties of Dublin: Its History, People and Future* (Dublin, 1973), 88.
14  Ibid., 90.
15  Alfred Barnard, *The Noted Breweries of Great Britain and Ireland: Volume 1* (London, 1889), 5.
16  Alfred Barnard, *The Whisky Distilleries of the United Kingdom* (London, 1887). Barnard's entry on Jones Road Distillery can be read in full on Whiskipedia at www.whiskipedia.com/barnard/jones-road/.
17  In Conor McCabe's *The Lost and Early Writings of James Connolly*, published by Iskra Books in 2024. A free PDF of this book is available to read at: https://www.iskrabooks.org/lost-and-early-writings.
18  L. M. Cullen, *An Economic History of Ireland since 1660* (Bristol, 1972), 156.
19  'The Whiskey', *Bentley's Miscellany* (London, 1840).
20  Paul Jennings, *The Local: A History of the English Pub* (Cheltenham, 2021), 87.
21  Ibid., 88.
22  *The Irish Citizen*, 1 October 1919.
23  John F. Quinn, *Father Mathew's Crusade: Temperance in Nineteenth-Century Ireland and Irish America* (Massachusetts, 2022), 126.
24  E. M. Mikhail, *Brendan Behan: Interviews and Recollections: Volume 2* (Dublin, 1982), 198.
25  Benedict Kiely, *The Waves Behind Us: Further Memoirs* (London, 2000), 121.
26  For more on Con Houlihan and Mulligan's see Declan Dunne's *Mulligan's: Grand Old Pub of Poolbeg Street* (Cork, 2015).
27  *Irish Independent*, 3 October 1997.

## CHAPTER 1

1   *The Sunday Times*, 23 April 2017.
2   Frank McDonald, *The Destruction of Dublin* (Dublin, 1985), 159.
3   Paul Rouse, 'Dan Donnelly', *Dictionary of Irish Biography*, Royal Irish Academy.

4   E. D. James, *The Life and Battles of Sir Dan Donnelly: Champion of Ireland* (New York, 1879), 1.

5   Patrick Myler, *Dan Donnelly 1788–1820: Pugilist, Publican, Playboy* (Dublin, 2010), 53.

6   *Dublin Penny Journal*, 24 August 1832.

7   Myler, *Dan Donnelly 1788–1820*, 74.

8   Samuel Haughton, *Memoirs of James Haughton* (Dublin, 1877), 127.

9   James, *The Life and Battles of Sir Dan Donnelly*, 24.

10  National Folklore Collection, The Schools' Collection, Vol. 0978, 43.

11  Jacinta Prunty, *Dublin Slums 1800–1925: A Study in Urban Geography* (Dublin, 2000), 91.

12  Myler, *Dan Donnelly 1788–1820*, 15.

## CHAPTER 2

1   Ernie O'Malley, *On Another Man's Wound* (Colorado, 1999), 62.

2   Thomas Bartlett entry on Theobald Wolfe Tone in the *Dictionary of Irish Biography*, see www.dib.ie/biography/tone-theobald-wolfe-a8590.

3   R. B. Madden, *The United Irishmen: Their Lives and Times* (Dublin, 1860), 224.

4   Martyn J. Powell, *The Politics of Consumption in Eighteenth-Century Ireland* (New York, 2005), 26.

5   Copy of sworn information concerning disloyal toasts made in Dublin public house, Chief Secretary's Office, National Archives of Ireland. CSO/RP/1822/2985.

6   Timothy Murtagh, *Irish Artisans and Radical Politics, 1776–1820: Apprenticeship to Revolution* (Liverpool, 2022), 31.

7   Seth Cotlar, *Tom Paine's America: The Rise and Fall of Transatlantic Radicalism in the Early Republic* (Virginia, 2011), 53.

8   Kevin Whelan, *The Tree of Liberty: Radicalism, Catholicism and the Construction of Irish Identity, 1760–1830* (Cork, 1996), 79.

9   Powell, *The Politics of Consumption in Eighteenth-Century Ireland*, 9.

10  Fergus Whelan, *May Tyrants Tremble: The Life of William Drennan, 1754–1822* (Dublin, 2020).

11  Madden, *The United Irishmen: Their Lives and Times*, 511.

12  Ibid., 94.

13  Seán Moylan, Bureau of Military History Witness Statement 838, Military Archives, Cathal Brugha Barracks.

14  Ruan O'Donnell, *Robert Emmet and the Rebellion of 1798* (Dublin, 2003), 55–6.

15  James Plunkett, *The Gems She Wore: A Book of Irish Places* (Dublin, 1972), 59.

16  Myles na gCopaleen's 1940 article on the pub trade for *The Bell* is reprinted in John Horgan (ed.), *Great Irish Reportage* (Dublin, 2014).

17  Richard Jones, *Haunted Inns of Britain and Ireland* (London, 2004); Paul Fenell, *Haunted: A Guide to Paranormal Ireland* (Dublin, 2016).

18  *Dublin Inquirer*, 14 March 2018.

19  John Edward Walsh, *Sketches of Ireland Sixty Years Ago* (Dublin, 1847), 152.

## CHAPTER 3

1   Jonathan Swift, quoted in Henry F. Berry, 'House and Shop Signs in Dublin in the Seventeenth and Eighteenth Centuries', *Journal of the Royal Society of Antiquaries of Ireland* (Vol. 40, No. 3), 81–98.

2   Henry Craik, *The Life of Jonathan Swift: Dean of St Patrick's Dublin* (London, 1882), 360.

3   John Stubbs, *Jonathan Swift: The Reluctant Rebel* (New York, 2017), 14–15.

4   Ibid.

5   Howard Williams (ed.), *English Letters and Letter-Writers of the Eighteenth Century* (London, 1886), 236.

6   Leo Damsrosch, *Jonathan Swift: His Life and His World* (Yale, 2013), 414.

7   Tara McConnell, '"Prodigious Fine Dinners": Drinking and dining with Jonathan Swift', in Dorothy Cashman, Máirtín Mac Con Iomaire (eds), *Irish Food History: A Companion* (Dublin, 2024), 318–48.

8. Martyn Cornell, 'Why Jonathan Swift said English porter was only fit for swine', *Zythophile*, Available at: https://zythophile.co.uk/2021/12/20/why-jonathan-swift-said-english-porter-was-only-fit-for-swine.
9. David Ryan, *Blasphemers and Blackguards: The Irish Hellfire Clubs* (Dublin, 2012), 48.
10. J. T. Gilbert, *A History of the City of Dublin: Volume Two* (Dublin, 1859), 15.
11. Ryan, *Blasphemers and Blackguards*, 49.
12. Massimo Introvigne, *Satanism: A Social History* (Leiden, 2016), 58.
13. Gilbert, *A History of the City of Dublin: Volume Two*, 59.
14. Sir Jonah Barrington, *Personal Sketches and Recollections of His Own Times* (London, 1876), 257.
15. Margaret Lincoln, *London and the 17th Century: The Making of the World's Greatest City* (Yale, 2021), 177.
16. Edward Forbes Robinson, *The Early History of Coffee Houses in England* (London, 1893).
17. Éamonn MacThomáis, *Me Jewel and Darlin' Dublin* (Dublin, 1977), 63. Éamonn's landmark history of the city was republished in 2024 to mark the fiftieth anniversary of its publisher, O'Brien Press. I authored a new introduction.
18. J. T. Gilbert, *A History of the City of Dublin: Volume One* (Dublin, 1854), 144.
19. Robert Burns, *The Poetical Works of Robert Burns: Volume 1* (London, 1821), 90.
20. *Irish Times*, 18 January 2016.

## CHAPTER 4

1. Owen McGee, *The Irish Republican Brotherhood from the Land League to Sinn Féin* (Dublin, 2005), 17.
2. John Devoy, *Recollections of an Irish Rebel: A Personal Narrative*, 102.
3. Eva Ó Cathaoir, *Soldiers of Liberty: A Study in Fenianism 1858–1908* (Dublin, 2018), 119–20.
4. Devoy, *Recollections of an Irish Rebel*, 133–4.
5. John O'Leary, *Recollections of Fenians and Fenianism, Volume II* (London, 1896), 246.
6. Devoy, *Recollections of an Irish Rebel*, 99.
7. Ibid.
8. These comments appear in the April 1867 edition of *All The Year Round*, a magazine edited by Charles Dickens.
9. William Chamney (ed.), 'The Fenian Conspiracy': Report of the Trials of Thomas F. Burke and others for High Treason, and Treason-Felony etc at the Special Commission, Dublin, held at the Court-House, Green Street, Dublin, Commencing 8 April 1867 (Dublin, 1869), 872.
10. Devoy, *Recollections of an Irish Rebel*, 65.
11. Breandán Mac Suibhne, Amy Martin, 'Fenians in the Frame: Photographing Irish Political Prisoners, 1865–68', *Field Day Review* (Vol. 1, 2005), 101–20.
12. Devoy, *Recollections of an Irish Rebel*, 183.
13. *Westmeath Independent*, 24 February 1866.
14. Ibid.
15. Terence Dooley, *The Greatest of the Fenians: John Devoy and Ireland* (Dublin, 2003), 56.
16. Ibid.
17. *Dundalk Democrat*, 16 March 1867.
18. For more on the Invincibles, see Julie Kavanagh, *The Irish Assassins: Conspiracy, Revenge and the Murders that Stunned an Empire* (London, 2021).
19. Blog post: 'Before Brogans was Brogans. A history of names', Publin.ie, see http://publin.ie/2018/before-brogans-was-brogans-a-history-of-names/.
20. Matthew Murtagh, Eugene Watters, *Infinite Variety: Dan Lowrey's Music Hall: 1878–97* (Dublin, 1975), 24.
21. David Fitzpatrick, *Harry Boland's Irish Revolution* (Cork, 2003), 18.
22. Dan Breen, Bureau of Military History Witness Statement 1739, Military Archives, Cathal Brugha Barracks.

## CHAPTER 5

1. *Irish Independent*, 6 March 1981.
2. Michael Barry, *Victorian Dublin Revealed: The Remarkable Legacy of Nineteenth-Century Dublin* (Dublin, 2011), 7.

3   *Evening Standard*, 9 February 1946.

4   Eamonn Casey, *The Dublin Pub Saunter* (Dublin, 1992), 94.

5   Turtle Bunbury, James Fennell, *The Irish Pub* (London, 2008), 15.

6   J. P. Donleavy, *J. P. Donleavy's Ireland* (London, 1986), 120.

7   Ibid., 21.

8   *Sunday Independent*, 23 October 1994.

## CHAPTER 6

1   Michael O'Riordan, *Connolly Column: The Story of the Irishmen who fought for the Spanish Republic 1936–1939* (Torfaen, 2005), 139.

2   Roger Joseph McHugh, *Dublin 1916: An Illustrated Anthology* (Michigan, 1976), 198.

3   R. R. Madden, *The United Irishmen, their Lives and Times* (London, 1860), 350.

4   *Irish Examiner*, 4 May 1916.

5   Kevin O'Shiel, Bureau of Military History Witness Statement 1770, Military Archives, Cathal Brugha Barracks.

6   William D. Daly, Bureau of Military History Witness Statement 291, Military Archives, Cathal Brugha Baracks.

7   Seán O'Casey, *Drums Under the Windows* (London, 1946), 235–6.

8   Quoted in Joseph McKenna, *Voices from the Easter Rising* (North Carolina, 2017), 74.

9   Michael Staines, Bureau of Military History Witness Statement 284, Military Archives, Cathal Brugha Barracks.

10  Leslie Price, Bureau of Military History Witness Statement 1754, Military Archives, Cathal Brugha Barracks.

11  Purcell's account appears in the *Sinn Féin Rebellion Handbook*, compiled by the *Weekly Irish Times* (1917 edition). His heroics are also explored by Las Fallon in *Firecall* magazine, 'Man of Fire: Captain Thomas Purcell'.

12  *Evening Telegraph*, 24 May 1917.

13  'The Women were worse than the Men', J. T. Gilbert Memorial Lecture delivered by Padraig Yeates. Available at: https://www.dublincity.ie/library/blog/19th-annual-sir-john-t-gilbert-lecture-transcript.

14  Frank Burke, Bureau of Military History Witness Statement 694, Military Archives, Cathal Brugha Barracks.

15  Gregory A. Schirmer, *Reviews and Essays of Austin Clarke* (Buckinghamshire, 1995), 148.

## CHAPTER 7

1   *Irish Examiner*, 14 March 1956.

2   Anne Dolan, 'Alfred Byrne', *Dictionary of Irish Biography*, Royal Irish Academy.

3   *The Irish Worker*, 4 January 1913.

4   Dermot Keogh, *The Rise of the Irish Working Class: The Dublin Trade Union Movement and Labour Leadership 1890–1914* (Dublin, 1982), 124.

5   *The Irish Worker*, 27 May 1911.

6   Diarmaid Ferriter, *A Nation of Extremes: The Pioneers in Twentieth-Century Ireland* (Dublin, 1999), 120.

7   *Irish Independent*, 3 March 2018.

8   Thomas Leahy, Bureau of Military History Witness Statement 660, Military Archives, Cathal Brugha Barracks.

9   Seamus de Burca, *The Soldier's Song: The Story of Peadar Kearney* (Dublin, 1958), 153.

10  Ibid.

11  Kearns, *Dublin Pub Life & Lore*.

12  Luke Kennedy, Bureau of Military History Witness Statement 165, Military Archives, Cathal Brugha Barracks.

13  Dan Breen, Bureau of Military History Witness Statement 1763, Military Archives, Cathal Brugha Barracks.

14  Jeremiah Frewen, Bureau of Military History Witness Statement 930, Military Archives, Cathal Brugha Barracks.

15  *Freeman's Journal*, 31 December 1920.

16  Michael O'Flanagan, Bureau of Military History Witness Statement 908, Military Archives, Cathal Brugha Barracks.

17  Annie O'Brien, Lily Curran, Bureau of Military History Witness Statement 805, Military Archives, Cathal Brugha Barracks.

18  Dying For A Pint, at www.dyingforapint.blogspot.com, is a brilliant resource for anyone researching or curious about the connection between the public house and violent death. The Northern Irish conflict, Dublin gangland killings, and more, are featured in detail.
19  De Burca, *The Soldier's Song*, 162.
20  *Evening Echo*, 4 October 1922.
21  Ibid., 163.
22  Caroline West, *Wrong Women: Selling Sex in Monto, Dublin's Forgotten Red Light District* (London, 2025), 2.
23  *Irish Press*, 25 November 1931.

## CHAPTER 8

1  Ulick O'Connor, *The Gresham Hotel, 1865–1965* (Dublin, 1985), 19.
2  Mary Colum and Padraic Colum, *The James Joyce We Knew* (London, 1959), 9.
3  John Ryan, *Remembering How We Stood* (Dublin, 2008), 42.
4  *Evening Herald*, 7 April 1971.
5  Frank Callanan, 'Timothy Michael Healy', *Dictionary of Irish Biography*, Royal Irish Academy.
6  W. B. Yeats, 'Come Gather Round Me Parnellites'. This poem was later published as a broadsheet by Cuala Press.
7  Flora H. Mitchell, *Vanishing Dublin* (Dublin, 1966), 1.
8  *T. P.'s Weekly*, 3 August 1906.
9  Rev. C. T. McCready, 'Howth: Its Objects of Antiquarian and General Interest', *Journal of the Royal Society of Antiquaries of Ireland* (Vol. 23, 1893).
10  The Duke of Buckingham and Chandos, *Memoirs of the Court of George IV, 1820–1830* (London, 1859), 194.
11  Joseph Sheridan Le Fanu, *The Cock and Anchor: Being a Chronicle of Old Dublin City* (Dublin, 1845), 45.
12  See Dublin By Pub review of The Bleeding Horse, www.dublinbypub.ie/pubs/bleeding-horse/#google_vignette.
13  Quoted in Frank Hopkins, *Hidden Dublin: Deadbeats, Dossers and Decent Skins* (Cork, 2008), 128.
14  Gilbert, *A History of the City of Dublin: Volume II*, 317.
15  Albert Perris, *A Ramble About Tallaght: History, People, Places* (Dublin, 2023).
16  Ibid.
17  Charles Dickens, *Bleak House* (London, 1892), 117.
18  Éamonn MacThomáis, *The Labour and the Royal* (Dublin, 1979), 37.
19  Dying For A Pint, 'The Deadman's Inn and More – Episode One' https://dyingforapint.blogspot.com/2016/06/the-deadmans-inn-and-more-episode-one.html.
20  Quoted in Georgina Louise Hambleton's *Christy Brown: The Life That Inspired My Left Foot* (Dublin, 2011). Chris Morash includes The Stone Boat in his *Dublin: A Writer's City* (Cambridge, 2023).

## CHAPTER 9

1  Bill Kelly, *Me Darlin' Dublin's Dead and Gone* (Dublin, 1987).
2  See 'Family Business is Best', RTÉ Archives. Available at www.rte.ie/archives/2024/0330/1438693-jackie-leonard-and-sons.
3  Kearns, *Dublin Pub Life & Lore*, 148.
4  Edna O'Brien, *Country Girl: A Memoir* (London, 2012), 83.
5  Gene Kerrigan, *Another Country: Growing Up in '50s Ireland* (Dublin, 1998).
6  *Evening Herald*, 23 January 2008.
7  *Sunday Independent*, 11 May 2008.
8  This 2003 feature is available to read from *Brand New Retro* at https://brandnewretro.ie/2014/10/03/early-house-pubs-dublin-2003-the-slate-25.
9  *Sunday Independent*, 21 March 2004.
10  *The Dubliner*, 16 February 2012.
11  *Irish Independent*, 30 June 2019.
12  *Evening Herald*, 6 March 1986.

13  Kevin C. Kearns, *Dublin Street Life & Lore: An Oral History* (Dublin, 1991), 30.
14  *Evening Herald*, 22 October 1982.
15  The society website is available at www.ddwps.omeka.net.
16  *Irish Times*, 26 March 2016.
17  See Dony McManus online at www.donymacmanus.com/the-art/the-linesman.
18  *Father Ted*, Season 2, Episode 8, 'Cigarettes and Alcohol and Rollerblading', 1996.
19  Ferriter, *A Nation of Extremes: The Pioneers in Twentieth-Century Ireland*, 127–8.
20  *Irish Press*, 19 June 1989.
21  *Evening Herald*, 17 April 1971.
22  *Irish Independent*, 11 May 2008.

## CHAPTER 10

1  *Theatre Ireland*, 1985.
2  *Irish Independent*, 22 May 2011.
3  'Alan Devlin Passes Away', *Come Here To Me!* Blog. See comments: https://comeheretome.com/2011/05/16/alan-devlin-passes-away.
4  *Evening Herald*, 27 March 1986.
5  This tale has even made it to the *Lonely Planet* guide to Dublin.
6  William Robert Rodgers, *Irish Literary Portraits* (London, 1972), 3–4.
7  Ibid.
8  O'Brien, *Country Girl: A Memoir*, 107.
9  *Sunday Independent*, 16 April 2006.
10  A. Norman Jeffares, *W. B. Yeats: A New Biography* (London, 2001), 42.

## CHAPTER 11

1  J. Bowyer Bell, *The Secret Army: A History of the IRA, 1916–1970* (Michigan, 1970), 101–2.
2  Patrick Byrne, *The Irish Republican Congress Revisited* (London, 1994), 10.
3  *Irish Examiner*, 5 December 1932.
4  *The Liberator*, 15 December 1932.
5  *Kerry Reporter*, 24 December 1932.
6  *Belfast Newsletter*, 18 January 1933.
7  *Irish Press*, 14 September 1933.
8  *Irish Press*, 15 September 1933.
9  *Irish Press*, 21 September 1933.
10  Ferriter, *A Nation of Extremes: The Pioneers in Twentieth-Century Ireland*, 109.
11  Ibid., 108.

## CHAPTER 12

1  Nicola Gordon Bowe, David Caron, Michael Wynne (eds), *Gazetteer of Irish Stained Glass* (Newbridge Kildare, 2024), 7.
2  Máire Nic Shiubhlaigh, *The Splendid Years: Recollection of Maire Nic Shiubhlaigh as Told to Edward Kenny* (Dublin, 1955), xvi.
3  *Irish Press*, 15 May 1990.
4  Nic Shiubhlaigh, *The Splendid Years*, 3.
5  *Belfast Newsletter*, 31 January 1907.
6  Mary Colum, *Life and the Dream: Memoirs of a Literary Life in Europe and America* (London, 1947), 138.
7  *Freeman's Journal*, 9 November 1908.
8  *Freeman's Journal*, 23 June 1915.
9  Denis Hayes's compensation claim for £200 11s 8d is contained in the Property Losses (Ireland) Committee files at National Archives of Ireland, PLIC/1/0255. Payment of £150 was recommended by Committee, one of the more significant payments made to a Dublin publican.
10  *Longford Leader*, 12 March 1982.
11  Colin Murphy, 'A new theatre in Dublin: Karl Shiels & the Theatre Upstairs', 15 February 2010. www.colinmurphy.ie/?p=521.
12  *Evening Herald*, 8 May 1992.
13  J. J. McCracken, 'Liberalism Under the Union: Three Generations of an Irish Liberal Family' in *Familia: Under Genealogical Review* (Belfast, 2001). This origin story emerges again in the *Irish Times*, 11 December 2024.
14  Paula Murphy, 'Modern Ireland in 100 Artworks 1925 – Monument to William Gladstone by John Hughes', *Irish Times*, 17 January 2015.

## CHAPTER 13

1. *Lee Miller in James Joyce's Dublin* (Dublin, 2014), 20.
2. Hayley Maitland, '"You Cannot Ration a Sense of Style": A Closer Look at British Vogue's Pivotal Role in the Second World War Effort', *Vogue*, 6 September 2024.
3. Lee Miller, 'St Malo', British *Vogue*, October 1944.
4. Ray Moseley, *Reporting War: How Foreign Correspondents Risked Capture, Torture and Death to Cover World War II* (Yale, 2017).
5. Curran's memoirs of Joyce were republished by UCD Press in 2022, marking the centenary of *Ulysses* (C. P. Curran, *James Joyce Remembered*). For discussion of Curran's photograph, see David Pierce, *Reading Joyce* (New York, 2013).
6. *Lee Miller in James Joyce's Dublin*, 18.
7. Stanislaus Joyce in the *Irish Digest* (Vol. 62, 1958).
8. Curran, *James Joyce Remembered*, 70.
9. Mary Colum, Padraic Colum, *Our Friend James Joyce* (London, 1959), 21.
10. Morrill Cody, *This Must Be the Place: Memoirs of Montparnasse by Jimmy 'The Barman' Charters* (New York, 1985), 35.
11. Quoted in Tony Gray, *Mr Smyllie, Sir* (Dublin, 1991), 74.
12. Ibid.
13. Anthony Cronin, *No Laughing Matter: The Life and Times of Flann O'Brien* (London, 1989), 90.
14. *Lee Miller in James Joyce's Dublin*, 20.
15. Ibid.
16. Ibid.
17. *Nationalist and Leinster Times*, 22 February 1947.
18. *Lee Miller in James Joyce's Dublin*, 21.
19. Ibid.
20. Ibid., 9.
21. 'Little Britain Street, Dublin 7' on daft.ie. Available at: https://www.daft.ie/commercial-property-for-sale/little-britain-st-dublin-7/1411970.
22. 'The Irish Times Pub 1973', RTÉ Archives, www.rte.ie/archives/2018/0327/950474-pearl-bar-a-journalists-pub.
23. *Irish Times*, 30 May 2022.

## CHAPTER 14

1. Beatrice Behan, *My Life With Brendan* (London, 1974), 59.
2. 'Cecil Ffrench Salkeld's natural talent', *Irish Arts Review* (Vol. 28, No. 1), 44.
3. Brian Trench has published on the Radical Club in *Irish Arts Review* and *History Ireland*. See Brian Trench, 'The Radical Club: A 1920s Forum for 'Progressive Cultural Activity', *History Ireland* (Vol. 27, No. 5), 44–7.
4. Behan, *My Life with Brendan*, 41.
5. *Irish Press*, 12 November 1986.
6. *Evening Herald*, 6 February 1965.
7. *Nationalist and Leinster Times*, 23 November 1946.
8. *Tipperary Star*, 29 January 1944.
9. Behan, *My Life with Brendan*, 49.
10. Donleavy, *J.P. Donleavy's Ireland*, 43.
11. Ibid., 44.
12. Desmond Fennell, *Bloomsday: A Day in the Life of Dublin* (Dublin, 1999), 33.

## CHAPTER 15

1. Cody, *This Must Be the Place: Memoirs of Montparnasse by Jimmie 'The Barman' Charters*, 2.
2. Sean Boyd, *Behind the Horseshoe Bar at Dublin's Shelbourne Hotel* (Dublin, 2009), 28.
3. *Irish Times*, 23 April 2016.
4. Elizabeth Bowen, *The Shelbourne* (London, 1951), 162.
5. Ibid., 177.
6. Bram Stoker, *Personal Reminiscences of Henry Irving* (London, 1907), 40.
7. Boyd, *Behind the Horseshoe Bar at Dublin's Shelbourne Hotel*, 29.
8. Michael O'Sullivan, *Brendan Behan: A Life* (Colorado, 1999), 215.

9   Jenny Uglow, *Hogarth: A Life and a World* (London, 2010), 423.

10   Boyd, *Behind the Horseshoe Bar at Dublin's Shelbourne Hotel*, 27.

11   Ibid.

12   Ibid.

13   Bernadine O'Neill, Michael O'Sullivan, *The Shelbourne and its People* (Dublin, 1999), 122.

14   *Sunday Independent*, 24 January 1993.

15   Ibid.

16   Boyd, *Behind the Horseshoe Bar at Dublin's Shelbourne Hotel*, 72.

## CHAPTER 16

1   Jim Davies, *The Book of Guinness Advertising* (London, 1998), 68.

2   Ibid., 73.

3   Ray Rivlin, *Jewish Ireland: A Social History* (Dublin, 2011), 9.

4   Harry Kernoff profile from *Irish Tatler and Sketch*, Capuchin Archives, IE CA CP/3/16/8/33.

5   *Irish Times*, 3 November 2016.

6   *Irish Examiner*, 26 May 2008.

7   *Tuam Herald*, 24 November 1951.

8   Pat Dargan, *Dublin Pubs* (Dublin, 2018).

9   Rivlin, *Jewish Ireland*, 164.

10   *Sunday Independent*, 20 December 2009.

11   *Irish Independent*, 15 November 1961.

12   Michael Kane, *Blind Dogs: A Personal History* (Dublin, 2023).

13   *Evening Herald*, 28 December 1974.

## CHAPTER 17

1   Joseph Sheridan Le Fanu, *The House by the Churchyard* (London, 1886), 1.

2   Le Fanu's Chapelizod ghost stories have been digitised and can be read at: https://www.askaboutireland.ie/aai-files/assets/libraries/dublin-city-public-libraries/reading-room/irish-language-legends/pdf-le-fanus-ghost-stories-of-chapelizod.pdf

3   See Barry McGovern's excellent entry in Motoko Fujita (ed.), *The Shadow of James Joyce: Chapelizod and Environs* (Dublin, 2011).

4   James Joyce, *Dubliners* (Dublin, 1914).

5   *Dublin: What's to be seen and how to see it; with excursions to the country and suburbs* (Dublin, 1888), 127.

6   Batt O'Connor, Bureau of Military History Witness Statement 330, Military Archives, Cathal Brugha Barracks.

7   John Brannigan (ed.), *A Bit of a Writer: Brendan Behan's Collected Short Prose* (Dublin, 2023), 260.

8   Thanks to *Brand New Retro*, who posted snippets of this feature on X.com.

9   A great history of this piece of music is available from FolkWorld.de at http://www.folkworld.de/33/e/inisheer.html.

10   Ken Larkin (ed.), *Ballyfermot Memories: A selection of stories and anecdotes and poetry of Ballyfermot* (Dublin, 2014), 46.

11   *Irish Independent*, 3 November 2022. *Dublin Inquirer*, 8 December 2017.

12   *The Guardian*, 23 November 2015.

13   Terry Moylan (ed.), *A Living Voice: The Frank Harte Song Collection* (Dublin, 2020), 270.

14   Ibid., 1.

15   Ole Vinding, Helge Irgens-Moller, Brookes Spencer, 'James Joyce in Copenhagen', *James Joyce Quarterly* (Vol. 14, No. 2), 173–84.

16   Peter Chrisp's 'A Pint in Earwicker's Pub' recalls his visit to the pub in 2013. His blog demystifies much of Joyce and is essential reading for anyone keen to understand Joyce better. Available at: https://peterchrisp.blogspot.com.

## CHAPTER 18

1   John Montague, *The Pear is Ripe: A Memoir* (Dublin, 2007), 76.

2   Frank Shovlin (ed.), *The Letters of John McGahern* (London, 2021).

3   Ibid.

4 Hugh McFadden (ed.), *Crystal Clear: The Selected Prose of John Jordan* (Dublin, 2006), 10.

5 Kearns, *Dublin Pub Life & Lore*, 65–6.

6 Pub Spy feature from *Sunday World* digitised by Brand New Retro, see www.brandnewretro.ie/tag/grogans-pub.

7 Ryan, *Remembering How We Stood*, ix.

8 Editorial, *The Bell* (Vol. 1, No. 1).

9 Ryan, *Remembering How We Stood*, 29.

10 Vivan Igoe, *A Literary Guide to Dublin: Writers in Dublin: Literary Associations and Anecdotes* (London, 1994), 294.

11 J. B. Lyons, *Oliver St John Gogarty* (London, 1976), 39.

12 Ryan, *Remembering How We Stood*, 30.

13 Anthony Cronin, *Dead as Doornails: A Chronicle of Life* (Dublin, 1975), 75.

14 *Irish Times*, 16 June 1954.

15 John Ryan (ed.), *A Bash in the Tunnel: James Joyce by the Irish* (Dublin, 1970), 20.

16 Cronin, *Dead as Doornails: A Chronicle of Life*, 124.

17 Antoinette Quinn, *Patrick Kavanagh: A Biography* (Dublin, 2003), 333.

18 Cronin, *Dead as Doornails: A Chronicle of Life*, 127.

19 Patrick Kavanagh's poem 'Joyce's Ulysses' is included in Bernard Benstock, *Pomes for James Joyce* (Dublin, 1982).

20 John McCourt, *Consuming Joyce: A Hundred Years of Ulysses in Ireland* (London, 2022), 162.

21 From RTÉ's 1979 'The Humours of Donnybrook' programme, available to view on the RTÉ Archives player.

22 Ryan, *Remembering How We Stood*, 124.

## CHAPTER 19

1 *Irish Press*, 12 May 1947.

2 Press Up, 'The Revival of a Cocktail Heritage', https://pressup.ie/news/cocktailrevival/.

3 *Evening Herald*, 7 September 1912.

4 Mallory O'Meara, *Girly Drinks: A World History of Women and Alcohol* (London, 2022), 146–7.

5 *Tipperary Star*, 15 December 1945.

6 *Southern Star*, 13 April 1940.

7 *Limerick Leader*, 28 September 1935.

8 J. P. Donleavy, *What They Did in Dublin with The Ginger Man, A Play* (Michigan, 1961), 27.

9 Graeme Thomson, *Cowboy Song: The Authorised Biography of Philip Lynott* (London, 2016). Pat Egan, *Backstage Pass: A Life in Show Business* (Dublin, 2023).

10 Jim Fitzpatrick, 'Philip Lynott Sculpture Post', https://jimfitzpatrick.com/philip-lynott-sculpture-post.

## CHAPTER 20

1 *Irish Independent*, 26 March 2011.

2 *The Peasant*, 29 August 1909.

3 Charles Booth, *Life and Labour of the People in London*, is digitised at Dictionary of Victorian London, https://www.victorianlondon.org/women/womendrinking.htm.

4 *The Toiler*, 8 November 1914.

5 *Irish Press*, 20 December 1979.

6 Ibid.

7 *Irish Independent*, 8 August 1974.

8 Ibid.

9 *Evening Herald*, 20 October 1977.

10 'Radio Review: Norris Trumps Duphy', *Magill* online, see: https://magill.ie/archive/radio-norris-trumps-dunphy.

11 *Irish Press*, 1 August 1974.

12 Kearns, *Dublin Pub Life & Lore*.

13 *Sunday Press*, 12 November 1989.

14 Ibid.

15 *Irish Independent*, 29 November 1991.

## CHAPTER 21

1 *Sunday Independent*, 11 May 1975.

2 *Sunday Independent*, 18 May 1975.

3 *Gay Community News*, August 1991.

4 *Irish Star*, 15 July 2023.

5   *Trinity News*, 21 May 1970.
6   *Irish Times*, 24 September 2016.
7   *Nonplus* (Number 1, October 1959).
8   *Gay Community News*, February 1996.
9   Éibhear Walshe, 'Wild(e) Ireland', in David Alderson, Fiona Becket, Scott Brewster, Virginia Crossman (eds), *Ireland in Proximity: History Gender Space* (London, 1999), 64–80, 73.
10  *Sunday Independent*, 29 September 1974.
11  Ibid.
12  *Sunday Independent*, 25 August 1985.
13  Páraic Kerrigan, *Reeling in the Queers: Tales of Ireland's LGBTQ Past* (Dublin, 2024), 97.
14  David Norris, *A Kick Against the Pricks: The Autobiography* (Dublin, 2012), 103.
15  'Reminders of Fortress Fownes' on *Come Here To Me*, 6 October 2016. Available at https://comeheretome.com/2016/10/06/reminders-of-fortress-fownes.
16  *Irish Independent*, 1 December 1987.
17  *Gay Community News*, April 1994. Historians of Dublin, LGBT history and more besides are indebted to *GCN* for their excellent and free online archive, at archive.gcn.ie.
18  *Evening Herald*, 13 August 2022.
19  Brian Dillon, 'The history of Bridie's Bar: One of Dublin's first openly gay bars', *GCN* online, 10 April 2019.
20  *Gay Community News*, October 1997.

## CHAPTER 22

1   Ronnie Drew, *Ronnie* (Dublin, 2008), 148.
2   Kane, *Blind Dogs: A Personal History*, 235–6.
3   Ibid.
4   Kiely, *The Waves Behind Us: Further Memoirs*, 121.
5   Kearns, *Dublin Pub Life & Lore* (Dublin, 1996).
6   Ronan Burtenshaw, 'Ireland's Red Troubadour', *Tribune*, 30 January 2019.
7   Des Geraghty, *Luke: A Memoir* (Dublin, 1994), 62.
8   Drew, *Ronnie*, 39.
9   *Irish Times,* 15 January 2000.
10  Quoted in Drew, *Ronnie*, 101.
11  *Sunday Independent*, 5 September 1971.
12  Ibid.
13  Quoted in Diarmaid Ferriter, *Ambiguous Republic: Ireland in the 1970s* (London, 2012), 580–1.
14  *Evening Press*, 6 May 1967.
15  John Glatt, *The Chieftains: The Authorised Biography* (London, 2012).
16  Brian Warfield, *The Ramblings of an Irish Ballad Singer* (Dublin, 2018), 128.
17  *Evening Herald*, 17 February 1967.
18  *Irish Times*, 24 April 2004.
19  Warfield, *Ramblings of an Irish Ballad Singer*, 124.
20  Drew, *Ronnie*, 101.
21  *Sunday Independent*, 4 February 2007.
22  *Spotlight*, April 1967.
23  Neil Hegarty, *Waking Up In Dublin* (Dublin, 2011).

## CHAPTER 23

1   *Irish Examiner*, 17 June 1954.
2   'Where gravediggers drank their pints', BBC travel feature, February 2022. https://www.bbc.com/travel/article/20161019-where-gravediggers-drank-their-pints.
3   Críostóir Ó Floinn, *Van Gogh Chocolates: Poems and Translations* (Dublin, 2000), 20.
4   The Downey's strike was international news, ending only with the death of the former owner. In *Tom Corkery's Dublin*, we learn that 'the men on picket duty at Downey's in Dún Laoghaire come in for a drink on the house at the invitation of the new management when the 14-year-old strike was settled'.
5   Quoted in Kearns, *Dublin Pub Life & Lore*, 61.
6   Ibid.
7   *Irish Independent*, 24 October 1959.
8   Tom Corkery, *Tom Corkery's Dublin* (Dublin, 1980), 75.
9   E. Taylor Atkins, *A History of Popular Culture in Japan: From the Seventeenth Century to the Present* (London, 2023), 238.

10. *South China Morning Post*, 8 August 2020.
11. *Evening Herald*, 29 May 1989.
12. *Evening Herald*, 18 July 1991.
13. *Evening Press*, 26 March 1991.
14. Ibid.
15. Maria Pramaggiore, *Irish and African American Cinema: Identifying Others and Performing Identities, 1980–2000* (New York, 2007), 112.

## CHAPTER 24

1. *Evening Echo*, 14 July 1984.
2. J. T. Gilbert, *A History of the City of Dublin: Volume III* (Dublin, 1859), 39.
3. Frederic Morton, 'Vienna's Evening Star', *Vanity Fair* (February 2013).
4. Ibid.
5. Mary Costello, 'Alfred Loos' Kärntner Bar: Reception, Reinvention, Reproduction' in Charlotte Ashby, Tag Gronberg, Simon Shaw-Millers (eds), *The Viennese Cafe and Fin-de-Siecle Culture* (Oxford, 2003), 138–57.
6. *Trinity News*, 22 November 1962.
7. Costello, 'Alfred Loos' Kärntner Bar: Reception, Reinvention, Reproduction', 142.
8. *Dublin Inquirer*, 2 August 2017.
9. Ibid.
10. Carl E. Schorske, *Fin-De-Siecle Vienna Politics and Culture* (New York, 2012), 306.
11. *Trinity News*, 7 June 1956.

## CHAPTER 25

1. *Irish Independent*, 19 October 1967.
2. Joseph Brady, *Dublin in the 1950s and 1960s* (Dublin, 2017).
3. See Karl Whitney's excellent article for *The Guardian*, 11 July 2017. Whitney is also the author of *Hidden City: Adventures and Explorations in Dublin*.
4. *Irish Independent*, 2 February 2014.
5. Pauric J. Dempsey, 'Patrick Belton', *Dictionary of Irish Biography*, Royal Irish Academy.
6. *Evening Herald*, 10 July 1970.
7. *Evening Herald*, 11 September 1970.
8. Christy Dignam, *My Crazy World: The Autobiography* (Dublin, 2019), 6–7.
9. *Magill*, 29 November 1982.
10. *Irish Independent*, 30 June 2015.

## CHAPTER 26

1. Myles na gCopaleen's 1940 article on the Dublin pub for *The Bell* is republished in John Horgan (ed.), *Great Irish Reportage* (Dublin, 2014).
2. Ibid.
3. *Irish Independent*, 6 January 1969.
4. Paul Jennings, *The Local: A History of the English Pub* (London, 2021), 219.
5. Roy Bulson, *Irish Pubs of Character* (Dublin, 1969). With thanks to Brand New Retro for the loan of this fascinating little book.
6. Brian J. Murphy, '"If it's eatin' and drinkin' you want, take a spoon and fork to a pint of stout": A brief history of food and the Irish pub', in Cashman, Mac Con Iomaire (eds), *Irish Food History: A Companion*, 716–43.
7. Tayto's website includes an interesting potted history and timeline of the company, as interesting for the design history dimension as the cultural and culinary history. In late 2024, Bobby Aherne produced a social history of the brand with Lilliput Press. www.taytocrisps.ie/history/.
8. Clair Wills, *The Best are Leaving: Emigration and Post-War Irish Culture* (London, 2015). Sean Sheridan, *A Mother's Tale* (London, 2022).
9. Ali Dunworth, *A Compendium of Irish Pints* (Dublin, 2024), 68.
10. *Sunday Independent*, 3 October 1999.
11. *Irish Independent*, 25 November 2000.
12. Richard Ryan, 'A Private Poet in the Public World: Some Personal Memories of Seamus Heaney', *Studies: An Irish Quarterly Review* (Vol. 104, No. 413), 8–15.
13. Quoted in Valentina Valentini, 'How a Dublin Pub Became a Haunt for Gravediggers and Ghosts Alike', *Atlas Obscura*, 29 October 2018.

14. See 'Here's how Ciaran makes it' at www.facebook.com/JohnKavanaghTheGravediggers/videos/coddlefancy-a-coddleheres-how-ciaran-makes-it/942186049160984.
15. This quotation is from Bourdain's travel show, *The Layover*. For more on Anthony Bourdain's time in Dublin, see the February 2024 episode of the 'Friends of Anthony Bourdain' podcast, featuring Ciaran Kavanagh from The Gravediggers.

## CHAPTER 27

1. Con Houlihan's article on St Patrick's Athletic appears in *The Lost Essays: Con Houlihan's Ireland*. It has also appeared in *The Saint*, match day programme of the club (Vol. 32, No. 4).
2. Ibid.
3. Ibid.
4. *The Kerryman*, 19 June 1998.
5. Ibid.
6. Richard McElligott, '"Degenerating from sterling Irishmen into contemptible West Britons": The GAA and Rugby in Kerry, 1885–1905', *History Ireland* (Vol. 19, No. 4), 28–31, 28.
7. *Evening Press*, 25 September 1978.
8. 'Coolest Neighbourhoods in the World', *Time Out*. http://www.timeout.com/travel/coolest-neighbourhoods-in-the-world.
9. Con Houlihan, *More Than a Game: Selected Sporting Essays* (Dublin, 2003).
10. Republished in *The Saint* (Vol. 32, No. 4).
11. Con Houlihan, *Windfalls* (Dublin, 1996), 11.
12. *Sunday Press*, 15 November 1992.
13. Scotch House, QRE Real Estate Advisers, https://qre.ie/properties/scotch-house-burgh-quay-dublin-2.
14. *Irish Independent*, 16 June 1994.
15. Kiely, *The Waves Behind Us: Further Memoirs*, 127.
16. *Evening Press*, 24 July 1990.
17. *Sunday Independent*, 17 May 2015.
18. *The Kerryman*, 8 August 2012.
19. *Sunday Independent*, 9 September 2007.
20. *Evening Press*, 21 August 1990.
21. Frank Kilfeather, *Changing Times: A Life in Journalism* (Dublin, 1997), 149.
22. Sean Creedon, 'Con Houlihan – A true giant amongst men', 2 April 2014. Published on *Terrace Talk*. https://www.terracetalk.com/articles/476/-Con-Houlihan--A-true-giant-amongst-men.
23. For more on Con Houlihan and St Patrick's Athletic, see Cian Manning, 'Con Houlihan: St Pat's Intellectual' on *Póg Mo Goal*. https://pogmogoal.com/league-of-ireland/con-houlihan-st-pats-intellectual/24151.

## CHAPTER 28

1. *Irish Examiner*, 19 May 1964.
2. Geraldine Walsh, introduction to Dublin Civic Trust's *The Irish House: An Teach Gaeleach: Public House, 1870–1968* (Dublin, 2009), 3.
3. Ibid., 11.
4. Ibid., 14.
5. Ibid., 34.
6. *Evening Herald*, 20 January 1966.
7. See A. C. Hepburn, *Catholic Belfast and Nationalist Ireland in the Era of Joe Devlin* (Oxford, 2008).

## CHAPTER 29

1. *Nenagh Guardian*, 11 June 1994.
2. 'Dublin's Freshest Sign Painter on the Revival of the Hand Painted Sign', TheTaste.ie, 2 September 2016.
3. *In Dublin*, February 1978. With thanks to the 'A Gentleman of Letters' Kevin Freeney page.
4. Ibid.
5. Clipping from the *Irish Times*, 1985. Thanks to 'A Gentleman of Letters'.
6. *Evening Herald*, 18 November 1892.
7. See PantiBar Facebook post at www.facebook.com/panti/posts/in-relation-to-this-in-todays-papers-httpmindependentieirish-newslas-vegasstyle-/1039036436106604.
8. *Irish Times*, 9 July 2016.

## CHAPTER 30

1. Kearns, *Dublin Pub Life & Lore*, 128.
2. *Evening Herald*, 14 October 1985.
3. 'About', Owen Walsh Art. www.owenwalshart.ie/about.
4. 'Reflections and Reviews', Owen Walsh Art. www.owenwalshart.ie/reflections-and-reviews.
5. *Evening Herald*, 14 October 1985.
6. *Sunday Independent*, 19 July 1992.
7. *Sunday Independent*, 19 March 1995.
8. Donleavy, *J. P. Donleavy's Ireland*, 121.
9. Ibid.
10. Interview with author, January 2025.
11. Ibid.
12. Ibid.
13. *Sunday World*, 6 November 2024.
14. Interview with author, January 2025.
15. *Irish Times*, 29 October 2005.

## CHAPTER 31

1. *Irish Independent*, 11 March 2011.
2. *The United Service Journal and Naval and Military Magazine*, 1837.
3. Murray Fraser, *John Bull's Other Homes: State Housing and British Policy in Ireland, 1883–1922* (Liverpool, 1996), 76.
4. Brendan Behan, *Confessions of an Irish Rebel* (London, 2008), 124.
5. Aaron Coultate, 'Inside Tokyo's audiophile venues', *Resident Advisor*. Available at: www.ra.co/features/2724.
6. *Irish Examiner*, 15 January 2025.
7. Interview with author, February 2025.
8. See Hatchett Sound website at www.hatchett.ie/about-1.
9. Interview with author, February 2025.

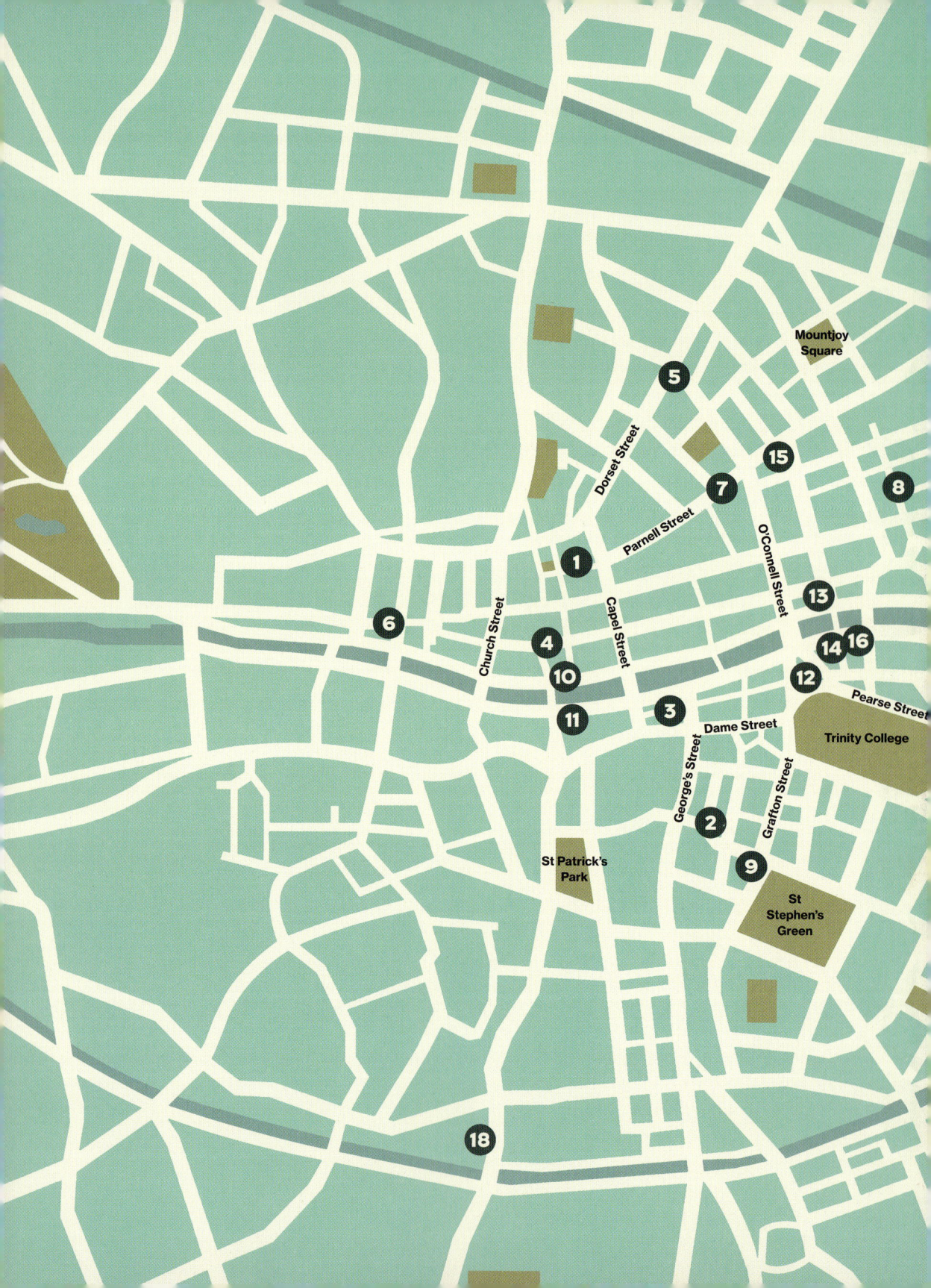

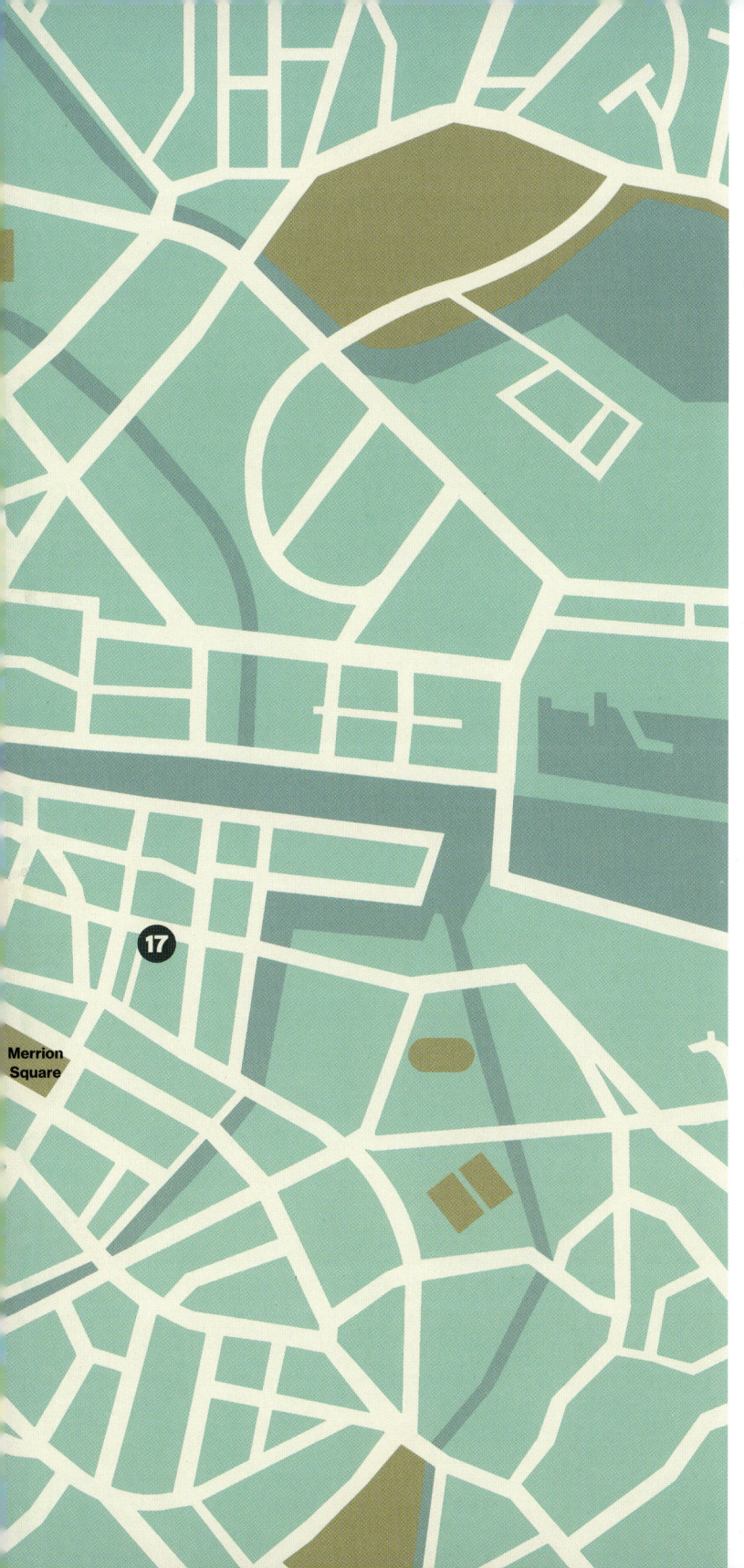

# SOME LOST PUBS OF DUBLIN

Many of these public houses feature in the book, and others are amongst the most sorely missed or unusual of the disappeared public house landscape.

1  Barney Kiernan's
2  Bartley Dunne's
3  Eagle Tavern
4  M. Hughes
5  Maye's
6  Museum Rest
7  Patrick Conway's
8  Philip Shanahan's
9  Rice's
10 The Chancery
11 The Irish House
12 The Pearl Bar
13 The Plough
14 The Scotch House
15 The Welcome Inn
16 The White Horse Inn
17 Widow Scallan's
18 Ye Olde Grinding Young

# INDEX OF PUBS

*All pubs are located in Dublin City unless otherwise stated*

*Lost pubs

1. The Abbey Tavern  220–1, 222
2. The Anglers Rest  182
3. Anseo  289
4. At the Sign of the Zodiac (now Bruxelles)  195–7
5. The Bailey  28, 103, 170, 188, 189, 190, 192–3
6. Bambrick's  130
7. The Bank on College Green  255, 258
8. Barney Kiernan's  17, 148–9, 150–1, 265
9. Bartley Dunne's  13, 200, 206–13
10. The Big Romance  290–1
11. The Bird Flanagan  12, 103, 109
12. The Black Lion  53
13. The Bleeding Horse  64, 106
14. The Bloody Stream  105
15. The Boar's Head  113, 122
16. Bowe's  99, 271–2
17. Brazen Head  12, 27, 28, 46–8, 50–1, 149, 216, 217
18. Brian Boru  204, 242
19. Bridie's Bar (The George)  213
20. Brogan's  70
21. The Capel (now Bar 1661)  117
22. The Chancery  115–16
23. Chaplin's  255
24. The Church  30, 31
25. The Cock and Punch Bowl  53, 56
26. Conway's  17, 18, 88
27. Cleary's  74, 271
28. The Cobblestone  114, 223, 226, 273
29. The Comet Bar  200
30. Corbett's  112–13
31. The Countess  120
32. Crown and Punch Bowl  53, 107
33. Cusack's  199, 201
34. Davy Byrne's  153–7, 168, 170, 173, 184, 193, 210, 258
35. Davy's (now The Portobello Bar)  87, 98
36. The Dawson Lounge  278–9
37. The Deadman's Inn  108, 131
38. The Dean Swift (now Jackie's)  55
39. Delaney's  114
40. Dice Bar  289–90
41. The Dog and Duck  107
42. Doheny & Nesbitt  258
43. The Dolphin Inn  241
44. Donoghue's  112
45. Downey's (Crumlin)  227
46. Downey's (Dún Laoghaire)  226
47. Dudley's  109
48. The Eagle Tavern (Cork Hill)  55–6
49. The Eagle Tavern (Eustace Street)  12, 42, 43, 107
50. The Embankment  13, 220–2
51. Fagan's  204, 205
52. Fassaugh House  17
53. Fidelity  31, 286–91
54. Five Lamps  202
55. The Flowing Tide  13, 80, 132–9
56. Four Provinces  109
57. The Fourth Corner  59
58. The Front Lounge (Street 66)  213
59. The George  208, 213
60. George Farrelly's  131
61. The Glen of Aherlow  180
62. The Globe (Cork Hill)  56
63. The Globe (South Great George's Street)  80
64. Goggins  190
65. Golden Bottle  50
66. The Gravediggers (John Kavanagh's)  180, 182, 226, 244–6,
67. Grogan's  13, 15, 28, 99, 173, 188, 226, 272, 276–85
68. H. Matthew's  287
69. Hacienda Market Bar  113–14
70. The Hairy Lemon  109, 272
71. Hanlon's Corner  114, 216
72. The Harold House  225, 259
73. Hoey's  66
74. The Hole in the Wall (formerly Nancy Hand's)  13, 103
75. The Hoop  56
76. Horse and Jockey  17, 254
77. Horseshoe and Magpie  107
78. The Horseshoe Bar (Shelbourne Hotel)  13, 158–65
79. Hourican's  17
80. The Hut  70
81. Hynes'  98
82. The International  12, 170
83. The Irish House (O'Meara's)  262–7
84. J. Connell's  131
85. J. J. Higgins  131
86. John Curran's  130
87. John Fallon's Capstan Bar  12, 38–9
88. Kenny's  59, 100
89. Kehoe's  75, 76–7, 79
90. The King's Inn  80
91. Kitty O'Shea  103–4
92. Lalor's (now The Landmark)  225, 227
93. Legal Eagle  115
94. The Liberty Belle  225
95. The Lincoln Inn  154
96. The Loft  208
97. The Long Hall  62, 65, 66, 70, 78
98. The Loos Bar (Trinity College Dublin)  230–3
99. The Lord Edward (formerly The Cunniam Tavern)  46, 243–4
100. Loughman's  289
101. Lowe's  59
102. The Lower Deck  228, 259
103. M. Hughes'  33, 117, 118
104. Maye's  167
105. McDaid's  4, 12, 30, 147, 170, 173, 187–9, 189, 195, 226, 277, 280, 281
106. McDonald's  131
107. McDonnell's  195
108. McNeill's  222
109. Molloy's  122–3

INDEX OF PUBS   319

110. Mooney's 100
111. The Morgue (The Tempelogue Inn) 107–8
112. Mulligan's 12, 28, 127, 146, 248–9, 252–3, 255, 257, 271, 292
113. Mullingar House 176, 184–5
114. The Museum Rest (formerly The Regal Bar) 287, 289
115. Nagle's (now Madigan's) 90
116. Neary's 73, 125–6, 168, 170, 204
117. Ned's 116
118. O'Beirne's 59
119. O'Donoghue's 11, 164, 214–17, 218–20, 222, 226
120. O'Neill's 255
121. The Oval Bar 83, 145
122. The Pádraig Pearse 118, 119–20
123. The Palace Bar 77, 142, 147, 258
124. PantiBar 268–9, 274–5
125. The Parliament Inn (now The Turk's Head) 208, 212–13
126. Pavilion Bar (Trinity College Dublin) 233
127. The Pearl 151
128. Peter's Pub 168, 170, 271
129. Pillsworth's 66
130. The Plough 137–38
131. Punch Bowl 107
132. Quinn's 59
133. Raven and Punch Bowl 107
134. Rice's 208–12
135. The Richmond House 251, 254
136. Roberts's 112
137. Rody Boland's 269, 270
138. Row Wines 291
139. Royal Oak 254
140. Ruggy O'Donoghue's (now The International) 145–6
141. Ryan's 77
142. The Scotch House 256
143. Shakespeare Tavern 107
144. Shamrock Lodge 205
145. (Philip) Shanahan's 97–101
146. Sheehan's 189
147. The Ship 86
148. Sinnott's 125
149. Slattery's 113, 122, 219, 246
150. The Stag's Head 79, 80
151. The Star Bar (formerly Larry Murphy's) 279
152. The Stone Boat 108, 109
153. The Strawberry Hall 176, 180, 182
154. Submarine Bar 238
155. The Swan 78–9, 98
156. Swift 55
157. Thomas Read's 80
158. Tom Kennedy's 225
159. Toner's 126, 127
160. Tower Bar 90
161. The Towers 13, 234–9
162. Turk's Head 13, 107, 212
163. Verdon Bar 94
164. The Viking (now Brogan's) 212–13
165. The Villager (formerly The Tap) 176, 183
166. The Victoria Tavern (now The Patriot's Inn) 74
167. Walsh's 76, 77, 205
168. Welcome Inn 17
169. White Bull Inn 50
170. The White Horse 116–17, 256, 258
171. Widow Scallan's 27, 120
172. The Windjammer 118, 120–1
173. The Wren's Nest 176, 178–80
174. Wrenn's (formerly O'Brien Bros, now Brogan's) 69
175. The Yacht Tavern 28
176. Ye Olde Grinding Young 104, 105

## OTHER PUBS MENTIONED

177. Admiral Duncan (London) 208
178. The American Bar (Kärntner Bar) (Vienna) 232–3
179. Bartley Dunne's (New York City) 208, 211
180. Bayardo Bar (Belfast) 27
181. Blakes of the Hollow (Enniskillen) 139
182. Brilliant Corners (London) 290
183. The Brogue Inn (Tralee) 255
184. The Devonshire Arms (London) 217
185. The Duncairn Arms (Belfast) 39
186. The Eagle (London) 242
187. Four Step Inn (Belfast) 27
188. The Fox & Anchor (London) 123
189. Hideout (Kilcullen) 39
190. Kelly's Cellars (Belfast) 267
191. McGurk's (Belfast) 27
192. McSorley's Ale House (New York City) 55
193. Mountainview Tavern (Belfast) 27
194. The Rights of Man (Lewes, UK) 47
195. Spiritland (London) 290
196. Swift Hibernian Lounge (New York City) 55
197. The Three Johns (London) 62
198. Tigh Neachtain (Galway) 139
199. Ye Olde Cheshire Cheese (London) 127